Essential

THAI

Speak Thai With Confidence

Michael Golding
& Benjawan Jai-Ua

Revised by
Scot Barmé

TUTTLE Publishing

Tokyo | Rutland, Vermont | Singapore

The Tuttle Story: "Books to Span the East and West"

Many people are surprised to learn that the world's largest publisher of books on Asia had its humble beginnings in the tiny American state of Vermont. The company's founder, Charles E. Tuttle, belonged to a New England family steeped in publishing.

Immediately after WW II, Tuttle served in Tokyo under General Douglas MacArthur and was tasked with reviving the Japanese publishing industry. He later founded the Charles E. Tuttle Publishing Company, which thrives today as one of the world's leading independent publishers.

Though a westerner, Tuttle was hugely instrumental in bringing a knowledge of Japan and Asia to a world hungry for information about the East. By the time of his death in 1993, Tuttle had published over 6,000 books on Asian culture, history and art—a legacy honored by the Japanese emperor with the "Order of the Sacred Treasure," the highest tribute Japan can bestow upon a non-Japanese.

With a backlist of 1,500 titles, Tuttle Publishing is more active today than at any time in its past—inspired by Charles Tuttle's core mission to publish fine books to span the East and West and provide a greater understanding of each.

Published by Tuttle Publishing, an imprint of Periplus Editions (HK) Ltd.

www.tuttlepublishing.com

Copyright © 2013 Periplus Editions

ISBN 978-0-8048-4244-0

First edition
16 15 14 13   8 7 6 5 4 3 2 1
1311HP

Printed in Singapore

TUTTLE PUBLISHING® is a registered trademark of Tuttle Publishing, a division of Periplus Editions (HK) Ltd.

Distributed by
North America, Latin America & Europe
Tuttle Publishing
364 Innovation Drive
North Clarendon, VT 05759-9436 U.S.A.
Tel: 1 (802) 773-8930
Fax: 1 (802) 773-6993
info@tuttlepublishing.com
www.tuttlepublishing.com

Japan
Tuttle Publishing
Yaekari Building, 3rd Floor, 5-4-12 Osaki
Shinagawa-ku, Tokyo 141 0032
Tel: (81) 3 5437-0171
Fax: (81) 3 5437-0755
sales@tuttle.co.jp
www.tuttle.co.jp

Asia Pacific
Berkeley Books Pte. Ltd.
61 Tai Seng Avenue #02-12,
Singapore 534167
Tel: (65) 6280-1330
Fax: (65) 6280-6290
inquiries@periplus.com.sg
www.periplus.com

Contents

Introduction

● **Welcome to the Tuttle Essential Language series, covering all of the most popular world languages. These books are basic guides in communicating in the language. They're concise, accessible and easy to understand, and you'll find them indispensable on your trip abroad to get you where you want to go, pay the right prices and do everything you've been planning to do.**

Each guide is divided into 15 themed sections and starts with a pronunciation table which explains the phonetic pronunciation to all the words and sentences you'll need to know, and a basic grammar guide which will help you construct basic sentences in your chosen language. At the end of the book is an extensive English–Thai word list.

Throughout the book you'll come across boxes with a beside them. These are designed to help you if you can't understand what your listener is saying to you. Hand the book over to them and encourage them to point to the appropriate answer to the question you are asking.

Other boxes in the book—this time without the symbol—give listings of themed words with their English translations.

For extra clarity, we have put all phonetic pronunciations of the foreign language terms in bold italic.

This book covers all subjects you are likely to come across during the course of a visit, from reserving a room for the night to ordering food and drink at a restaurant and what to do if your car breaks down or you lose your money. With over 2,000 commonly used words and essential sentences at your fingertips you can rest assured that you will be able to get by in all situations, so let **Essential Thai** become your passport to learning to speak with confidence!

Pronunciation guide

You'll no doubt be wanting to dive straight in and get your Thai language working for you as quickly as possible. There are, however, some points to note, not the least of which is that Thai is a tonal language and has some sounds in it that might sound strange to the western ear. Hence the purpose of this section: firstly, to give you some idea as to how Thai is pronounced and, secondly, to show you how the tones work. This is a good point to ask your Thai friend to give some assistance with both pronunciation and tone—you'll note that this dictionary has every word in Thai script as well as a romanized phonetic Thai for exactly this purpose.

Romanized phonetic Thai

English is such a complex language to write—many vowel sounds can be produced using the letter "e" for example (mother, women, they, he, etc.). Thai romanized phonetics, on the other hand, are straightforward once you learn the basic rules. It's worth pointing out that the system is important when Thai is "written" in English. Even the word *Thai* itself shows this: the **h** represents an expelling of air after the **t**. It is not "thigh"! There are six new consonants and vowels to learn and a re-jigging of some old ones—we'll place them in slash marks for now to show they are in romanized phonetic Thai; however, the words in the dictionary are given without the slashes. The new vowels are **aeh** (air), **aw** (or), **oeh** (er) and **ueh** (ueh). All these are explained in more detail below.

Vowels

Standard five. The main point to note is that the five Thai vowels (a e i o u) are pronounced as in Spanish or Italian: /**aa**/ *car*, /**eh**/ *hey*, /**ii**/ *free*, /**oh**/ *oh*, and /**uu**/ *true*; they are written doubly to show that they are pronounced long. They are all pure vowels, so shouldn't have traces of other vowels creeping in. Ask your Thai friend to pronounce them for you, and note that the /**oh**/ requires the lips to be brought forward somewhat.

New ones. For the four new ones, try to mimic your friend as much as possible. Some of the sounds may be quite funny, so make the most of them! /**aeh**/ is pronounced as in *tare*; /**aw**/ as in *born*, but without sounding the *r*; /**oeh**/ as in *skirt*, but feel it under your chin; and /**ueh**/ is said by imagining there's a twig across your mouth, by clenching your teeth and making *ueh* noises! You'll get them easily with practice. Just have a go, and try to closely copy your friend's pronunciation.

Mixed vowels. There are many vowel combinations, but they sound as you see them. Have your friend say the following combinations for you (short and long) and try to mimic the sounds:

with a:	/**ia**/	/**ua**/	/**uea**/		
with o:	/**ao**/	/**eo**/	/**aeo**/	/**iao**/	
with i:	/**ai**/	/**oi**/	/**oei**/	/**ui**/	/**uai**/	/**ueai**/
with u:	/**iu**/ (sounds like the "ew" in *few*)				

Consonants

End sounds—live or sonorant. These sounds are pronounced just as in English; they are "live," so are easy to say. Try /**man**/, /**mang**/, /**mam**/, /**mai**/ (rhymes with *Thai*) and /**mao**/ (as in *mouth*).

End sounds—stops. Thai stop sounds are not "pronounced," they just finish or stop. For example, say /**mat**/, but leave your tongue on the roof of your mouth as you get to the *t*. The same for /**mak**/, /**map**/ and a new ending: /**maa**/ which is produced by just leaving the mouth open after starting.

Initial sounds. The majority of Thai starting sounds are like those in English, with a few missing and a couple tossed in. However, the romanized phonetics treat some letters differently from what you may be used to. The /**c**/ is similar to a *j*, and /**k**/ is pronounced like a *g* to help it match a pattern. That pattern is given next.

Is there air produced or not? Place your palm in front of your mouth and say *tie* (quite hard and distinctly) and then *die*. You should feel a puff of air for the first word—we show this with an *h* after the letter. So /**thai**/ as in *tie*, /**khai**/ as in *kite* and /**phai**/ as in *pie* all give a puff of air and are called aspirated letters. Those which do not produce as much air (if any) are /**dai**/ as in *die*, /**kai**/ as in *guy* and /**pai**/ as in *by*, but not voiced and with the lips pressed together to start. /**p**/ is one of the two new-sound consonants.

New-sound consonants. Thai has two new sounds: /**p**/ and /**t**/, which appear between /**ph**/ and /**b**/, and between /**th**/ and /**d**/ respectively. To help hear the difference, note that /**b**/ and /**d**/ are "voiced"—you have to voice a sound to say them.

The /**ph**/ and /**th**/ are like the English *p* in *possible* and *t* in *terrific*. They are certainly not pronounced as in *phone* or *thing*! So, we note that Phuket in the south of Thailand is actually pronounced /**phuukèt**/ (*poohget*)!

The phonetic /**p**/ is pronounced by starting with the lips slightly pressed together (as some people show when dissatisfied), then "explode" them open and say /**puu**/ (rhymes with *zoo*), which means a crab.

The /**t**/ is pronounced by starting with the tongue pressed behind the front teeth, then released to say the word. Try /**tii**/ (rhymes with *see*), which means to hit.

Practice, practice, practice these new consonants by saying /**ph**/, /**p**/, /**b**/ over and over to feel the difference on your lips. Do the same for /**th**/, /**t**/ and /**d**/. It helps to give them a vowel like /**ii**/ (as with /**tii**/) /**uu**/ or better /**aw**/, as this is the vowel the Thais give them.

Tones

English has tones, but you may not have noticed them. We use them to extend meaning, but the word itself doesn't change. For example, Mum wants to call James back home after he has run up the street: "/**céh-ehms**/!". James arrives, covered in dust: "/**cêhms**/! Where've you been?". The matter is still about James, but the intonation suggests a different meaning. In Thai, a change in intonation will change the meaning of a word, for example, from close to far, and from being pretty to being bad luck!

Thai has five tones: mid, low, falling, high and rising. After the mid tone (no mark), these are represented by the symbols ` , ^ , ´ and ˇ. Rising and falling tones are the most important. For a rising tone, start low and raise the pitch of your voice. Suppose someone has called you and you respond "*me-ee*" or /*mǐi*/ (a bear) in the romanized phonetics as you question whether they mean you or not. To make a falling tone, start high in pitch and drop it, like throwing a pebble away from you as in "*wow!*" which would be /*wâo*/ (a strung kite) in phonetics. You'll get used to the low, mid and high tones as you go. Ask your Thai friend to show you and, once again, practice, practice.

Some Thai word examples

Short or long vowels. Thai vowels can be either short or long. In romanized phonetic Thai, short vowels are represented by a single letter, long vowels by double letters, for example:

/*lék*/ (to be small), /*lêhk*/ (number)

/*láe*/ (and), /*laeh*/ (to look)

/*khim*/ (Kim), /*khiim*/ (pliers)

/*khong*/ (probably), /*khóhng*/ (to be curved)

/*lóe*/ (to be messy), /*lôehk*/ (to finish up)

/*lúk*/ (to get up), /*lûuk*/ (son, daughter)

/*khûen*/ (to go up), /*khuehn*/ (to give back)

Initial consonants. There are some differences in pronunciation: the *h* showing aspiration; /*c*/ for a *j*; /*k*/ for a *g*; and the new sounds /*p*/ and /*t*/. However, the rest of the consonants are as said in English—any tiny differences are attributable to accent, and we all have an accent of some form or other! There is one tricky one: /*ng*/, which sounds like the *ng* in the middle of *singing*. Look at and study the following examples carefully:

/*khohn*/ (base of a tree; pronounced *cone*), /*kohn*/ (to shave; pronounced *goan*)

/*phâi*/ (cards; pronounced like *pie*, but with a falling tone), /*pai*/ (to go; pronounced by exploding the lips and sounding something like the *py* in *spy*)

/*thaang*/ (a way or path; pronounced *tarng* but without the *r* sounded), /*tàang*/ (to differ; same vowel, but the initial consonant pronounced with the tongue from behind the teeth and the tone going low)

/*ìm*/ (to be full; pronounced like *him* without the *h* and with a low tone)

/*ciin*/ (Chinese; pronounced *jean*, but the *j* is actually more like *tj*)

/*nguu*/ (snake; pronounced *ngoo* to rhyme with *zoo*)

Different tones. Standard Thai tones can be represented in pitch as follows:

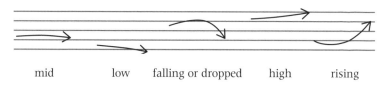

mid   low   falling or dropped   high   rising

Thais understand the five tones as being in this order, and counted 0, 1, 2, 3 and 4. Ask your Thai friend to say /*maa*/ /*màa*/ /*mâa*/ /*máa*/ /*mǎa*/ (มา หม่า ม่า ม้า หมา). The first, fourth and fifth words mean come, horse, dog. There's a popular brand of Thai noodle called /*maa mâa*/. You'll get there with practice!

The following sentence uses words that all have a mid tone:

/*mii*/ /*khon*/ /*thoh*/ /*maa*/ /*wan*/ /*can*/
someone phoned on Monday
มีคนโทร.มาวันจันทร์

These examples have a low tone:

/*dèk*/ /*yàak*/ /*àan*/ /*khào*/ /*bài*/ /*sìi*/
the child wants to read the news at four o'clock
เด็กอยากอ่านข่าวบ่ายสี่

These have a falling tone:

/*mâe*/ /*mâi*/ /*dâi*/ /*wâa*/ /*hâi*/ /*rîip*/
Mum didn't say to hurry
แม่ไม่ได้ว่าให้รีบ

These words have a high tone:

/kháo/ /mák/ /khít/ /cháa/ /tháng/ /cháo/
they usually think slowly all morning
เขามักคิดช้าทั้งเช้า

These words have a rising tone:

/nǔu/ /thǎam/ /mǎw/ /sǎwng/ /sǎam/ /hǒn/
the kid asked the doctor a few times
นูถามหมอสองสามหน

Final consonants. Last of all, there is the matter of final conso-nants. Some Thais say that their language has "no final sou-;" but there *are* final consonants, even though sometimes they're hard to make out. The stops: /p/ /t/ and /k/ may take time to hear. Once you can pronounce them, you'll start to hear them yourself (and vice versa!).

The words below are arranged into groups of final consonants—try to say them the "Thai" way:

/p/: /kòp/ (a frog), /tàwp/ (to answer), /bìip/ (to squeeze),
/sàwp/ (to test)

/t/: /kòt/ (to press), /tàt/ (to cut), /bàat/ (baht), /sǎmphâat/
(to interview)

/k/: /kók/ (a tap), /tòk/ (to fall), /bòehk/ (to withdraw money),
/sák/ (to wash clothes)

no final /kâw/ (well…), /tò/ (table), /bàw/ (cushion), /sà
[náam]/ (swimming pool)

/m/: /kôm/ (bend over), /taam/ (to follow), /bǔm/ (dented),
/sâwm/ (fork)

/n/: /khon/ (person), /thon/ (to put up with), /bun/ (merit,
virtue), /sǎwn/ (to teach)

/ng/: /khong/ (probably), /thíng/ (to throw away), /baang/
(to be thin), /sòng/ (to send)

/o/: /khâo/ (to enter), /thâo/ (to equal), /bao/ (lightweight),
/sǎo/ (young woman)

/i/: /khwai/ (water buffalo), /thǎi/ (to reverse), /bài/ (often),
/sài/ (to put on)

Important Things to Note

The phrases in this book are straightforward once you've familiarized yourself with the romanized phonetics. However, a few basic points concerning language usage and grammar need to be understood.

Male or Female Speaking

In everyday polite Thai speech gender specific words for the first person singular pronouns ("I"/"me") are used. In the case of males this is the word *phǒm* (which also has a separate meaning "hair," or, more specifically, "the hair on the head"). Females when referring to themselves use the word dichán. The word *chán* is sometimes also used as a first person pronoun for both men and women and some examples used in this book employ this term. However, when you first begin to speak Thai it is best to use the gender specific terms *phǒm* and *dichán* mentioned above.

As for the English first person collective pronouns—"we," "us," and "our"—use the Thai word *rao*.

With regard to the second person pronoun—"you"—use the Thai word *khun*, and for the third person pronouns—"he/his," "her/ hers" and "their/theirs" use the word *kháo*.

It should be pointed out that Thai has a far more complex system of personal pronouns than indicated here. Pronouns can be, and are, used in many ways to convey the speaker's attitude towards another person: for example, to show deference, intimacy, or anger. However, it is beyond the scope of this book to go into detail about this particular aspect of Thai language and culture.

Another key area of the Thai language, indeed one of fundamental importance, is the use of gender specific words known as polite particles. These are used at the end of an utterance to indicate politeness, respect and courtesy. When asking or answering a question a male will use the word *khráp*. For example a male being asked his name would say (in Thai of course) "my name is…*khráp*." In the case of females the use of polite particles is slightly more complex. When asking a question a female will say *khá* (that is with a high tone). In answering a question or making a statement a female will use the same polite particle, but with a falling tone, *khâ*.

Here is perhaps the first Thai expression most people learn: the common polite form of greeting for "Hello, Good morning, Good afternoon" etc. (it is not time specific).

For a man: *sawàt dii khráp*

And for a woman: *sawàt dii khâ*

Whenever using examples from this book (some of which don't include polite particles) please remember to use the appropriate gender specific term. Failing to do so makes your question or answer seem brusque or abrupt, not pleasing to the ear. In Thailand it is always better to err on the side of politeness.

Basic grammar

Grammar is basically sentence or language "rules." Knowing a few basic rules will allow you to create and develop your communicative ability in the Thai language. One of the best things about Thai is that it shares the English pattern of "subject-verb-object," where subjects and objects are mainly nouns and pronouns, and the verbs tell what these are doing or what action is being performed. We'll have a look at these separately.

Parts of speech

Nouns. Thai nouns do not have an article ("a" or "the") and there is no plural form (most commonly made in English by adding an "s"). A noun names a person or thing as well as people and things. For example, "a book" is **nǎngsǔeh**, as are "books" and "the books." You might think that this will be confusing, but Thai has its own way of indicating number (of people, objects, etc.), the main one being the use of a noun's *classifier*. Every noun has a classifier that allows us to count it. A simple rule is "noun-number-classifier." Say we are counting books on a bookshelf; now the classifier for books is **lêm** (and the word for "one" is **nùeng**), so one book would be **nǎngsǔeh nùeng lêm**; two books **nǎngsǔeh sǎwng lêm**; ten books **nǎngsǔeh sìp lêm**, and so on.

Pronouns. See the section **Male or Female Speaking** on page 12.

Adjectives. In Thai the adjective comes after the noun it describes, so "a hot day" becomes "day hot" or **wan ráwn**. Adjectives in English are coupled with the verb "to be" to produce a sentence such as "It's hot." In Thai, however, the "to be" is left off. For example, "to be hot" is simply **ráwn**. And a range of different forms such as —"it's hot," "I'm hot," "we're hot"—are all conveyed by the one word: **ráwn**. An added noun or pronoun will make the meaning more precise, but often it isn't necessary.

Verbs. The verb is the most important part of speech in Thai. A sentence can comprise just a single verb (as demonstrated in above in the case of *ráwn*). The Thai verb "to go" is *pai*. "I go," "you go," "he/she goes," "we go" and "they go" are all conveyed by the single, unchanging verb *pai*. But to clearly mark tense (past, present and future) other helping words are generally used, although context is also an indicator of meaning.

For past tense, add *láeo* to the verb: *pai láeo* ("she's gone," "they've gone," etc.); *tham láeo* ("he's done it," "it's [the job] finished already" etc.) where *tham* means "to do" or "to make." Note that *láeo* means something like "already." There are other ways of indicating the past, such as adding a "timeframe" such as *mûea-waan* (yesterday), *hòk mohng* (six o'clock); *aathít thîi láeo* (last week): e.g. *mûea-waan phǒm/dichán pai hòk mohng* ("Yesterday I went at six o'clock").

For the present tense, the verb is often left as is, e.g. *phǒm/ dichán pai thîao* ("I'm going out"), *kháo àan nǎngsǔeh-phim* ("She reads/She's reading the newspaper"). To indicate more precisely that someone is presently doing something (i.e. the continuous tense) the word *kamlang* is used before the verb: *kháo kamlang thaan aahǎan yen* ("He/she is having dinner").

As for the future tense, use the future indicator *cà* before the verb: *phǒm cà pai chiang mài* ("I'm going to Chiang Mai"). Or also add a timeframe to emphasize *when*: *phǒm cà pai chiang mài phrûng níi* ("I'm going to Chiang Mai tomorrow"). Note that the timeframe can either be at the beginning or the end of the sentence: *phrûng níi phǒm cà pai chiang mài* ("Tomorrow I'm going to Chiang Mai")—its position is only one of emphasis to show when or who more clearly (as in English).

Variations

There are variations in many of the examples provided, each is marked with a "/". As with *phǒm/dichán* (male "I"/female "I") and *khráp/khâ*, only one part should be used. The words are clear when whole phrases are given as alternatives as in *nîi làe/thǔeng láeo* ("here we are/we're here"), but with longer phrases the choice is shown as underlined, e.g. *khàp reo khûen/cháa long nòi dâi mái khráp/khá* ("Could you *speed up/ slow down* a little?"), where the variation is between **reo khûen** (*speed up*) and **cháa long** (*slow down*). Note that the variations are separated by a space in the Thai script.

A final tip

Thai has an ever-increasing number of English loanwords, although they are pronounced in a distinctively Thai manner and may not even sound like English. A mobile (or cell) phone, for example, is **moh-bai** in Thai. So, if you don't know the name of something (generally of a modern or contemporary nature), try to "Thai-ify" its English name, e.g. "bill" (at a restaurant) = **bin**; "room service" = **ruum soehwít**; "computer" = **khawm** and **so on**. Many "brand names" should also be pronounced in the Thai way as well, e.g. "Fanta" becomes **faentâa**, and Pepsi **páepsîi**. It's often the Thai-ified English words that catch you out when you speak with a Thai person—they're the ones you don't expect.

1 The Basics

1. The Basics

1.1 Personal details

surname	*naam sakun* นามสกุล
first name	*chûeh tua* ชื่อตัว
initials	*chûeh yâw* ชื่อย่อ
address (street/number)	*thîi yùu (thanŏn/bâan lêhk thîi)* ที่อยู่ (ถนน/บ้านเลขที่)
postal (zip) code/town	*mueang/rahàt praisanii* เมือง/รหัสไปรษณีย์
sex (male/female)	*phêht (chai/yĭng)* เพศ (ชาย/หญิง)
nationality/citizenship	*sănchâat/chúea chât* สัญชาติ/เชื้อชาติ
date of birth	*wan duean pii kòeht* วันเดือนปีเกิด
place of birth	*sathăan thîi kòeht* สถานที่เกิด
occupation	*aachîip* อาชีพ
marital status	*sathâanáphâap sŏmrót* สถานภาพสมร
married, single	*tàeng-ngaan/sòht* แต่งงาน/โสด
widowed	*mâi* ม่าย
(number of) children	*lûuk (camnuan) khon* ลูก (จำนวน) คน

– two children	*lûuk sǎwng khon* ลูกสองคน
passport/identity card/ driving license number	*nangsǔeh dern thaang/bàt pracam tua/lêhk thîi bai khàp khìi* หนังสือเดินทาง/บัตรประจำตัว/ เลขที่ใบขับขี่
place and date of issue	*sathǎan thîi láe wan thîi àwk bàt* สถานที่และวันที่ออกบัตร
signature	*laai sen* ลายเซ็น

1.2 Today or tomorrow?

What day is it today?	*wan níi wan arai* วันนี้วันอะไร
Today's Monday	*wan níi wan can* วันนี้วันจันทร์
– Tuesday	*wan angkhaan* วันอังคาร
– Wednesday	*wan phút* วันพุธ
– Thursday	*wan pharúehàtsabodee* วันพฤหัสบดี
– Friday	*wan sùk* วันศุกร์
– Saturday	*wan sǎo* วันเสาร์
– Sunday	*wan aathít* วันอาทิตย์
in January	*nai duean mókkaraakhom* ในเดือนมกราคม
since February	*tâng tàeh duean kumphaaphan* ตั้งแต่เดือนกุมภาพันธ์

in spring	*nai ruéduu bai mái phlì* ในฤดูใบไม้ผลิ
in summer	*nai rúeduu ráwn* ในฤดูร้อน
in autumn	*nai rúeduu bai mái rûang* ในฤดูใบไม้ร่วง
in winter	*nai rúeduu năo* ในฤดูหนาว
2013	*pee khaw săw săwng phan sìp săam* ปี ค.ศ. สองพันสิบสาม
the twentieth century	*sàttawát thîi yîi sìp* ศตวรรษที่ยี่สิบ
the twenty-first century	*sàttawát thîi yîi sìp èt* ศตวรรษที่ยี่สิบเอ็ด
What's the date today?	*wan níi wan thîi thâorài* วันนี้วันที่เท่าไหร่
Today's the 24th	*wan níi wan thîi yîi sìp sìi* วันนี้วันที่ยี่สิบสี่
Monday 3 November	*wan can thîi săam duean phrúetsacikaayon* วันจันทร์ที่สามเดือนพฤศจิกายน
in the morning	*tawn cháo* ตอนเช้า
in the afternoon	*tawn bài* ตอนบ่าย
in the evening	*tawn yen* ตอนเย็น
at night	*tawn klaang khuehn* ตอนกลางคืน
this morning	*cháo níi* เช้านี้
this afternoon	*bàii níi* บ่ายนี้

this evening	*yen níi* เย็นนี้
tonight	*khuehn níi* คืนนี้
last night	*mûea khuehn níi* เมื่อคืนนี้
this week	*sàpdaa níi* สัปดาห์นี้
next month	*duean nâa* เดือนหน้า
last year	*pii thîi láeo* ปีที่แล้ว
next…	*…nâa* …หน้า
in…days/weeks/months/ years	*nai…wan/sàpdaa/duean/pii* ใน…วัน/สัปดาห์/เดือน/ปี
…weeks ago	*…sàpdaa thîi láeo* …สัปดาห์ที่แล้ว
day off	*wan yùt* วันหยุด

1.3 What time is it?

What time is it?	*kìi mohng láeo* กี่โมงแล้ว
It's nine o'clock	*kâo mohng cháo* เก้าโมงเช้า
– five past ten	*sìp mohng hâa naathii* สิบโมงห้านาที
– a quarter past eleven	*sìp èt mohng sìp hâa naathii* สิบเอ็ดโมงสิบห้านาที
– twenty past twelve	*thîang yîi sìp* เที่ยงยี่สิบ

– half past one	*bài mohng khrûeng*	
	บ่ายโมงครึ่ง	
– twenty-five to three	*bài săwng mohng săam sìp hâa naathii*	
	บ่ายสองโมงสามสิบห้านาที	
– a quarter to four	*bài săam mohng sìi sìp hâa*	
	บ่ายสามโมงสี่สิบห้า	
– ten to five	*bài sìi mohng hâa sìp*	
	บ่ายสี่โมงห้าสิบ	
– It's midday (twelve noon)	*thîang wan*	
	เที่ยงวัน	
It's midnight	*thîang khuehn*	
	เที่ยงคืน	
half an hour	*khrûeng chûamohng*	
	ครึ่งชั่วโมง	
What time?	*kìi mohng*	
	กี่โมง	
What time can I come by?	*chán maa dâi tawn kìi mohng*	
	ฉันมาได้ตอนกี่โมง	
At…	*tawn*	
	ตอน…	
After…	*lăng*	
	หลัง…	
Before…	*kàwn*	
	ก่อน…	
Between…and…(o'clock)	*ra-wàang…kàp…(naalíkaa/mohng)*	
	ระหว่าง…กับ…(นาฬิกา/โมง)	
From…to…	*càak…thŭeng…*	
	จาก…ถึง…	
In…minutes	*nai…naathii*	
	ใน…นาที	
– an hour	*nùeng chûamohng*	
	หนึ่งชั่วโมง	

– ...hours	*...chûamohng*	...ชั่วโมง
a quarter of an hour	*sìp hâa naathii*	สิบห้านาที
three quarters of an hour	*sìi sìp hâa naathii*	สี่สิบห้านาที
too early/late	*reo pai/cháa pai*	เร็วไป/ช้าไป
on time	*trong wehlaa*	ตรงเวลา

1.4 One, two, three...

0	*sǔun*	ศูนย์
1	*nùeng*	หนึ่ง
2	*sǎwng*	สอง
3	*sǎam*	สาม
4	*sìi*	สี่
5	*hâa*	ห้า
6	*hòk*	หก
7	*cèt*	เจ็ด
8	*pàeht*	แปด
9	*kâo*	เก้า
10	*sìp*	สิบ
11	*sìp èt*	สิบเอ็ด
12	*sìp sǎwng*	สิบสอง
13	*sìp sǎam*	สิบสาม
14	*sìp sìi*	สิบสี่
15	*sìp hâa*	สิบห้า
16	*sìp hòk*	สิบหก

17	*sìp cèt*	สิบเจ็ด
18	*sìp pàeht*	สิบแปด
19	*sìp kâo*	สิบเก้า
20	*yîi sìp*	ยี่สิบ
21	*yîi sìp èt*	ยี่สิบเอ็ด
22	*yîi sìp sǎwng*	ยี่สิบสอง
30	*sǎam sìp*	สามสิบ
31	*sǎam sìp èt*	สามสิบเอ็ด
32	*sǎam sìp sǎwng*	สามสิบสอง
40	*sìi sìp*	สี่สิบ
50	*hâa sìp*	ห้าสิบ
60	*hòk sìp*	หกสิบ
70	*cèt sìp*	เจ็ดสิบ
80	*pàeht sìp*	แปดสิบ
90	*kâo sìp*	เก้าสิบ
100	*nùeng rói*	หนึ่งร้อย
101	*(nùeng) rói nùeng, rói èt*	(หนึ่ง) ร้อยหนึ่ง
110	*(nùeng) rói sìp*	(หนึ่ง) ร้อยสิบ
120	*(nùeng) rói yîi sìp*	(หนึ่ง) ร้อยยี่สิบ
200	*sǎwng rói*	สองร้อย
300	*sǎam rói*	สามร้อย
400	*sìi rói*	สี่ร้อย
500	*hâa rói*	ห้าร้อย
600	*hòk rói*	หกร้อย
700	*cèt rói*	เจ็ดร้อย
800	*pàeht rói*	แปดร้อย
900	*kâo rói*	เก้าร้อย

1,000	*nùeng phan*	หนึ่งพัน
1,100	*nùeng phan nùeng rói*	หนึ่งพันหนึ่งร้อย
2,000	*sǎwng phan*	สองพัน
10,000	*nùeng mùehn*	หนึ่งหมื่น
100,000	*nùeng sǎehn*	หนึ่งแสน
1,000,000	*nùeng láan*	หนึ่งล้าน
1st	*thîi nùeng*	ที่หนึ่ง
2nd	*thîi sǎwng*	ที่สอง
3rd	*thîi sǎam*	ที่สาม
4th	*thîi sìi*	ที่สี่
5th	*thîi hâa*	ที่ห้า
6th	*thîi hòk*	ที่หก
7th	*thîi cèt*	ที่เจ็ด
8th	*thîi pàeht*	ที่แปด
9th	*thîi kâo*	ที่เก้า
10th	*thîi sìp*	ที่สิบ
11th	*thîi sìp èt*	ที่สิบเอ็ด
12th	*thîi sìp sǎwng*	ที่สิบสอง
13th	*thîi sìp sǎam*	ที่สิบสาม
14th	*thîi sìp sìi*	ที่สิบสี่
15th	*thîi sìp hâa*	ที่สิบห้า
16th	*thîi sìp hòk*	ที่สิบหก
17th	*thîi sìp cèt*	ที่สิบเจ็ด
18th	*thîi sìp pàeht*	ที่สิบแปด
19th	*thîi sìp kâo*	ที่สิบเก้า
20th	*thîi yîi sìp*	ที่ยี่สิบ
21st	*thîi yîi sìp èt*	ที่ยี่สิบเอ็ด
22nd	*thîi yîi sìp sǎwng*	ที่ยี่สิบสอง

30th	*thîi săam sìp*	ที่สามสิบ
100th	*thîi nùeng rói*	ที่หนึ่งร้อย
1,000th	*thîi nùeng phan*	ที่หนึ่งพัน
once	*nùeng thii, thii nùeng*	หนึ่งที, ทีหนึ่ง
twice	*săwng thii*	สองที
double	*săwng thâo*	สองเท่า
triple	*săam thâo*	สามเท่า
half	*khrûeng*	ครึ่ง
a quarter	*sèht nùeng sùan sìi*	เศษหนึ่งส่วนสี่
a third	*nùeng nai săam*	หนึ่งในสาม
some/a few	*baang/săwng săam*	บาง/สองสาม

2 + 4 = 6   *săwng bùak sìi thâo kàp hòk*
สองบวกสี่ เท่ากับ หก

4 – 2 = 2   *sìi lóp săwng thâo kàp săwng*
สี่ลบสอง เท่ากับ สอง

2 x 4 = 8   *săwng khuun sìi thâo kàp pàeht*
สองคูณสี่ เท่ากับ แปด

4 ÷ 2 = 2   *sìi hăan dûai săwng thâo kàp săwng*
สี่หารด้วยสอง เท่ากับ สอง

even/odd   *lêhk khûu/lêhk khîi*
เลขคู่/เลขคี่

total   *tháng mòt*
ทั้งหมด

6 x 9   *hòk khuun kâo*
หกคูณเก้า

1.5   The weather

| Is the weather going to be good/bad? | *aakàat ca dii khûen/yaé lông* |
| | อากาศจะ ดีขึ้น/แย่ลง |

Is it going to get colder/hotter?	*aakàat man ca yen long/ráwn khûen* อากาศมันจะ เย็นลง/ร้อนขึ้น
What temperature is it going to be?	*unhàphuum ca thâorài* อุณหภูมิจะเท่าไหร่
Is it going to rain?	*fŏn ca tòk mái* ฝนจะตกไหม
Is there going to be a storm?	*ca mii phaayú mái* จะมีพายุไหม
Is it going to flood?	*náam ca thûam mái* น้ำจะท่วมไหม
Is it going to be humid?	*aakàat ca òp âo mái* อากาศจะอบอ้าวไหม
Is it going to be cloudy?	*ca mii mêhk mâak mái* จะมีเมฆมากไหม
Is it going to be foggy?	*màwk ca long mái* หมอกจะลงไหม
Is there going to be a thunderstorm?	*ca mii fŏn fáa khánawng mái* จะมีฝนฟ้าคะนองไหม
The weather's changing	*aakàat kamlang plìan* อากาศกำลังเปลี่ยน
It's going to be cold	*aakàat ca yen* อากาศจะเย็น
What's the weather going to be like today/tomorrow?	*wan níi/phrung níi aakàat ca pen yang-ngai* วันนี้/พรุ่งนี้ อากาศจะเป็นอย่างไร

อากาศเย็นยะเยือก *aakàat yen ya-yûeak* bleak	กี่องศา *kìi ong-săa* degree(s) as in temperature	อากาศดี *aakàat-dii* fine
มืดมัว *mûed-mua* dark or gloomy	เย็นและชื้น *yen láe chúen* cool and damp	ร้อนมาก *ráwn mâak* very hot

อากาศแจ่มใส
aakàat càem-săi
clear

ฝนตกปอยปอย
fŏn-tòk pòe pòe
light rain

ลูกเห็บ
lûuk-hèp
hail

เย็นสบาย
yen sabai
(comfortably) cool

ฝนตกหนัก
fŏn-tòk nàk
a downpour/heavy rain

อบอ้าว
òb-âo
muggy

อากาศไม่จัด
aakàat mâi càt
mild

น้ำค้างแข็ง
náam-kháang khăeng
frost/frosty

มรสุม
morasŭm
monsoon

ลมแรง
lom raeng
strong winds

ฝนตกเป็นบางแห่ง
fŏn-tòk pen baang hàeng
scattered showers

ฝนตกหนัก
fŏn-tòk nàk
heavy rain

พายุเฮอริเคน
phayú hurikhen
hurricane

(ลม) ปานกลาง/แรง/แรงมาก
(lom) paan klaang/raeng/raeng mâak
moderate/strong/very strong wind(s)

ฝนตก
fŏn-tòk
rain

ลมกรรโชก
lom kan-chôok
gusts of wind

มีน้ำค้างแข็งตอนกลางคืน
mii náam-khăeng tawn klaang khuen
overnight frost

พายุ
phayú
storm

วันแดดออก
wan dàet àwk
(a) sunny day

ร้อนอบอ้าว/เปียกชื้น
ráwn òb-âo/pìak chúen
sweltering/muggy

แดดออก
dàet àwk
sunny

คลื่นความร้อน
khlûen khwaam-ráwn
heatwave

ฟ้าใส/เมฆครึ้ม/ฝนจะตก
fáa săi/mêhk khrúem/fŏn cà tòk
clear skies/cloudy or overcast/it will rain

ลม
lom
wind

หมอก/หมอกจัด
màwk/màwk-càt
fog/foggy

อึดอัด
ùet-àt
stifling

 ## Here, there...

See also 5.1 Asking directions

here, over here/there, over there	*thîi nîi, trong nîi/thîi nân, trong nân* ที่นี่, ตรงนี้/ที่นั่น, ตรงนั้น
somewhere/nowhere	*sák hàeng/mâi mii sák hàeng* สักแห่ง/ไม่มีสักแห่ง

everywhere	*thúk hàeng* ทุกแห่ง
far away/nearby	*klai/klâi* ไกล/ใกล้
(on the) right/(on the) left	*thaang khwǎa/thaang sái* ทางขวา/ทางซ้าย
to the right/left of	*yàu khâng khwǎa/khâng sái khǎwng…* อยู่ข้างขวา/ข้างซ้าย ของ…
straight ahead	*trong pai* ตรงไป
via	*phàan* ผ่าน
in/to	*nai/pai yang* ใน/ไปยัง
on	*bon* บน
under	*tâi* ใต้
against	*trong khâam* ตรงข้าม
opposite/facing	*trong khâam/trong khâam kàp* ตรงข้ม/ตรงข้ามกับ
next to	*tìt kàp* ติดกับ
near	*klâi* ใกล้
in front of	*dân nâa* ด้านหน้า
in the center	*trong klaang* ตรงกลาง
forward	*pai khâng nâa* ไปข้างหน้า

down	*long*
	ลง
up	*khûen*
	ขึ้น
inside	*khâng nai*
	ข้างใน
outside	*khâng nâwk*
	ข้างนอก
behind	*khâng lăng*
	ข้างหลัง
at the front	*dân nâa*
	ด้านหน้า
at the back	*thîi khâng lăng*
	ที่ข้างหลัง
in the north	*thaang nŭea*
	ทางเหนือ
to the south	*thaang tâi*
	ทางใต้
from the west	*càak thaang ta-wan tòk*
	จากทางตะวันตก
from the east	*càak thaang ta-wan àwk*
	จากทางตะวันออก
to the…of	*yùu thaang…khăwng…*
	อยู่ทาง…ของ

 1.7 **What does that sign say?**

See 5.2 Traffic signs

ให้เช่า	ไฟฟ้าแรงสูง	น้ำร้อน/น้ำเย็น
hâi châo	*fai-fáa raeng sŭung*	*náam ráwn/náam yen*
for rent/hire	high voltage	hot water/cold water

โรงแรม
rong-raem
hotel

ระวังสุนัขขดุ
rawang sunák du
beware of the dog

(ไม่ใช่) น้ำดื่ม
(mâi chái) náam duem
(not) drinking water

หยุด
yùt
stop

เบรคฉุกเฉิน
brèk chùk-chǒen
emergency brake

สำนักงานบริการข้อมูลนัก
ท่องเที่ยว
*sam nák ngan bôrîkan khôr
moon nák tong teaw*
tourist information bureau

ไม่ใช้แล้ว
mâi chái láew
not in use

ที่แลกเปลี่ยน
thîi lâek-plìan
(a place to) exchange

ปฐมพยาบาล/อุบัติเหตุและ
เหตุฉุกเฉิน(โรงพยาบาล)
*patǒm phayaabaan/ùbatihèt
láe hèt chùk-chǒen (rong
phayaabaan)*
first aid/accident and
emergency (hospital)

ผลัก
phlàk
push

คนเก็บเงิน
khon kèp ngoen
cashier

ดึง
dueng
pull

ห้ามล่าสัตว์/ตกปลา
hâam lâa sàt/tòk plaa
no hunting/fishing

บันไดหนีไฟ/บันไดเลื่อน
ban-dai nǐi fai/ban-dai lûen
fire escape/escalator

ที่ขายตั๋ว
thîi khǎi tǔa
ticket office

ขายหมดแล้ว
khǎi mòt láew
sold out

ทางออก(ฉุกเฉิน)
thaang awk (chùk-chǒen)
(emergency) exit

ตำรวจ
tamrùat
police

ทางเข้า (ฟรี)
thaang khâo (frii)
entrance (free)

สียังไม่แห้ง
sǐi yang mâi hâeng
wet paint

ห้องน้ำ
hâwng-náam
bathroom(s)

ประชาสัมพันธ์
pracha-sǎmphan
information

งดสูบบุหรี่/งดทิ้งขยะ
ngòt sùup burìi/ngòt tíng khayà
no smoking/no littering

ขาย
khǎi
for sale

ตารางเวลา
ta-raang wehlaa
timetable

กรุณาอย่า รบกวน/จับ
karuna yàa róp-kuan/càp
please do not disturb/touch

เต็ม
tem
full

เสีย
sǐa
out of order/broken

อันตราย/อันตรายจากไฟ/
อันตรายต่อชีวิต
*antarai/antarai càak fai/antarai
tòr chiwít*
danger/fire hazard/danger to
life

ไปรษณีย์
praisanii
post office

โรงพยาบาล
rong phayabaan
hospital

ไม่ว่าง
mâi wâang
engaged/busy

คนเดินเท้า
khon durn tháo
pedestrian

อันตราย	จอง	หน่วยดับเพลิง
antarai	*cawng*	*nùai dàp phloeng*
danger/	to reserve/to book	fire department
dangerous		
	ห้องรับรอง	ตำรวจ (เทศบาล)
ทางเข้า	*hông rup rông*	*tàmrûat (thétsabaan)*
thaang khâo	waiting room	(municipal) police
entrance		
	ตำรวจจราจร	ปิด (วันหยุด/ปรับปรุง)
ห้ามเข้า	*tàmrûat ja ra jorn*	*pìt (wan yùt/pràp prung)*
hâam khâo	traffic police	closed (for holiday/
no access/no		refurbishment)
entry		

1.8 Legal holidays

● **The most important legal holidays** in Thailand are the following: (those marked with a † change from year to year; also note if a public holiday falls on either a Saturday or Sunday the following Monday becomes a holiday):

January 1, New Year's Day   *wan pii mài*   วันปีใหม่

†March 5, Maka Puja   *wan maakhá buuchaa*   วันมาฆบูชา
The day 1,250 of the Lord Buddha's disciples gathered to listen to his first sermon

April 6, Chakri Day   *wan jàkrii*   วันจักรี
The founding of the present dynasty in Bangkok in 1782

April 13-15, Songkran festival; Chiang Mai New Year festival
wan sǒngkraan   วันสงกรานต์
Days that are the hottest and driest of the year, celebrated with water throwing

May 5, Coronation Day   *wan chàt mongkhon*   วันฉัตรมงคล
The crowning day of the present king—King Bhumibol Adulyadej—high-ranking government officials pay their respects to the king at the Grand Palace

†May 7, Royal Ploughing Ceremony Day *wan phûeht mongkhon* วันพืชมงคล

An auspicious Hindu-Brahman ceremony held at Sanam Luang (Pramane Ground) that marks the beginning of the rice-planting season

†June 2, Visakha Puja *wan wísǎakhà buuchaa* วันวิสาขบูชา

A very important Buddhist holiday marking the birth, enlightenment and death of Buddha; candle-lit processions occur at Thai temples

†July 31, Asalaha Puja *wan aasǎanhà buuchaa* วันอาสาฬหบูชา

The beginning of the Buddhist lent. Every Thai Buddhist male spends at least three months as a monk. Lent is often the period chosen, as its three months occur over the rainy season when monks are to remain in their temples

†August 1, Buddhist Lent Day *wan khâo phansǎa* วันเข้าพรรษา

When monks enter a "rains retreat", staying in their temples to strictly attend to religious duties

August 12, Mother's Day; the birthday of H.M. Queen Sirikit
wan chalǒehm phrá-chonamá phansǎa sǒmdèt phrá-naang-câo phrá-boromáâatchinii-nâat วันเฉลิมพระชนมพรรษา
สมเด็จพระนางเจ้าฯ พระบรมราชินีนาถ

October 23, Chulalongkorn Day *wan piyá mahǎarâat* วันปิยมหาราช

Celebrates the reign of King Chulalongkorn (r.1873–1910) who passed away on this day in 1910

†October 28, Ork Phansa *wan àwk phansǎa* วันออกพรรษา

Marks the end of the rains retreat and the start of the *kathin* period when people present new saffron robes to the monks

November 26, Loi Krathong *wan lawi krathong* วันปิยมหาราช

A beautiful Thai water festival offering the opportunity to see your cares and woes "float away" in a **krathong** made of leaves, a candle, some coins and flower petals

December 5, the birthday of H.M. the King   *wan chalŏehm phrá-chonamá phansăa phrá-bàat sŏmdèt phrá-câo yùu hŭa*
วันเฉลิมพระชนมพรรษา พระบาทสมเด็จ พระเจ้าอยู่หัว

Much of the celebrations are centred around the Grand Palace and along Ratchadamnoen Avenue in Bangkok

December 10, Constitution Day   *wan rátthàthammánuun*
วันรัฐธรรมนูญ

December 25, Christmas Day   *wan khrís(t)mâat*   วันคริสต์มาส

Not a Thai festival, but many shops in the larger cities recognize the celebration of Christmas for the traveler

December 31, New Year's Eve   *wan sîn pii*   วันสิ้นปี

Celebrated as the end of the year for most Thai matters (the old Thai New Year is celebrated at Songkran)

1.9 Telephone alphabets

Pronouncing the alphabet: Thais use the English names to refer to the letters of the Roman alphabet:

a (eh)	เอ	*eh*	n (en)	เอ็น	*en*
b (bee)	บี	*bii*	o (o)	โอ	*oh*
c (see)	ซี	*sii*	p (pee)	พี	*phii*
d (dee)	ดี	*dii*	q (kew)	คิว	*khiu*
e (ee)	อี	*ii*	r (ah)	อาร์	*aa*
f (eff)	เอฟ	*èf*	s (ess)	เอส	*ès*
g (jee)	จี	*cii*	t (tee)	ที	*thii*
h (hait)	เอช	*èht*	u (yew)	ยู	*yuu*
i (ai)	ไอ	*ai*	v (vee)	วี	*wii*
j (jay)	เจ	*ceh*	w (doubleyew)	ดับเบิลยู	*dàbboenyuu*
k (kay)	เค	*kheh*	x (ex)	เอ็กซ์	*èk*
l (el)	แอล	*aehl*	y (wai)	วาย	*wai*
m (em)	เอ็ม	*em*	z (zet)	เซ็ด	*séd*

2 Meet and Greet

2. Meet and Greet

● **It is usual in Thailand** to "wai" (*wâi*) on meeting someone and when taking one's leave. The "wai" involves putting the hands together in a prayer-like gesture and bringing them up towards the tip of the nose or, in the case of greeting a significant or powerful individual, to the bridge of the nose. You "wai" a superior or an elderly person whom you respect, as well as monks. Thais generally "wai" their colleagues and bosses at work when they first meet them each day and on leaving at the end of the day. If someone "wais" you just a smile, and perhaps a nod of the head, is sufficient. It is perhaps better to avoid "wai-ing" others until you develop a good sense of Thai cultural practice. At that point the "wai" should come to you naturally.

Thais tend not to complain, at least face to face with someone, as westerners often do. If you wish to criticize something, it's often better to say nothing and just take things in your stride.

2.1 Greetings

Hello/Good morning, Khun James (formal)	*sawàt dii khun cehm* สวัสดี คุณเจมส์
Hello/Good morning, Khun Anitra	*sawàt dii khun anítraa* สวัสดี คุณอนิทรา
Hello, Somsri (informal)	*sawàt dii sŏmsĭi* สวัสดีสมศรี
Hi, Peter	*sawàt dii piitêh* สวัสดีปีเตอร์
Good morning, madam	*sawàt dii maadaam* สวัสดีมาดาม
Good afternoon, sir	*sawàt dii thân* สวัสดีท่าน
Good afternoon/evening	*sawàt dii* สวัสดี

Hello/Good morning	*sawàt dii* สวัสดี
How are you?/ How are things?	*sabaai dii loěh/pen yang-ai* สบายดีหรือ/เป็นยังไง
Fine, thank you, and you?	*sabaai dii khàwp khun; láeo khun lâ* สบายดี ขอบคุณ แล้วคุณล่ะ
Very well, and you?	*sabaai dii; láeo khun lâ* สบายดี แล้วคุณล่ะ
In excellent health/ In great shape	*sùkhaphâap dii yîam/khǎeng raehng dii* สุขภาพดีเยี่ยม/แข็งแรงดี
So-so	*rûeai rûeai* เรื่อยๆ
Not very well	*mâi khôi sabai* ไม่ค่อยสบาย
(It's) Not bad/ It's OK	*kôr dee na* ก็ดีนะ
I'm going to leave	*pai lá ná* ไปละนะ
I have to be going, someone's waiting for me	*tâwng pai lá ná; mii khon raw yùu* ต้องไปละนะ มีคนรออยู่
Good-bye	*laa kàwn* ลาก่อน
See you soon	*phóp kan reo reo níi ná* พบกันเร็วๆนี้นะ
See you in a little while	*dǐao phóp kan ná* เดี๋ยวพบกันนะ
Sweet dreams	*fǎn dii ná* ฝันดีนะ
Good night	*raatrii sawàt* ราตรีสวัสดิ์
All the best	*chôhk dii* โชคดี

Have fun	*sanùk ná* สนุกนะ
Good luck	*chôhk dii* โชคดี
Have a nice vacation	*thîao hâi sanùk ná* เที่ยวให้สนุกนะ
Bon voyage/ Have a good trip	*doehn thaang doi plàwt phai ná* เดินทางโดยปลอดภัยนะ
Thank you, the same to you	*khàwp khun; khun dûai* ขอบคุณ คุณด้วย
Say hello to/Give my regards to… (formal)	*sòng khwaam khít thŭeng pai yang…* ส่งความคิดถึงไปยัง…
Say hello to… (informal)	*fàak sawàt dii…* ฝากสวัสดี…

2.2 Asking a question

Who?	*khrai* ใคร
Who's that?/Who is it?/ Who's there?	*nân khrai/khrai ná/khrai yùu thîi nân* นั่นใคร/ใครน่ะ/ใครอยู่ที่นั่น
(Pardon me) What did you say	*arai ná* อะไรนะ
What is there to see?	*mii arai hâi duu* มีอะไรให้ดู
What category of hotel is it?	*rohng raehm kìi dao* โรงแรมกี่ดาว
Where?	*thîi năi ná* ที่ไหนนะ
Where's the bathroom?	*hâwng náam yùu thîi năi* ห้องน้ำอยู่ที่ไหน

Where are you going?	*khun ca pai nǎi* คุณจะไปไหน
Where are you from?	*khun maa càak nǎi* คุณมาจากไหน
What?/How?	*arai ná/yang-ai ná* อะไรนะ/ยังไงนะ
How far is that?	*klai khâeh nǎi* ไกลแค่ไหน
How long does that take?	*naan khâeh nǎi* นานแค่ไหน
How long is the trip?	*dern thaang naan thâorài* เดินทางนานเท่าไหร่
How much?	*thâorài* เท่าไหร่
How much is this?	*nîi thâorài* นี่เท่าไหร่
What time is it?	*kìi mohng láeo* กี่โมงแล้ว
Which one(s)?	*an nǎi* อันไหน
Which glass is mine?	*kâeo nǎi khǎwng chán* แก้วไหนของฉัน
When?	*mûea rài* เมื่อไหร่
When are you leaving?	*khun ca pai mûearài* คุณจะไปเมื่อไหร่
Why?	*tham mai* ทำไม
Could you…?	*chûai…nòi dâi mái* ช่วย…หน่อยได้ไหม
Could you come with me please?	*karunaa maa kàp chán dâi mái* กรุณามากับฉันได้ไหม

Could you help me/ give me a hand please?	*chuâi chán nòi dâi mái/karunaa chûai chán nòi* ช่วยฉันหน่อยได้ไหม/กรุณาช่วยฉันหน่อย
Could you point that out to me/show me please?	*chuâi chíi hâi duu nòi dâi mái/karunaa chíi hâi duu nòi* ช่วยชี้ให้ดูหน่อยได้ไหม/กรุณาชี้ให้ดูหน่อย
Could you reserve/book me some tickets please?	*karunaa sǎmrawng/cawng tǔa hâi nòi dâi mái* กรุณา สำรอง/จอง ตั๋วให้หน่อยได้ไหม
Could you recommend another hotel?	*náe-nam rohng raehm ùehn hâi nòi dâi mái* แนะนำโรงแรมอื่นให้หน่อยได้ไหม
Do you know…?	*khun rúucàk…mái khá/khráp* คุณรู้จัก…ไหมคะ/ครับ
Do you know whether…?	*khun rûu mai waá…* คุณรู้ไหมว่า…
Do you have…?	*khun mii…mái khá/khráp* คุณมี…ไหมคะ/ครับ
Do you have a…for me?	*khun mii…hâi chàn mài* คุณมี…ให้ฉันไหม
Do you have a vegetarian dish please?	*khun mii aahǎan ceh mái* คุณมีอาหารเจไหม
I would like…	*chán yàak…* ฉันอยาก…
I'd like a kilo of apples, please	*chán yàak dâi áeppôen nùeng kiloh* ฉันอยากได้แอปเปิ้ลหนึ่งกิโล
Can/May I?	*dâi mái* …ได้ไหม
Can/May I take this away?	*chán ao nîi pai dâi mái* ฉันเอานี่ไปได้ไหม

Can I smoke here?	*chán sùup burìi thîi nîi dâi mái*
	ฉันสูบบุหรี่ที่นี่ได้ไหม
Could I ask you something?	*khǎw thǎam arai nòi dâi mái*
	ขอถามอะไรหน่อยได้ไหม

2.3 How to reply

Yes, of course	*dâi, nâeh nawn*
	ได้ แน่นอน
No, I'm sorry	*mâi dâi; sǐa cai dûai*
	ไม่ได้ เสียใจด้วย
Yes, what can I do for you?	*ca hâi chán tham arai hâi khun*
	จะให้ฉันทำอะไรให้คุณ
Just a moment, please	*sák khrûu ná*
	สักครู่นะ
No, I don't have time now	*mâi dâi, tawn níi chán mâi mii wehlaa*
	ไม่ได้ ตอนนี้ฉันไม่มีเวลา
No, that's impossible	*pen pai mâi dâi*
	เป็นไปไม่ได้
I think so/I think that's absolutely right	*chán khít wâa thùuk tâwng thîi sùt*
	ฉันคิดว่าถูกต้องที่สุด
I think so too/I agree	*chán wâa yàang nán dûai/chán hěn duâi*
	ฉันว่าอย่างนั้นด้วย/ฉันเห็นด้วย
I hope so too	*chán wǎng wâa yàang nán dûai*
	ฉันหวังว่าอย่างนั้นด้วย
No, not at all/Absolutely not	*mâi loei/mâi nâeh nâeh*
	ไม่เลย/ไม่แน่ๆ
No, no one	*mâi mii khrai*
	ไม่มีใคร
No, nothing	*mâi mii arai*
	ไม่มีอะไร

That's right	*thùuk láeo*
	ถูกแล้ว
Something's wrong	*mii arai phìt pòkàtì*
	มีอะไรผิดปกติ
I agree (don't agree)	*chán hěn dûai (mâi hěn dûai)*
	ฉันเห็นด้วย (ไม่เห็นด้วย)
OK/it's fine	*ok/dii láeo*
	โอเค/ดีแล้ว
OK, all right	*ok/tòk long*
	โอเค/ตกลง
Perhaps/maybe	*baang thii/àat ca*
	บางที/อาจจะ
I don't know	*chán mâi rúu*
	ฉันไม่รู้

2.4 Thank you

Thank you	*khàwp khun*
	ขอบคุณ
That's all right	*mâi pen rai*
	ไม่เป็นไร
Thank you very much/ Many thanks	*khàwp khun mâak/khàwp khun cing cing*
	ขอบคุณมาก/ขอบคุณจริงๆ
Very kind of you	*khun cai dii mâak*
	คุณใจดีมาก
My pleasure	*yin dii ráp chái*
	ยินดีรับใช้
I enjoyed it very much	*chán sanùk mâak*
	ฉันสนุกมาก
Thank you for…	*khàwp khun sǎmràp…*
	ขอบคุณสำหรับ…

| That was so kind of you | *khun mâi khuan tâwng/khun mii nam jai mâk mâk*
คุณไม่ควรต้อง/คุณมีน้ำใจมากมาก |

2.5 I'm sorry

Excuse me/pardon me/ sorry	*khǎw thôht* ขอโทษ
Sorry, I didn't know that...	*khǎw thôht, chán mâi rúu...* ขอโทษ ฉันไม่รู้...
I really do apologize	*chán khǎw thôht jing jing* ฉันขอโทษจริงๆ
I'm sorry	*sǐa cai dûai* เสียใจด้วย
I didn't mean it/It was an accident	*chán mâi dâi tâng cai/man pen ùbatìhèht* ฉันไม่ได้ตั้งใจ/มันเป็นอุบัติเหตุ
That's all right/Don't worry about it	*mâi pen rai/mâi tâwng hùang* ไม่เป็นไร/ไม่ต้องห่วง
Never mind/Forget it	*mâi pen rai/luehm sá thòe* ไม่เป็นไร/ลืมเสียเถอะ
It could happen to anyone	*mun àat kòeht kàp khrai kôr dâi* มันอาจเกิดขึ้นกับใครก็ได้

2.6 What do you think?

Which do you prefer/ like best?	*khun yàak dâi/châwp an nǎi mâak thîi sùt* คุณ อยากได้/ชอบ อันไหนมากที่สุด
What do you think?	*khun khít wâa yang-ngai* คุณคิดว่าอย่างไร
Don't you like dancing?	*khun mâi châwp tên ram lǒeh* คุณไม่ชอบเต้นรำหรือ
I don't mind	*chán mâi rangkìat* ฉันไม่รังเกียจ

Well done!	*kèng mâak* เก่งมาก!
Not bad!	*mâi leo* ไม่เลว!
Great!/Marvelous!	*wísèht* วิเศษ!
We're in luck	*pûck raâw chôk dee jing jing* พวกเราโชคดีจริงจริง
You're lucky	*khun chôhk dii* คุณโชคดี!
I'm (not) very happy with…	*chán (mâi) khâwi phaw cai rûeang…* ฉัน (ไม่) ค่อยพอใจเรื่อง…
I'm glad that…	*chán dii cai thîi* ฉันดีใจที่…
I'm having a great time	*chán kamlang sanùk mâak* ฉันกำลังสนุกมาก
I can't wait till tomorrow/ I'm looking forward to tomorrow	*chán raw thǔeng phrûng níi mâi dâi/ chán jah raw wan phrûng níi* ฉันรอถึงพรุ่งนี้ไม่ได้/ฉันจะรอวันพรุ่งนี้
I hope it works out	*chán wǎng wâa jah dâi phǒn* ฉันหวังว่าจะได้ผล
How awful/terrible!	*yâeh mâak* แย่มาก!
It's frightening/scary/ horrible!	*nâa klua* น่ากลัว
What a pity/shame!	*nâa sǒngsǎan* น่าสงสาร!
How disgusting!	*nâa rangkìat* น่ารังเกียจ!
What nonsense/How silly!	*mâi khâo rûeang* ไม่เข้าเรื่อง!

I don't like it/them	*chán mâi châwp man* ฉันไม่ชอบมัน
I'm bored to death	*chán bùea ja tai* ฉันเบื่อจะตาย
I'm fed up	*chán thon mâi whai leaw* ฉันทนไม่ไหวแล้ว
This is no good	*mâi dii loei* ไม่ดีเลย
This is not what I expected	*nîi mâi châi thîi chán khít wái* นี่ไม่ใช่ที่ฉันคิดไว้

3 Small Talk

3. Small Talk

3.1 Introductions

May I introduce myself?	*chán khǎw náe-nam tua ehng ná* ฉันขอแนะนำตัวเองนะ
My name's…	*chán chûeh…* ฉันชื่อ…
I'm…	*chán…* ฉัน…
What's your name?	*khun chûeh arai* คุณชื่ออะไร
May I introduce…?	*chán khǎw náe-nam…* ฉันขอแนะนำ…
This is my wife/husband	*nîi phanrayaa/sǎamii chán* นี่ ภรรยา/สามี ฉัน
This is my daughter/son	*nîi lûuk sǎo/lûuk chai chán* นี่ ลูกสาว/ลูกชาย ฉัน
This is my mother/father	*nîi khun mâeh/khun phâw chán* นี่ คุณแม่/คุณพ่อ ฉัน
This is my fiancée/fiancé	*nîi khûu mân chán* นี่คู่หมั้นฉัน
This is my friend	*nîi phûean chán* นี่เพื่อนฉัน
How do you do	*yin dii thîi dâi rúucàk* ยินดีที่ได้รู้จัก
Hi, pleased to meet you	*sawàt dii, yin dii thîi dâi phóp khun* สวัสดี ยินดีที่ได้พบคุณ
Where are you from?	*khun pen khon thîi nái* คุณเป็นคนที่ไหน
I'm American	*chán pen khon amehríkan* ฉันเป็นคนอเมริกัน

What city do you live in?	*khun yùu mueang nǎi* คุณอยู่เมืองไหน
In... near...	*nai... klâi...* ใน… ใกล้…
Have you been here long?	*khun maa thîi nîi naan láeo lǒeh* คุณมาที่นี่นานแล้วหรือ
A few days	*sǎwng sǎam wan* สองสามวัน
How long are you staying here?	*khun jah yùu thîi nîi naan thâorài* คุณจะอยู่ที่นี่นานเท่าไหร่
We're (probably) leaving tomorrow/in two weeks	*rao (khong) ca klàp phrûng níi/iik sǎwng aathít* เรา (คง) จะกลับพรุ่งนี้/อีกสองอาทิตย์
Where are you staying?	*khun phák thîi nǎi* คุณพักที่ไหน
I'm staying in a hotel/an apartment	*chán phák thîi rohng raehm/apartment* ฉันพักที่ โรงแรม/อพาร์ตเมนท์
At a campsite	*thîi camp* ที่แคมป์
I'm staying with friends/relatives	*chán phák kàp phûean/yâat* ฉันพักกับ เพื่อน/ญาติ
Are you here on your own?	*khun maa thîi nîi khon diao lǒeh* คุณมาที่นี่คนเดียวหรือ
Are you here with your family?	*khun maa thîi nîi kàp khrâwp khrua lǒeh* คุณมาที่นี่กับครอบครัวหรือ
I'm on my own	*chán maa khon diao* ฉันมาคนเดียว
I'm with my partner/wife/husband	*chán maa kàp fhann/gig/phanráyaa/sǎamii khǎwng chán* ฉันมากับ แฟน/กิ๊ก/ภรรยา/สามี ของฉัน
– with my family	*kàp khrâwp khrua khǎwng chán* กับครอบครัวของฉัน

– with relatives	*kàp yâat* กับญาติ
– with a friend/friends	*kàp phûean/phûean phûean* กับ เพื่อน/เพื่อน ๆ
Are you married?	*khun tàeng-ngaan láeo rúe yang* คุณแต่งงานแล้วหรือยัง
Are you engaged?/Do you have a boyfriend/girlfriend?	*khun mân láeo rúe yang/khun mii faen rúe plào* คุณหมั้นแล้วหรือยัง/ คุณมีแฟนหรือเปล่า
That's none of your business (formal/informal)	*mâi châi thúrá khǎwng khun/thúrá mâi châ* ไม่ใช่ธุระของคุณ/ธุระไม่ใช่
I'm married	*chán tàeng-ngaan láeo* ฉันแต่งงานแล้ว
I'm single	*chán sòht* ฉันโสด
I'm not married	*chán yang mâi tàeng-ngaan* ฉันยังไม่แต่งงาน
I'm separated	*chán yâehk kan* ฉันแยกกัน
I'm divorced	*chán yàa láeo* ฉันหย่าแล้ว
I'm a widow/widower	*chán phen maé mhai/pôh mhai* ฉันเป็น แม่ม้าย/พ่อม้าย
I live alone/with someone	*chán yùu khon diao/kàp khon ùehn* ฉันอยู่ คนเดียว/กับคนอื่น
Do you have any children/grandchildren?	*khun mii lûuk/lǎan mái* คุณมีลูก/หลานไหม
How old are you?	*khun aayú thâorài* คุณอายุเท่าไหร่
How old is she/he?	*thor/kháo aayú thâorai* เธอ/เขา อายุเท่าไหร่

I'm…(years old)	*chán aayú…pii* ฉันอายุ…ปี
She's/he's…(years old)	*kháo aayú…pii* เขาอายุ...ปี
What do you do for a living?	*khun tham ngaan arai* คุณทำงานอะไร
I work in an office	*chán tham ngaan nai office* ฉันทำงานในสำนักงาน
I'm a student	*chán pen nákrian* ฉันเป็นนักเรียน
I'm unemployed	*chán wâang ngaan* ฉันว่างงาน
I'm retired	*chán kasǐan láeo* ฉันเกษียณแล้ว
I'm on a disability pension	*chán ráp ngoen bamnaan khon phíkaan* ฉันรับเงินบำนาญคนพิการ
I'm a housewife	*chán pen mâeh bâan* ฉันเป็นแม่บ้าน
Do you like your job?	*khun châwp ngaan khun mái* คุณชอบงานคุณไหม
Most of the time	*wehlaa sùan yài* เวลาส่วนใหญ่
Mostly I do, but I prefer vacations	*sùan yài chán tham, tàe chán châwp pai thîao mâak kwàa* ส่วนใหญ่ฉันทำแต่ฉันชอบไปเที่ยวมากกว่า

3.2 I beg your pardon?

I don't speak any/ I speak a little…	*chán mâi phûut…/chán phûut…nít nòi* ฉันไม่พูด…ฉันพูด…นิดหน่อย
I'm American	*chán pen khon amehríkan* ฉันเป็นคนอเมริกัน

Do you speak English?	*khun phûut phaasǎa angkrit dâi mái* คุณพูดภาษาอังกฤษได้ไหม
Is there anyone who speaks…?	*mii khrai phûut phaasǎa…bâang mái* มีใครพูดภาษา...บ้างไหม
I beg your pardon/What?	*arai ná* อะไรนะ
I (don't) understand	*chán (mâi) khâojai* ฉัน (ไม่) เข้าใจ
Do you understand me?	*khun khâojai chán mái* คุณเข้าใจฉันไหม
Could you repeat that, please?	*chûay phûut ìik thii dâi mái* ช่วยพูดอีกทีได้ไหม
Could you speak more slowly, please?	*chûay phûut chá cháa dâi mái* ช่วยพูดช้าๆ ได้ไหม
What does that mean?/ that word mean?	*nân/kham nán mǎi khwaam wâa arai* นั่น/คำนั้น หมายความว่าอะไร
It's more or less the same as…	*man khwaam mǎi mǔean kàp…* มันความหมายเหมือนกับ…
Could you write that down for me, please?	*chûay khǐan hâi chán dâi mái* ช่วยเขียนให้ฉันได้ไหม
Could you spell that for me, please?	*chûay sakòt hâi chán dâi mái* ช่วยสะกดให้ฉันได้ไหม

(See 1.9 Telephone alphabet)

Could you point that out in this phrase book, please?	*chûay chíi nai nangsǔeh níi hâi chán dâi mái* ช่วยชี้ในหนังสือนี้ให้ฉันได้ไหม
Just a minute, I'll look it up	*dǐao, chán ca hǎa hâi* เดี๋ยว ฉันจะหาให้
I can't find the word/ the sentence	*chán hǎa kham/prayòhk mâi jhor* ฉันหา คำ/ประโยค ไม่เจอ
How do you say that in…?	*khun phûut yang-ngai nai phaasǎa…* คุณพูดยังไงในภาษา…

How do you pronounce that?	*khun àwk síang yang-ai* คุณออกเสียงยังไง

3.3 Starting/ending a conversation

Could I ask you something?	*khǎw thǎam arai nòi dâi mái* ขอถามอะไรหน่อยได้ไหม
Excuse/Pardon me	*khǎw thôht* ขอโทษ
Could you help me please?	*chuâi chán nòi dâi mái* ช่วยฉันหน่อยได้ไหม
Yes, what's the problem?	*dâi, mii panhǎa arai* ได้ มีปัญหาอะไร
What can I do for you?	*jah hâi chûai arai* จะให้ช่วยอะไร
Sorry, I don't have time now	*sǐa cai, tawn níi chán mâi mii wehlaa* เสียใจ ตอนนี้ฉันไม่มีเวลา
Do you have a light (match)?	*khun mii máikhìit mái* คุณมีไม้ขีดไหม
May I join you?	*chán pai dûai dâi mái* ฉันไปด้วยได้ไหม
Could you take a picture of me/us?	*chûai thài rûup hâi chán/rao nòi dâi mái* ช่วยถ่ายรูปให้ ฉัน/เรา หน่อยได้ไหม
I want to be alone/ Leave me alone	*khǎw chán yùu khon diao/plòi chán* ขอฉันอยู่คนเดียว/ปล่อยฉัน
Get lost	*pai hâi phón* ไปให้พ้น
Go away or I'll scream	*pai klai klai, mâi ngán chán jah ráwng dang dang* ไปไกล ๆ ไม่งั้นฉันจะร้องดังๆ

3.4 A chat about the weather

See also 1.5 The weather

It's so hot/cold today!	*wan níi ráwn/yen jang* วันนี้ร้อน/เย็นจัง
Isn't it a lovely day?	*wan níi aakàat dii mâak ná* วันนี้อากาศดีมากนะ
It's so windy/What a storm!	*lom raehng/phaayú raehng* ลมแรง/พายุแรง
All that rain/fog!	*duu fǒn sí/duu màwk sí* ดูฝนซิ/ดูหมอกซิ
It's so foggy!	*màwk long jad* หมอกลงจัด
Has the weather been like this for long?	*aakàat pen yàang níi naan láeo lǒeh* อากาศเป็นอย่างนี้นานแล้วหรือ
Is it always this hot/cold here?	*thîi nîi ráwn/nǎo yàang níi samǒeh lǒeh* ที่นี่ ร้อน/หนาว อย่างนี้เสมอหรือ
Is it always this dry/humid here?	*thîi nîi aakàat hâehng/òp âo yàang níi samǒeh lǒeh* ที่นี่อากาศ แห้ง/อบอ้าว อย่างนี้เสมอหรือ

3.5 Hobbies

Do you have any hobbies?	*khun mii ngaan adirèhk mái* คุณมีงานอดิเรกไหม
I like knitting/reading/photography	*chán châwp thàk níttìng/àan nangsǔeh/thài rûup* ฉันชอบ ถักนิตติ้ง/อ่านหนังสือ/ถ่ายรูป
I enjoy listening to music	*chán châwp fang phlehng* ฉันชอบฟังเพลง

I like listening to Korean pop on my MP3 player.	*chán châwp fang phleng póp kao-lii nai em-phi săam khăwng chán*
	ฉันชอบฟังเพลงป็อปเกาหลีในเอ็นพี3 ของฉัน
I play the guitar/piano	*chán lên guitar/piano*
	ฉันเล่นกีตาร์/เปียโน
I like the cinema	*chán châwp duu năng*
	ฉันชอบดูหนัง
I like traveling/playing sports/fishing/ going for a walk	*chán châwp thâwng thîao/lên kiilaa/ tòk plaa/pai doehn lên*
	ฉันชอบ ท่องเที่ยว/เล่นกีฬา/ ตกปลา/ไปเดินเล่น

3.6 Invitations

Are you doing anything tonight?	*khuehn níi khun tham arai rúe plào*
	คืนนี้คุณทำอะไรหรือเปล่า
Do you have any plans for today/this afternoon/ tonight? (formal/informal)	*wan níi/bài níi/khuehn níi mii phăehn ca tham arai*
	วันนี้/บ่ายนี้/คืนนี้ มีแผนจะทำอะไร
Would you like to go out with me?	*khun yàak àwk pai thîao kàp chán mái*
	คุณอยากออกไปเที่ยวกับฉันไหม
Would you like to have lunch/dinner with me?	*khun yàak pai thaan aahăan klaang wan/aahăan yen kàp chán mái*
	คุณอยากไปทาน อาหารกลางวัน/ อาหารเย็น กับฉันไหม
Would you like to go dancing with me?	*khun yàak pai tên ram kàp chán mái*
	คุณอยากไปเต้นรำกับฉันไหม
Would you like to come to the beach with me?	*khun yàak pai chai thaleh kàp chán mái*
	คุณอยากไปชายทะเลกับฉันไหม
Would you like to come and see some friends with us?	*khun yàak pai hăa phûean kàp raw mái*
	คุณอยากไปหาเพื่อนกับเราไหม

Would you like to come into town with us?	*khun yàak khâo mueang kàp rao mái* คุณอยากเข้าเมืองกับเราไหม
Shall we dance?	*tên ram mái* เต้นรำไหม
– sit at the bar?	*pai nâng thîi baa mái* ไปนั่งที่บาร์ไหม
– get something to drink?	*pai hǎa arai dùehm mái* ไปหาอะไรดื่มไหม
– go for a walk?	*pai doehn lên mái* ไปเดินเล่นไหม
– go for a drive?	*pai khàp rót lên mái* ไปขับรถเล่นไหม
Yes, all right	*pai tòklong* ไป ตกลง
Good idea	*pen khwaam khít thîi dii* เป็นความคิดที่ดี
No, thank you	*mâi pai khàwp khun* ไม่ไป ขอบคุณ
Maybe later	*dǐao àat jah pai* เดี๋ยวอาจจะไป
I don't feel like it	*chán mâi rúusùek yàak pai* ฉันไม่รู้สึกอยากไป
I don't have time	*chán mâi mii wehlaa* ฉันไม่มีเวลา
I already have a date	*chán mii nát láeo* ฉันมีนัดแล้ว
I'm not very good at dancing/volleyball/swimming	*chán tên ram/lên wawnlehbawn/wâi náam mâi kèng* ฉัน เต้นรำ/เล่นวอลเล่ย์บอล/ ว่ายน้ำ ไม่เก่ง

3.7 Paying a compliment

You look great!	*khun tàeng tua sǔai jang* คุณแต่งตัวสวยจัง
I like your car!	*chán châwp rót khun* ฉันชอบรถคุณ
I like your water ski outfit!	*chán châwp chút sakii náam khǎwng khun* ฉันชอบชุดสกีน้ำของคุณ
You are very nice	*khun pen khon dii mâak* คุณเป็นคนดีมาก
What a good boy/girl!	*dèk dii arai yàang níi!* เด็กดีอะไรอย่างนี้!
You're a good dancer	*khun tên ram kèng mâak* คุณเต้นรำเก่งมาก
You're a very good cook	*khun tham aahǎan kèng mâak* คุณทำอาหารเก่งมาก
You're a good soccer player	*khun lên fútbawn kèng mâak* คุณเล่นฟุตบอลเก่งมาก

3.8 Intimate comments/questions

I like being with you	*chán châwp yùu kàp khun* ฉันชอบอยู่กับคุณ
I've missed you so much	*chán khít thǔeng khun lǔea koehn* ฉันคิดถึงคุณเหลือเกิน
I dreamt about you	*chán fǎn thǔeng khun* ฉันฝันถึงคุณ
I think about you all day	*chán khít thǔeng khun tháng wan* ฉันคิดถึงคุณทั้งวัน
I've been thinking about you all day	*chán khít thǔeng khun talàwt wan* ฉันคิดถึงคุณตลอดวัน

You have such a sweet smile	*khun yím wǎan cang* คุณยิ้มหวานจัง
You have such beautiful eyes	*taa khun sǔai lǔea koehn* ตาคุณสวยเหลือเกิน
I'm very fond of you	*chán châwp khun mâak* ฉันชอบคุณมาก
I love you	*chán rák khun* ฉันรักคุณ
I love you too	*chán rák khun dûai* ฉันรักคุณด้วย
I don't feel as strongly about you	*chán mâi rúusùek arai mâak kàp khun* ฉันไม่รู้สึกอะไรมากกับคุณ
I already have a girlfriend/ boyfriend	*chán mii faehn láeo* ฉันมีแฟนแล้ว
I'm not ready for that	*chán yang mâi phráwm nai rûeang nán* ฉันยังไม่พร้อมในเรื่องนั้น
I don't want to rush into it	*chán yang mâi yàak rîip ráwn* ฉันยังไม่อยากรีบร้อน
Take your hands off me	*ao mueh khun àwk pai* เอามือคุณออกไป
Okay, no problem	*tòklong, mâi mii panhǎa* ตกลง ไม่มีปัญหา
Will you spend the night with me?	*khun ca kháang kàp chán mái khuehn níi* คุณจะค้างกับฉันไหมคืนนี้
I'd like to go to bed with you	*chán yàak ca nawn kàp khun* ฉันอยากจะนอนกับคุณ
Only if we use a condom	*thâa rao chái thǔng yaang, thâo nán* ถ้าเราใช้ถุงยางเท่านั้น
We have to be careful about AIDS	*rao tâwng rawang rôhk èhd* เราต้องระวังโรคเอดส์
That's what they all say	*nân thîi kháo phûut kan* นั่นที่เขาพูดกัน

We shouldn't take any risks	*rao mâi khuan sìang* เราไม่ควรเสี่ยง
Do you have a condom?	*khun mii thǔng yaang mái* คุณมีถุงยางไหม
No? Then the answer's no	*mâi mii lǒeh, thâa ngán mâi dâi* ไม่มีหรือ ถ้างั้นไม่ได้

3.9 Congratulations and condolences

Happy birthday	*sùksǎn wan kòeht* สุขสันต์วันเกิด
Many happy returns	*khǎw hâi mii khwaam sùk mâak mâak* ขอให้มีความสุขมาก ๆ
Please accept my condolences	*khǎw sadaehng khwaam sǐa cai dûai* ขอแสดงความเสียใจด้วย
My deepest sympathy	*chán sǐa cai yàang sùt súeng* ฉันเสียใจอย่างสุดซึ้ง

3.10 Arrangements

When will I see you again?	*chán jah dai phóp khun iik mûea rhai* ฉันจะได้พบคุณอีกเมื่อไหร่
Are you free over the weekend? (informal)	*khun wâang mái, sǎo aathít níi* คุณว่างไหมเสาร์อาทิตย์นี้
What's the plan, then?	*thâa ngán mii phǎehn arai* ถ้างั้นมีแผนอะไร
Where shall we meet?	*rao ca phóp kan thîi nǎi* เราจะพบกันที่ไหน
Will you pick me/us up?	*khun ca maa ráp chán/rao mái* คุณจะมารับฉัน/เราไหม
Shall I pick you up?	*chán pai ráp khun, dee mai* ฉันไปรับคุณดีไหม

| I have to be home by… | *chán tâwng klàp bâan kàwn*
ฉันต้องกลับบ้านก่อน… |
| I don't want to see you anymore | *chán mâi tâwngkaan phóp khun ìik loei*
ฉันไม่ต้องการพบคุณอีกเลย |

3.11 Being the host(ess)

See also 4 Eating out

Can I offer you a drink? (formal/informal)	*khun ca dùehm arai mái/hǐu náam mái* คุณจะดื่มอะไรไหม/หิวน้ำไหม
What would you like to drink?	*khun yàak dùehm arai* คุณอยากดื่มอะไร
Something non-alcoholic, please	*arai thîi mâi mii alcohol* อะไรที่ไม่มีแอลกอฮอล
Would you like a cigarette/cigar?	*khun yàak sùup <u>burìi/cigar</u> mái* คุณอยากสูบ บุหรี่/ซิการ์ ไหม
I don't smoke	*chán mâi sùup* ฉันไม่สูบ

3.12 Saying good-bye

Can I take you home?	*chán pai sòng khun thîi bâan dâi mái* ฉันไปส่งคุณที่บ้านได้ไหม
Can I write to you?	*chán khǐan thǔeng khun dâi mái* ฉันเขียนถึงคุณได้ไหม
Can I call you?	*chán thoh hǎa khun dâi mái* ฉันโทร.หาคุณได้ไหม
Will you write to me?	*khun ca khǐan thǔeng chán mái* คุณจะเขียนถึงฉันไหม
Will you call me?	*khun ca thoh hǎa chán mái* คุณจะโทร.หาฉันไหม
Can I send you an email?/ Can I email you?	*chán sòng ii-mei hǎa khun dâi mái* ฉันส่งอีเมล์หาคุณได้ไหม

Can I have your address/ phone number?	*khǎw thîi yùu/boeh thohrasàp khǎwng khun dâi mái*
	ขอ ที่อยู่/เบอร์โทรศัพท์ ของคุณได้ไหม
Do you have an email address?	*khun mii thîi yùu ii-mei mái*
	คุณมีที่อยู่อีเมล์ไหม
Can I have your email address?	*chán khǎw thîi yùu ii-mei khǎwng khun dâi mái*
	ฉันขอที่อยูอีเมล์ของคุณได้ไหม
Thanks for everything	*khàwp khun sǎmràp thúk sìng thúk yàang*
	ขอบคุณสำหรับทุกสิ่งทุกอย่าง
It was a lot of fun	*sanùk mâak*
	สนุกมาก
Say hello to…	*fàak sawàt dii…*
	ฝากสวัสดี…
All the best/Good luck	*chôhk dii*
	โชคดี
When will you be back?	*khun jah klàp maa ìik mûearài*
	คุณจะกลับมาอีกเมื่อไหร่
I'll be waiting for you	*chán jah raw khun*
	ฉันจะรอคุณ
I'd like to see you again	*chán yàak phóp khun ìik*
	ฉันอยากพบคุณอีก
I hope we meet again soon	*chán wǎng wâa rao ca phóp kan ìik reo reo níi*
	ฉันหวังว่าเราจะพบกันอีกเร็วๆ นี้
Here's our address. If you're ever in the United States…	*nîi thîi yùu khǎwng rao, thâa khun pai america…*
	นี่ที่อยู่ของเรา ถ้าคุณไปอเมริกา…
You'd be more than welcome	*chán yindii tâwn ráp yàang tem thîi*
	ฉันยินดีต้อนรับอย่างเต็มที่

4 Eating Out

4. Eating Out

● **Eating establishments**

Many Thais "snack all day," and the noodle shops (*ráan kǔai tǐao*) and smaller eating places (*ráan aahǎan*) are open much of the day, and often late into the night. Restaurants (*ráan aahǎan*) usually open for lunch and dinner. In Bangkok, as in the west, there are specific restaurants for seafood (*aahǎan thaleh*), steak (*núea wua*), as well as international styles, the main being German (*yoehraman*), Italian (*itaalii*) and French (*farangsèht*). A growing trend for snacking is in the coffee shop serving beautiful cakes (*ráan kaafaeh khǎi khanǒm khéhk*), and also at the donut parlors (*ráan khǎi dohnát*).

Mealtimes

Monks eat only twice in a day (early morning and just before midday), but on the whole, Thais eat three main meals (*sǎam múeh*) a day:

Breakfast (*aahǎan cháo*), is eaten sometime between 5 and 8 am. Many Thais get up very early to go to work, and some give food to the monks on their dawn food round. Breakfast is often a rice porridge (*cóhk*), but can also be a rice dish. Some Thais like the western or farang-style breakfast of fried eggs (*khài dao*), grilled or fried frankfurters (*sâi kràwk thâwt*) and some toast (*khanǒm pang pîng*) with coffee (*kaafaeh*).

Lunch (*aahǎan klaang wan*) is usually eaten at food shops/small restaurants near offices, or for students, in canteens at schools and universities. Some students and workers upcountry take their lunch in a food carrier (*pintoh*) packed with two or three dishes (*kàp khâo*) e.g. stir-fried chicken with bean sprouts (*kài phàt thùa ngâwk*) or stir-fried meat with ginger and vegetables (*núea phàt phrík khǐng*), and some rice (*khâo sǔai*).

Dinner (*aahǎan yen*) is eaten around 6 or 7 pm, and often involves more "formal" Thai food, e.g. a soup, a curry dish or spicy salad, perhaps a fish dish and a range of Thai condiments. Most notable of Thai foods are the hot and spicy sour soup with prawns and mushrooms (*tôm yam kûng*); the various curries: red (*kaehng daehng*), green (*kaehng khǐao*), masuman (*mátsamân*); and Pat Thai (*phàt thai*)—thin rice noodles with tofu, egg, meat and vegetables.

In restaurants

Because food is relatively cheap in Thailand, it's common for Thai families to eat out. The meal will often consist of many and various dishes from which the family or group shares. Thai restaurants range from the smaller inexpensive places serving common dishes, to interesting but sometimes expensive venues serving specialties or having particular gimmicks, e.g. waiters on roller skates or tables set around water. Additional charges may include service charge topped by the ubiquitous Value Added Tax (VAT) (*phasǐi muunlákhâa phôehm*).

4.1 At the restaurant

I'd like to reserve a table for seven o'clock, please	*khǎw cawng tó sǎmràp tawn nùeng thûm khâ/khráp* ขอจองโต๊ะสำหรับตอนหนึ่งทุ่มค่ะ/ครับ
A table for two, please	*tó sǎmràp sǎwng khon khâ/khráp* โต๊ะสำหรับสองคนค่ะ/ครับ
We've (We haven't) reserved	*rao (mâi dâi) jhong* เรา (ไม่ได้) จอง

คุณจองไว้หรือเปล่า *khun jhong wái rǔe-plao*	Do you have a reservation?
ชื่ออะไรคะ/ครับ *chûeh aria khá/khráp*	What name please?

เขตสูบบุหรี่ *khèet sùup burìi*	Smoking
เขตปลอดบุหรี่ *khèet plode burìi*	Non-smoking
ทางนี้ค่ะ/ครับ *thaang níi khâ/khráp*	This way, please
โต๊ะนี้จองแล้ว *tó níi jhong láeo*	This table is reserved
อีกสิบห้านาทีจะมีโต๊ะว่างค่ะ/ครับ *ìik sìp-hâa naa-thi jah mii tó wâang khâ/khráp*	We'll have a table free in fifteen minutes
คอยได้ไหมคะ/ครับ *khoi dâi mái khá/khráp*	Would you mind waiting?

Is the restaurant open yet?	*ráan aahǎan pòeht rúe yang* ร้านอาหารเปิดหรือยัง
What time does the restaurant open?/What time does the restaurant close?	*ráan aahǎan pòeht kìi mohng/ráan aahǎan pìt kìi mohng* ร้านอาหารเปิดกี่โมง/ ร้านอาหารปิดกี่โมง
Can we wait for a table?	*rao raw tó wâang dâi mái* เรารอโต๊ะว่างได้ไหม
Do we have to wait long?	*rao tâwng raw naan mái* เราต้องรอนานไหม
Is this seat taken?	*thîi nîi khon nâng rúe yang* ที่นี่มีคนนั่งหรือยัง
Could we sit here/there?	*rao nâng thîi nîi/thîi nân dâi mái* เรานั่ง ที่นี่/ที่นั่น ได้ไหม
Can we sit by the window?	*rao nâng khâng nâatàang dâi mái* เรานั่งข้างหน้าต่างได้ไหม
Are there any tables outside?	*mii tó khâng nâwk mái* มีโต๊ะข้างนอกไหม

Do you have another chair for us?	*khǎw kâo-ìi ìik tua nueng khâ/khráp*
	ขอเก้าอี้อีกตัวหนึ่งค่ะ/ครับ
Do you have a highchair?	*mii kâo-ìi dèk mái khâ/khráp*
	มีเก้าอี้เด็กไหมคะ/ครับ
Is there a socket for this bottle-warmer?	*mii plák sǎmràp thîi ùn khùat nom mái khâ/khráp*
	มีปลั๊กสำหรับที่อุ่นขวดนมไหมคะ/ครับ
Could you warm up this bottle/jar for me? (in the microwave)	*khun chuâi ùn khùat nom/aahǎan khùat hâi nàwi dâi mái (nai maikhrohwéhf)*
	คุณช่วยอุ่น ขวดนม/อาหารขวด ให้หน่อยได้ไหม (ในไมโครเวฟ)
Not too hot, please	*mâi ráwn càt ná khá/khráp*
	ไม่ร้อนจัดนะคะ/ครับ
Is there somewhere I can change the baby's diaper?	*mii thîi plìan phâa âwm dèk mái khá/khráp*
	มีที่เปลี่ยนผ้าอ้อมเด็กไหมคะ/ครับ

4.2 Ordering

Where are the restrooms?	*hâwng náam yùu thîi nǎi khá/khráp*
	ห้องน้ำอยู่ที่ไหนคะ/ครับ
Waiter/Waitress!	*náwng*
	น้อง
Madam/Sir	*khun khá/khráp*
	คุณ ค่ะ/ครับ
We'd like something to eat/drink	*rao yàak hǎa arai thaan/dùehm nòi*
	เราอยากหาอะไร ทาน/ดื่ม หน่อย
Could I have a quick meal?	*khǎw aahǎan dùan nòi dâi mái*
	ขออาหารด่วนหน่อยได้ไหม
We don't have much time	*rao mâi mii wehlaa mâak nák*
	เราไม่มีเวลามากนัก
We'd like to have a drink first	*rao khǎw khrûeang dùehm kàwn ná*
	เราขอเครื่องดื่มก่อนนะ

Could we see the menu/ wine list, please?

khǎw duu mehnuu/rai-kaan wai nòi dâi mái khá/khráp

ขอดู เมนู/รายการไวน์ หน่อยได้ไหมคะ/ครับ

Do you have a menu in English?

khun mii mehnuu pen phaasǎa angkrît mái

คุณมีเมนูเป็นภาษาอังกฤษไหม

Do you have a dish of the day?

khun mii aahǎan phísèht wan níi mái

คุณมีอาหารพิเศษวันนี้ไหม

We haven't made a choice yet

rao yang mâi dâi lûeak khâ/khráp

เรายังไม่ได้เลือกค่ะ/ครับ

What do you recommend?

khun náe-nam arai bâang

คุณแนะนำอะไรบ้าง

What are the local specialities/your specialities?

mii aahǎan arai phísèht khǎwng thîi níi/ khǎwng khun ehng

มีอาหารอะไรพิเศษ ของที่นี่/ ของคุณเอง

I like strawberries/olives

chán châwp satrawboehrîi/mákàwk

ฉันชอบ สตรอเบอรี่/มะกอก

I don't like meat/fish

chán mâi châwp núea/plaa

ฉันไม่ชอบ เนื้อ/ปลา

What's this?

níi arai

นี่อะไร

Does it have…in it?

sài…rúe plào

ใส่…หรือเปล่า

Is it stuffed with…?

yát sâi dûai…châi mái

ยัดไส้ด้วย…ใช่ไหม

What does it taste like?

rót châat mǔean arai

รสชาติเหมือนอะไร

Is this a hot or a cold dish?

caan níi ráwn rúe yen

จานนี้ร้อนหรือเย็น

Is this sweet?

níi wǎan mái

นี่หวานไหม

Is this hot/spicy?	*nîi phèt mái* นี่เผ็ดไหม
Do you have anything else, by any chance?	*khun mii arai ìik mái* คุณมีอะไรอีกไหม
I'm on a salt-free diet	*chán mâi thaan kluea* ฉันไม่ทานเกลือ
I can't eat pork	*chán thaan mǔu mâi dâi* ฉันทานหมูไม่ได้
I can't have sugar	*chán thaan námtaan mâi dâi* ฉันทานน้ำตาลไม่ได้
I'm on a fat-free diet	*chán mâi thaan khǎi man* ฉันไม่ทานไขมัน
I can't have spicy food	*chán thaan aahǎan phèt mâi dâi* ฉันทานอาหารเผ็ดไม่ได้
We'll have what those people are having	*rao ao bàehp thîi phûak kháo kamlang* *thaan kan* เราเอาแบบที่พวกเขากำลังทานกัน
I'd like…	*chán ao…* ฉันเอา…
We're not having an entrée	*rao mâi ao aahǎan wâang* เราไม่เอาอาหารว่าง

คุณจะทานอะไร *khun cà thaan aria*	What would you like (to eat)?
คุณตัดสินใจหรือยัง *khun tàt-sǐn-jai rǔe-yang*	Have you decided?
คุณอยากดื่มก่อนไหม *khun yàak dùehm kàwn mái*	Would you like a drink first?
คุณอยากดื่มอะไร *khun yàak dùehm aria*	What would you like to drink?

…หมดแล้ว *(beer)…mòt láeo*	We've run out of…(e.g. beer)
ทานให้อร่อยนะคะ/ครับ *than hâi aròi ná khá/khráp*	Enjoy your meal/Bon appétit
ทุกอย่างเรียบร้อยไหม *thúk yang rîap rói mái*	Is everything all right?
ขอเก็บโต๊ะนะคะ/ครับ *khǎw kèp tó ná khá/khráp*	May I clear the table?

Could I have some more bread/rice, please?
khǎw khanǒm pang/khâo ìik dâi mái khá/khráp
ขอ ขนมปัง/ข้าว อีกได้ไหมคะ/ครับ

Could I have another bottle of water/wine/beer, please?
khǎw náam/wai/bia ìik khùat dâi mái khá/khráp
ขอ น้ำ/ไวน์/เบียร์ อีกขวดได้ไหมคะ/ครับ

Could I have another portion of…, please?
khǎw…ìik nòi dâi mái khá/khráp
ขอ…อีกหน่อยได้ไหมคะ/ครับ

Could I have the salt and pepper, please?
khǎw kluea kàp phrík thai nòi dâi mái khá/khráp
ขอเกลือกับพริกไทยหน่อยได้ไหมคะ/ครับ

Could I have a napkin, please?
khǎw kradàat chét mueh nòi dâi mái khá/khráp
ขอกระดาษเช็ดมือหน่อยได้ไหมคะ/ครับ

Could I have a teaspoon, please?
khǎw cháwn chaa nòi dâi mái khá/khráp
ขอช้อนชาหน่อยได้ไหมคะ/ครับ

Could I have an ashtray, please?
khǎw thîi khìa burii nòi dâi mái khá/khráp
ขอที่เขี่ยบุหรี่หน่อยได้ไหมคะ/ครับ

Could I have some matches, please?
khǎw máikhìit nòi dâi mái khá/khráp
ขอไม้ขีดหน่อยได้ไหมคะ/ครับ

Could I have some toothpicks, please?	*khǎw mái cîm fan nòi dâi mái khá/khráp* ขอไม้จิ้มฟันหน่อยได้ไหมคะ/ครับ
Could I have a glass of water, please?	*khǎw náam kâeo nùeng dâi mái khá/khráp* ขอน้ำแก้วหนึ่งได้ไหมคะ/ครับ
Could I have a straw please?	*khǎw làwt dùut nòi dâi mái khá/khráp* ขอหลอดดูดหน่อยได้ไหมคะ/ครับ
Enjoy your meal/Bon appetit!	*thaan aahǎan hâi aràwi ná khá/khráp* ทานอาหารให้อร่อยนะคะ/ครับ
You too!	*khun dûai ná* คุณด้วยนะ
Cheers!	*chai yoh* ไชโย
The next round's on me	*râwp nâa chán líang* รอบหน้าฉันเลี้ยง
Could we have a "doggy bag," please?	*khǎw hǎw klàp bâan dâi mái khá/khráp* ขอห่อกลับบ้านได้ไหมคะ/ครับ

 4.3 **The bill**

See also 8.2 Settling the bill

How much is this dish?	*caan níi thâorài* จานนี้เท่าไหร่
Could I have the bill, please?	*kid thong duey ka/krap* คิดตังด้วยค่ะ/ครับ
All together	*thángmòt* ทั้งหมด
Everyone pays separately/ let's go Dutch	*tàang khon tàang cài/yâehk kan cài* ต่างคนต่างจ่าย/แยกกันจ่าย
Could we have the menu again, please?	*khǎw mehnuu ìik dâi mái khá/khráp* ขอเมนูอีกได้ไหมคะ/ครับ

The…is not on the bill	*mâi dâi yùu nai bin*
	…ไม่ได้อยู่ในบิล…
It's on me today (my treat)	*wan níi dichán/phŏm pen châw múe khá/khráp*
	วันนี้ดิฉัน/ผม เป็นเจ้ามือเองค่ะ/ครับ
Thank you for the meal	*khàwp khun sǎmràp aahǎan múe níi khá/khráp*
	ขอบคุณสำหรับอาหารมื้อนี้ค่ะ/ครับ

4.4 Complaints

Westerners tend to make a complaint or complain in order to improve the food or service, at least for the next person or, perhaps, for their next visit. Thais, on the other hand, rarely complain in this manner. You might see Thai body language expressed when someone is dissatisfied, but they will often accept what is done/given to them without comment. Instead of causing a fuss or showing distaste, Thais are unlikely to revisit a place that has displeased them. The following phrases are for those who feel the need to complain…

It's taking a very long time	*chái wehlaa naan mâak*
	ใช้เวลานานมาก
We've been here an hour already	*rao raw pen chûamohng láeo*
	เรารอเป็นชั่วโมงแล้ว
This must be a mistake	*nîi tâwng mii arai phìt*
	นี่ต้องมีอะไรผิด
This is not what I ordered	*nîi mâi châi thîi sàng*
	นี่ไม่ใช่ที่สั่ง
I ordered…	*chán sàng…*
	ฉันสั่ง…
There's a dish missing	*hǎi pai caan nueng*
	หายไปจานหนึ่ง
This is broken/not clean	*nîi hàk/mâi sa-àat*
	นี่ หัก/ไม่สะอาด

The food's cold	*aahǎan yen chûeht* อาหารเย็นชืด
The food's not fresh	*aahǎan mâi sòt* อาหารไม่สด
The food's too salty/ sweet/spicy	*aahǎan khem pai/wǎan pai/phèt pai* อาหาร เค็มไป/หวานไป/เผ็ดไป
The meat's too rare	*núea dìp pai* เนื้อดิบไป
The meat's overdone	*núea sùk pai* เนื้อสุกไป
The meat's tough	*núea nǐao* เนื้อเหนียว
The meat is off/has gone bad	*núea sǐa/mii klìn* เนื้อ เสีย/มีกลิ่น
Could I have something else instead of this?	*khǎw arai yàang ùehn thîi mâi châi nîi dâi mái* ขออะไรอย่างอื่นที่ไม่ใช่นี่ได้ไหม
The bill/this amount is not right	*bin/jum nuan níi mâi thùuk tâwng* บิล/จำนวน นี้ไม่ถูกต้อง
We didn't have this	*rao mâi mii nîi* เราไม่มีนี่
There's no toilet paper in the restroom	*mâi mii kradàat chamrá nai hâwng náam* ไม่มีกระดาษชำระในห้องน้ำ
Will you call the manager, please?	*chûai rîak phûu jad khan hâi nòi khá/ khráp* ช่วยเรียกผู้จัดการให้หน่อยค่ะ/ครับ

4.5 Paying a compliment

That was a wonderful meal	*aahǎan aròi mâak* อาหารอร่อยมาก
The food was excellent	*aahǎan yod yîam* อาหารยอดเยี่ยม

The...in particular was
delicious

doey chapháw...aròi mâak
โดยเฉพาะ...อร่อยมาก

4.6 The menu

ขนมปัง
khanŏm-pang
bread

ขนมเค้ก
khanŏm khék
cakes

ของหวาน
khăwng wăan
dessert

ซอสพริก
sàwt phrík
chili sauce

แกง
kaeng
curry

ปลา
plaa
fish

เครื่องดื่ม
khrûeng–dùehm
drinks

คอร์สแรก
khaw râek
first course

ไอศครีม
ais-khriim
ice-cream

น้ำปลา
náam plaa
fish sauce

ผลไม้
phŏnlamái
fruit

ข้าว
khâaw
rice

เมนูหลัก
mae nu lâhk
main course

เนื้อ
néua
meat (red meat, not pork)

อาหารเคียง
aahăan khiang
side dishes

สลัด
salàt
salad

ค่าบริการ
khâa borikaan
service charge/cover charge

อาหารพิเศษ
aahăan phisèt
specialities

ซุป
súp
soup

ภาษี/แว็ท
phasĭi
VAT (tax)

ผัก
phàk
vegetables

อาหารว่าง
aahăan wâang
entrée/starter/hors d'oeuvres

4.7 List of dishes and drinks

Soups and entrées

Curry puffs	*karìi páp* กะหรี่ปั๊บ
Chicken in pandanus leaves	*kài hàwi bai toei* ไก่ห่อใบเตย
Chicken satay	*kài saté* ไก่สะเต๊ะ
Pork (and often prawn) toasts	*khanǒm pang nâa mǔu* ขนมปังหน้าหมู
Spicy minced meat	*lâap núea* ลาบเนื้อ
Sweet crisp beef	*núea wǎn* เนื้อหวาน
Fried stuffed crab	*puu cǎa* ปูจ๋า
Green papaya salad	*sôm tam* ส้มตำ
Spicy fish cakes	*thâwt man plaa* ทอดมันปลา
Mildly spicy coconut and galangal soup with chicken	*tôm khàa kài* ต้มข่าไก่
Hot and sour prawn soup	*tôm yam kûng* ต้มยำกุ้ง
Prawn salad with mint and lemon grass	*yam kûng* ยำกุ้ง
Eggplant salad	*yam mákhǔea phǎo* ยำมะเขือเผา
Thai beef salad	*yam núea* ยำเนื้อ

| Squid salad | *yam plaa mùek* |
| | ยำปลาหมึก |

Main meals

Steamed fish curry served in a small banana leaf container	*hàw mòk plaa*
	ห่อหมกปลา
Stir-fried chicken with chilli and basil	*kài phàt bai kapraw*
	ไก่ผัดใบกะเพรา
Stir-fried chicken with ginger	*kài phàt khĭng*
	ไก่ผัดขิง
Stir-fried chicken with cashew nuts	*kài phàt mét mámûang hĭ mmáphaan*
	ไก่ผัดเม็ดมะม่วงหิมพานต์
Thai barbecued (BBQ) chicken	*kài yâang*
	ไก่ย่าง
Corn and prawn soup	*kaehng cùeht khâo phôht àwn*
	แกงจืดข้าวโพดอ่อน
Yellow prawn curry	*kaehng karìi kûng*
	แกงกะหรี่กุ้ง
Chicken green curry	*kaehng khĭao wăan kài*
	แกงเขียวหวานไก่
Pumpkin and coconut soup	*kaehng liang fák thawng*
	แกงเลียงฟักทอง
Musaman beef curry	*kaehng mátsamân núea*
	แกงมัสมั่นเนื้อ
Jungle curry beef	*kaehng pàa núea*
	แกงป่าเนื้อ
Rice with steamed chicken	*khâo man kài*
	ข้าวมันไก่
Rice with red pork	*khâo mŭu daehng*
	ข้าวหมูแดง
Fried rice with prawns	*khâo phàt man kûng*
	ข้าวผัดมันกุ้ง

Pineapple fried rice	*khâo phàt sapparót* ข้าวผัดสับปะรด
Rice soup with prawns	*khâo tôm kûng* ข้าวต้มกุ้ง
Seafood and rice soup	*khâo tôm pó tàehk* ข้าวต้มโป๊ะแตก
Stuffed omelette, generally served with minced pork	*khài yát sâi* ไข่ยัดไส้
Stuffed seafood omelette	*khài yát sâi aahǎan thaleh* ไข่ยัดไส้อาหารทะเล
Fried noodles with gravy-like sauce	*kǔai tǐao râat nâa* ก๋วยเตี๋ยวราดหน้า
Sweet crispy fried noodles	*mìi kràwp* หมี่กรอบ
Crisp pork	*mǔu kràwp* หมูกรอบ
Thai sweet and sour pork	*mǔu phàt prîao wǎan* หมูผัดเปรี้ยวหวาน
Sweet pork	*mǔu wǎan* หมูหวาน
Stir-fried beef with oyster sauce	*núea phàt námman hǎwi* เนื้อผัดน้ำมันหอย
Mild chicken curry with coconut milk	*phanaehng kài* แพนงไก่
Stir-friend Thai green vegetable (*phàk bûng*) with garlic	*phàt phàk bûng* ผัดผักบุ้ง
Stir-fried mixed vegetables	*phàt phàk ruam mít* ผัดผักรวมมิตร
Chili beef	*phàt phèt núea* ผัดเผ็ดเนื้อ
Stir-fried seafood with basil	*phàt phèt thaleh* ผัดเผ็ดทะเล

Stir-fried noodles with soy sauce	*phàt sii-íu* ผัดซีอิ๊ว
Thai fried noodles	*phàt thai* ผัดไทย
Stir-fried bean sprouts	*phàt thùa ngâwk* ผัดถั่วงอก
Baked chicken wings	*pìik kài òp* ปีกไก่อบ
Crispy deep-fried fish with chili	*plaa kràwp râat phrík* ปลากรอบราดพริก
Squid with garlic and black pepper	*plaa mùek krathiam phrík thai* ปลาหมึกกระเทียมพริกไทย
Sweet and sour stir-fried fish	*plaa phàt prîao wǎan* ปลาผัดเปรี้ยวหวาน
Hot seafood soup	*pó tàehk* โป๊ะแตก
Chili crab	*puu phàt phrík* ปูผัดพริก
Beef with oyster sauce	*núea phàt námman hǎwi* เนื้อผัดน้ำมันหอย
Fried corn cakes	*thâwt man khâo phôht* ทอดมันข้าวโพด
Chicken and coconut soup	*tôm khàa kài* ต้มข่าไก่
Spicy tofu salad	*yam tâo hûu* ยำเต้าหู้

Desserts

Mangoes with sticky rice	*khâo nǐao mámûang* ข้าวเหนียวมะม่วง
Sticky rice with Thai custard	*khâo nǐao sǎngkhayaa* ข้าวเหนียวสังขยา

Banana pancakes	*khanŏm klûai* ขนมกล้วย
Coconut and agar agar cake	*khanŏm tàkôh* ขนมตะโก้
Steamed coconut pudding	*khanŏm thûai* ขนมถ้วย
Bananas in coconut cream	*klûai bùat chii* กล้วยบวดชี
Bananas in syrup	*klûai chûeam* กล้วยเชื่อม
Fried bananas	*klûai thâwt* กล้วยทอด
Lychees in custard sauce	*líncìi lawi mêhk* ลิ้นจี่ลอยเมฆ
Thai custard	*săngkhayaa* สังขยา
Thai custard served in a hollowed out piece of pumpkin	*săngkhayaa fák thawng* สังขยาฟักทอง
Baked coconut custard	*săngkhayaa máphráo àwn* สังขยามะพร้าวอ่อน
Coconut custard with jackfruit	*săngkhayaa nâa khanŭn* สังขยาหน้าขนุน
Pomelo in light syrup	*sôm-oh lawi kâeo* ส้มโอลอยแก้ว
Coconut jelly	*wún kathí* วุ้นกะทิ
Coconut ice-cream	*ais(a)khriim kathí* ไอศครีมกะทิ
Custard apple ice-cream	*ais(a)khriim nòi-nàa* ไอศครีมน้อยหน่า

Drinks

Coffee	**kaafaeh** กาแฟ
– strong	**kàeh** แก่
– weak	**mâi kàeh** ไม่แก่
– with cream	**sài khriim** ใส่ครีม
– with sugar	**sài námtaan** ใส่น้ำตาล
Hot black coffee	**kaafaeh dam ráwn** กาแฟดำร้อน
Tea	**náam chaa** น้ำชา
– with milk	**sài nom** ใส่นม
– with sugar	**sài námtaan** ใส่น้ำตาล
Ginger drink	**náam khǐng** น้ำขิง
Longan juice	**náam lamyai** น้ำลำไย
Papaya drink	**náam málákaw** น้ำมะละกอ
Lime juice drink	**náam manao** น้ำมะนาว
Young coconut juice	**náam máphráo àwn** น้ำมะพร้าวอ่อน
Orange juice	**náam sôm khán** น้ำส้มคั้น

Sugarcane juice	*náam âwi* น้ำอ้อย
Iced sweet Thai-style black coffee	*ohlíang* โอเลี้ยง
Hot black coffee	*ohyúa* โอยั้วะ

Nibbles

Curry puffs	*karìi púp* กะหรี่ปั๊ป
French fries/chips	*man thâwt* มันทอด
Potato crisps/chips	*man thâwt kràwp* มันทอดกรอบ
Tapioca with pork filling	*sǎakhuu sâi mǔu* สาคูไส้หมู
Fried tofu/beancurd	*tǎo hûu thâwt* เต้าหู้ทอด

5 Getting Around

5. Getting Around

5.1 Asking directions

Excuse me, could I ask you something?	*khǎw thôht, khǎw thǎam arai nòi dâi mái khá/khráp* ขอโทษ ขอถามอะไรหน่อยได้ไหมคะ/ครับ
I've lost my way	*chán lǒng thaang* ฉันหลงทาง
Is there a...around here?	*thǎeo níi mii...bâang mái* แถวนี้มี...บ้างไหม
Is this the way to...?	*nîi thaang pai...châi mái* นี่ทางไป...ใช่ไหม
Could you tell me how to get to...?	*chûai bàwk thaang pai...nòi dâi mái khá/khráp* ช่วยบอกทางไป...หน่อยได้ไหมคะ/ครับ
What's the quickest way to...?	*pai...thaang nǎi reo thîi sùt* ไป...ทางไหนเร็วที่สุด
How many kilometers is it to...?	*pai...kìi kilo* ไป...กี่กิโล
Could you point it out on the map?	*chûai chíi nai phǎehn thîi hâi nòi dâi mái* ช่วยชี้ในแผนที่ให้หน่อยได้ไหม

ฉันไม่ทราบ ฉันไม่รู้จักทางแถวนี้ *chán mâi sâap/chán mâi rúu-jàk thaang thǎeo níi*	I don't know/I don't know my way around here
คุณกำลังไปผิดทาง *khun kamlang pai phìt thaang*	You're going the wrong way

คุณต้องกลับไปที่…
khun tâwng klàp pai thîi…

You have to go back to…

จากที่นั่นตามป้ายไป
jàak thîi nân taam pâai pai

From there on just follow the signs

พอถึงที่นั่น ถามอีก
phaw thǔeng thîi nân thǎam ìik

When you get there, ask again

ตรงไป
trong pai
Go straight ahead

เลี้ยวซ้าย
líao sái
Turn left

เลี้ยวขวา
líao khwǎa
Turn right

ตามไป
taam pai
Follow

ข้าม
khâam
Cross (a road)

ป้ายชี้ไปที่…
pâi chíi pai thîi
(a) sign pointing to
(a place/estination)

ไฟจราจร
fai daeng
traffic lights

อุโมงค์
u-moong
the tunnel

ป้ายหยุด
pâi yùt
"stop" sign

ตึก
tùek
building

แม่น้ำ
mâe-náam
river

ทางข้าม
thaang khâam
crossing (ie. over
the road/railway
track)

ถนน
thanǒn
road/street

ที่มุมถนน
thîi mum thanǒn
at/on the corner

สะพานลอย
saphaan loi
overpass

สะพาน
saphaan
bridge

สี่แยก/ถนนตัดกัน
sìi yâek
(four-way) intersection/
crossroads

ลูกศร
lûuk sǎwn
an arrow (symbol)

5.2 Traffic signs

ระวัง
rawang
beware/danger

ทางรถในบ้าน
thaang rót nai bâan
driveway

ที่จอดรถจำกัดเวลา
thîi càwt rót cam-kàt wehlaa
parking for a limited period

เปลี่ยนเลน
plìan len
change lanes

อันตราย
antarai
danger(ous)

ถนนปิด
thanǒn pìt
road closed

ทางโค้ง
thaang khóong
curves

ทางออก
thaang àwk
exit

ห้ามโบกรถ
hâam bòok rót
no hitchhiking

รถบรรทุกหนัก
rót banthúk nàk
heavy trucks

ชิดขวา/ซ้าย
chit khwǎa/sái
keep right/left

ห้ามเข้า
hâam khâw
no entry

เขตควบคุม
*khèt khûap-
khum*
control zone

ทางเบี่ยง
thaang bìang
detour

หยุด
yùt
stop

ทางข้ามรถไฟ
thaang khâam rót-fai
rail crossing

ความเร็วสูงสุด
khwaam reo sǔung sùt
maximum speed

ทางม้าลาย
thaang máa-lai
pedestrian crossing

บัตรจอดรถ
bàt càwt rót
parking sticker

ห้ามเลี้ยวขวา/ซ้าย
hâam líao khwǎa/sái
no right/left turn

รถเดินทางเดียว
rót doehn thaang diao
one way

อย่าขวางทาง
yàa khwǎang thaang
do not obstruct

ความสูงที่รถลอดได้
*khwaam sǔung thîi rót
lâwt dâi*
maximum headroom

ระวัง หินตก
rawang hǐn tòk
beware, falling rocks

จอดชั่วคราว
jhod chûa khraaw
temporary parking

ถนนที่ถูกกั้น
thanǒn thîi thùuk kân
road blocked

งานซ่อมถนน
ngaan sâwm thanǒn
road works

มีสิทธิ์ไปก่อนที่สุดถนน
*mii sìt pai kàwn thîi sùt
thanǒn*
right of way at end of road

ช่องทางฉุกเฉิน
châwng thaang chùk-chǒehn
emergency lane

ทางแคบ
thaang khâep
narrow section of road/road
narrows

ไหล่ถนนที่แซงไม่ได้
lài thanǒn thîi saeng mâi dâi
impassable shoulder

ห้ามเข้า/ห้ามคนเดินเท้า
*hâam khâw/hâam khon
doehn tháo*
no entry/no pedestrian
access

ป้ายแสดงสิทธิ์จอดรถ
(ติดกระจกหน้ารถ)
*pâi sadaeng sìt càwt rót (tìt
kracòk nâa rót)*
parking permit (on front
windscreen)

ห้ามผ่าน/ห้ามจอด
hâam phàan/hâam càwt
no thoroughfare/no
parking

อู่ซ่อมรถ/ที่จอดรถมีคนเฝ้า
*ùu sâwm rót/thîi jhod rót mii
khon fâw*
garage (for car/vehicle
repairs)/supervised
parking lot

พื้นผิวขรุขระ/ไม่เรียบ
*phúen-phǐw khrù-khrà/mâi
rîap*
broken/uneven surface

เกาะกลางถนน
kòh klaang thanǒn
traffic island

ปั๊มน้ำมัน
pâm náam-man
service station/ gas station

เปิดไฟหน้า
pòeht fai nâa
turn on the headlights

สี่แยก
sìi yâek
intersection/ crossroads

เขตห้ามจอดรถ (สองข้างถนน)
khèt hâam càwt rót (sǎwng khâang thanǒn)
tow-away area (both sides of the road)

จ่ายค่าผ่านทาง
càai khâa phàan thaang
toll payment

ขับช้าๆ
khàp cháa-cháa
slow down (drive slowly)

ทางที่มีสิทธิ์ไปก่อน
thaang thîi mii sìt pai kàwn
right of way

ฝนหรือน้ำแข็ง…กม
fǒn rǔe náam-khǎeng… kiiloo-mét
rain or ice for (number of)…km

หน่วยช่วยเหลือข้างถนน (บริการรถเสีย)
nùai chûai-lǔe-a khâang thanǒn (borikaan rót sǐa)
road assistance (breakdown service)

ที่จอดรถเสียเงิน/ที่จอดรถสำรองเพื่อ
thîi càwt rót sǐa ngoen/thîi càwt rót sǎmrong phêua
paid car park/reserved parking for

5.3 The car

See the diagram on page 87

● **Particular traffic regulations**

Thais drive on the left as in UK, Ireland, Hong Kong, Singapore, and Australia.

For **car and motorbike**: you'll need your own driving license as well as an international one, issued outside Thailand, valid for the type of vehicle you are going to drive.

Trailer: these are rare in Thailand. It's best to hire a small truck (*rót kabà lék*) and driver (*khon khàp*) to carry large items. For smaller items, a utility (*rót sǎwng thǎeo*) will do.

Emergency equipment is not compulsory by any means, but you'd be wise to take a bulb kit, fire extinguisher and first-aid kit.

Roads upcountry are generally sealed, but you'll need to be wary of ten-wheeled trucks (*rót sìp láw*) that tend to hog the highway.

If your hired car should break down, phone the number displayed on, or near the dashboard, or refer to the car hire company's documentation. Broken down or parked vehicles must be parked on the side, or shoulder, of the road and display a warning sign. Your car's rear lights must be used to provide a warning for other road users after nightfall.

Speed limits: on super highways are up to 110 km/h, on major highways the limit is 100 km/h, reducing to 80 km/h where signposted. The limit is 60 km/h in urban areas.

The gas station

Major international oil companies operate gas stations throughout Thailand. These are open 24 hours on main highways, but if they are far from the major roads, stations open around 5 am and close at about 8 pm. Gas stations rarely have repair shops on their premises, but can perform simple servicing and change tires if required.

จีพีเอส	รถยนต์ไฮบริด	รถยนต์ไฟฟ้า
GPS (cii phii es)	*rót-yon hai-brìd*	*rót-yon fai-fáa*
GPS	hybrid car	electric car

How many kilometers to the next gas station, please?	*ìik kìi kiloh thǔeng pám námman kháng nâa*
	อีกกี่กิโลถึงปั๊มน้ำมันข้างหน้า
I would like…liters of	*chuâi toehm…lít*
	ช่วยเติม…ลิตร
– super	*suupôeh*
	ซูเปอร์
– leaded	*námman sǎan takùa*
	น้ำมันสารตะกั่ว
– unleaded	*námman rái sǎan takùa*
	น้ำมันไร้สารตะกั่ว

The parts of a car
(the diagram shows the numbered parts)

1	battery	แบ็ตเตอรี	*bàettoehrii*
2	rear light	ไฟท้าย	*fai thái*
3	rear-view mirror	กระจกส่องหลัง	*kracòk sàwng lăng*
	backup light	ไฟเสริม	*fai sŏehm*
4	aerial	เสาอากาศ	*săo aakàat*
	car radio	วิทยุติดรถยนต์	*wítthayú rót yon*
5	gas tank	ถังน้ำมัน	*thăng námman*
6	spark plugs	หัวเทียน	*hŭa thian*
	fuel filter/pump	ปั้มน้ำมัน	*pám námman*
7	side mirror	กระจกส่องข้าง	*kracòk sàwng khâang*
8	bumper	กันชน	*kan chon*
	carburettor	คาร์บูเรเตอร์	*khaabuurehtôeh*
	crankcase	ห้องเพลาข้อเหวี่ยง	*hâwng phlao khâw wìang*
	cylinder	ลูกสูบ	*lûuk sùup*
	ignition	ไฟเครื่องยนต์	*fai khrûeang yon*
	warning light	สัญญาณเตือน	*sănyaan tuean*
	generator	เครื่องกำเนิดไฟฟ้า	*khrûeang kamnòeht fai fáa*
	accelerator	คันเร่ง	*khan rêng*
	handbrake	เบรคมือ	*brèhk mueh*
	valve	ลิ้นปิดเปิด	*lín pìt pòeht*
9	muffler	หม้อพักไอเสีย	*mâw phák ai sĭa*
10	trunk	กระโปรงหลัง	*kraprohng lăng*
11	headlight	ไฟหน้า	*fai nâa*
	crank shaft	เพลาข้อเหวี่ยง	*phlao khâw wìang*
12	air filter	หม้อกรองอากาศ	*mâw krawng aakàat*
	fog lamp	ไฟตัดหมอก	*fai tàt màwk*
13	engine block	เครื่องยนต์	*khrûeang yon*
	camshaft	เพลาลูกเบี้ยว	*phlao lûuk bîao*
	oil filter/pump	เครื่องกรอง/เครื่องสูบ น้ำมันหล่อลื่น	*khrûeang krawng/khrûeang sùup námman làwi lûehn*
	dipstick	ก้านวัดระดับน้ำมันหล่อลื่น	*kâan wát radàp námman làw lûehn*
	pedal	แป้น	*pâehn*
14	door	ประตู	*pratuu*
15	radiator	หม้อน้ำ	*moh náam*

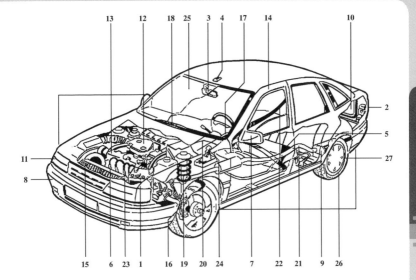

16	brake disc	จานเบรก	*caan brèhk*
	spare wheel	ยางอะไหล่	*yaang alài*
17	indicator	สัญญาณไฟเตือน	*sǎnyaan fai tuean*
18	windshield	กระจกหน้า	*kracòk nâa*
	wiper	ที่ปัดน้ำฝน	*thîi pàt nám fǒn*
19	shock absorbers	โช้คอัป	*chók àb*
	sunroof	หน้าต่างหลังคารถ	*nâatàang lǎngkhaa rót*
	spoiler	ร่องระบายอากาศ	*râwng rabai aakàat*
	starter motor	แกนพวงมาลัย	*kaehn phuang maalai*
20	steering column	พวงมาลัย	*phuang maalai*
21	exhaust pipe	ท่อไอเสีย	*thâw ai sǐa*
22	seat belt	เข็มขัดนิรภัย	*khěm khàt niráphai*
	fan	พัดลม	*phátlom*
23	distributor	จานจ่ายไฟ	*caan cài fai*
	cables	สายเคเบิล	*sǎi khehbôen*
24	gear shift	คันเกียร์	*khan kia*
25	windshield	กระจกหน้ารถ	*kracòk nâa rót*
	water pump	เครื่องสูบน้ำ	*khrûeang sùup náam*
26	wheel	ล้อ	*láw*
27	hubcap	จานปิดดุมล้อรถ	*caan pìt dum láw rót*
	piston	ลูกสูบ	*lûuk sùup*

– diesel	*diesel* ดีเซล
…liter worth of gas	*gas…lít* แก๊ซ…ลิตร
Fill it up, please	*toehm tem khâ/khráp* เติมเต็มค่ะ/ครับ
Could you check…?	*chûai trùat…hâi nòi khâ/khráp* ช่วยตรวจ…ให้หน่อยค่ะ/ครับ
– the oil level	*rádàp námman khrûeang* ระดับน้ำมันเครื่อง
– the tire pressure	*lom láw* ลมล้อ
Could you change the oil, please?	*chûai plàan námman khrûeang hâi nòi khâ/khráp* ช่วยเปลี่ยนน้ำมันเครื่องให้หน่อยค่ะ/ครับ
Could you clean the windshield, please?	*chûai chét kracòk nâa hâi nòi khâ/khráp* ช่วยเช็ดกระจกหน้าให้หน่อยค่ะ/ครับ
Could you wash the car, please?	*chûai láang rót hâi nòi khâ/khráp* ช่วยล้างรถให้หน่อยค่ะ/ครับ

5.5 Breakdowns and repairs

My car has broken down, could you give me a hand?	*rót sĭa, chûai nòi dâi mái khâ/khráp* รถเสีย ช่วยหน่อยได้ไหมคะ/ครับ
I have run out of gas	*námman mòt khâ/khráp* น้ำมันหมดค่ะ/ครับ
I've locked the keys in the car	*chán luehm kuncaeh wái nai rót khâ/khráp* ฉันลืมกุญแจไว้ในรถค่ะ/ครับ

The car/motorbike/ moped won't start	*rót/mawtôehsai/càkrayaan yon satàat mâi tìt* รถ/มอเตอร์ไซค์/จักรยานยนต์ สตาร์ตไม่ติด
Could you contact the breakdown service for me, please?	*chûai tìt tàw bawríkaan rót sĭa hâi nòi dâi mái khâ/khráp* ช่วยติดต่อบริการรถเสียให้หน่อยได้ ไหมคะ/ครับ
Could you call a garage for me, please?	*chûai thoh hăa ùu sâwm rót hâi nòi dâi mái khâ/khráp* ช่วยโทร.หาอู่ซ่อมรถให้หน่อยได้ ไหมคะ/ครับ
Could you give me a lift…?	*chûai pai sòng thîi…hâi nòi dâi mái khâ/khráp* ช่วยไปส่ง…ให้หน่อยได้ไหมคะ/ครับ
– to the nearest garage?	*ùu sâwm rót thîi klâi thîi sùt* อู่ซ่อมรถที่ใกล้ที่สุด
– to the nearest town?	*mueang thîi klâi thîi sùt* เมืองที่ใกล้ที่สุด
Can we hire a moped/ car around here?	*rao châo càkrayaan yon/rót thăeo níi dâi mái* เราเช่า จักรยานยนต์/รถ แถวนี้ได้ไหม
Could you tow me to a garage?	*chûai lâak rót pai thîi ùu nòi dâi mái* ช่วยลากรถไปที่อู่หน่อยได้ไหม
There's probably something wrong with…	*khong ca mii arai phìt pòkkatì kàp…* คงจะมีอะไรผิดปกติกับ...
Can you fix it?	*khun sâwm dâi mái* คุณซ่อมได้ไหม
Could you fix my tire?	*khun sâwm yaang rót hâi nòi dâi mái* คุณซ่อมยางรถให้หน่อยได้ไหม
Could you change this wheel?	*khun plìan láw níi hâi nòi dâi mái* คุณเปลี่ยนล้อนี้ให้หน่อยได้ไหม

Can you fix it so it'll get me to…?	*khun sâwm hâi nòi dâi mái khâ/ khráp, chán ca dâi pai thîi…* คุณซ่อมให้หน่อยได้ไหมคะ/ครับ ฉันจะได้ไปที่…
Which garage can help me?	*ùu nǎi sâwm dâi khâ/khráp* อู่ไหนซ่อมได้คะ/ครับ
When will my car/bicycle be ready?	*rót/cakrayaan khǎwng phǒm/dichán ca sèt mûearài* รถ/จักรยาน ของผมจะเสร็จเมื่อไหร่
Have you finished?	*khun tham sèt láeo lǒeh* คุณทำเสร็จแล้วหรือ
Can I wait for it here?	*chán raw thîi nîi dâi mái* ฉันรอที่นี่ได้ไหม
How much will it cost?	*thángmòt thâorài* ทั้งหมดเท่าไหร่
Could you itemize the bill?	*chûai câehng rai lá-ìat khǎwng bin nòi dâi mái* ช่วยแจ้งรายละเอียดของบิลหน่อยได้ไหม
Could you give me a receipt for insurance purposes?	*khǎw bai sèt pai hâi prakan nòi dâi mái khâ/khráp* ขอใบเสร็จไปให้ประกันหน่อยได้ไหมคะ/ครับ

5.6 Bicycles/motorbikes

See the diagram on page 93

● **Bikes** can be hired in most Thai towns. Don't expect much consideration for bikes on the roads, however. Motorcycles may be tuned to be slightly noisy and to emit a certain amount of exhaust. Be aware that there are new pollution laws, and associated crackdowns by Thai police are common. There are no special speed limits for motorcycles; the same limits as cars apply, but you have to wear a crash helmet. Two (and sometimes more) can ride the same bike along with considerable baggage/goods in some cases, although such behavior is not recommended for the tourist!

ผมไม่มีอะไหล่รถ/จักรยานของคุณ *phǒm mâi mii alài rót/càkrayaan khǎwng khun*	I don't have parts for your car/bicycle
ผมต้องสั่งอะไหล่มาจากที่อื่น *phǒm tâwng sàng alài maa càak thîi èun*	I have to get the parts from somewhere else
ผมต้องสั่งอะไหล่มา *phǒm tâwng sàng alài maa*	I have to order the parts
จะใช้เวลาครึ่งวัน *jà chai wehlaa khrûeng wan*	That'll take half a day
จะใช้เวลาหนึ่งวัน *jà chai wehlaa nùeng wan*	That'll take a day
จะใช้เวลาสองสามวัน *jà chai wehlaa sǎwng sǎam wan*	That'll take a few days
จะใช้เวลาหนึ่งอาทิตย์ *jà chai wehlaa nùeng aathít*	That'll take a week
รถคุณพังจนไม่คุ้มที่จะซ่อม *rót khun phang jhon mâi khúm thîi cà sâwm*	Your car is a write-off
ซ่อมไม่ได้ *sâwm mâi dâi*	It can't be repaired
รถ/มอเตอร์ไซค์/จักรยานยนต์/ จักรยานจะเสร็จตอน...โมง *rót/mo-toer-sai/jakkrayanyone jah sèt tawn...moong*	The car/motorbike/bicycle will be ready at ...o'clock

5.7   Renting a vehicle

| I'd like to rent a… | *chán yàak châo…*
ฉันอยากเช่า... |

The parts of a bicycle
(the diagram shows the numbered parts)

1	rear light	ไฟหลัง	*fai lăng*
2	rear wheel	ล้อหลัง	*láw lăng*
3	(luggage) carrier	ที่ใส่สัมภาระ	*thîi sài sămphaará*
4	fork	ตะเกียบล้อ	*takìap láw*
5	bell	กระดิ่ง	*kradìng*
	inner tube	ยางใน	*yaang nai*
	tire	ยาง	*yaang*
6	peddle crank	คันถีบ	*khan thìip*
7	gear change	ที่เปลี่ยนเกียร์	*thîi plìan kia*
	wire	ขี่ลวด	*sîi lûat*
	generator	จานจ่ายไฟ	*caan càai fai*
	bicycle trailer	ที่ซ้อนท้าย	*thîi sâwn thái*
	frame	โครง	*khrohng*
8	wheel guard	กระบังล้อ	*krabang láw*
9	chain	โซ่	*sôh*
	chain guard	กระบังโซ่	*krabang sôh*
	speedometer	มาตราวัดความเร็ว	*mâatraa wát khwaam reo*
	child's seat	อานนั่งสำหรับเด็ก	*aan năng sămràp dèk*
10	headlight	ไฟหน้า	*fai nâa*
	bulb	หลอดไฟ	*láwt fai*
11	pedal	คันถีบ	*khan thìip*
12	pump	กระบอกสูบลม	*krabàwk sùup lom*
13	reflector	แผ่นสะท้อนแสง	*phàen satháwn săehng*
14	brake shoe	ส่วนห้ามล้อที่บีบกับล้อ	*sùan hâam láw thîi bìip kàp láw*
15	brake cable	สายเบรค	*săi brèhk*
16	anti-theft device	เครื่องมือกันขโมย	*khrûeang mueh kan khamoi*
17	carrier straps	สายผูกสัมภาระ	*săi phùuk sămphaará*
	tachometer	เครื่องวัดความเร็ว	*khrûeang wát khwaam reo*
18	spoke	ซี่ลวดล้อ	*sîi lûat láw*
19	mudguard	บังโคลนล้อหลัง	*bang khlohn láw lăng*
20	handlebar	คันบังคับเลี้ยว	*khan bangkháp líao*
21	chain wheel	เฟืองล้อขับ	*fueang láw khàp*
	toe clip	ที่รัดเท้า	*thîi rát tháo*
22	crank axle	แกนข้อเหวี่ยง	*kaehn khâw wìang*
	drum brake	ระบบเบรกแบบดรัม	*rabo-p brèhk bàehp dram*

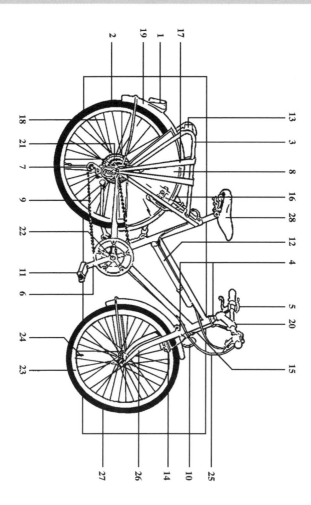

23	rim	ขอบล้อ	*khàwp láw*
24	valve	ลิ้นปิดเปิด	*lín pìt po-eht*
25	gear cable	สายเกียร์	*săi kia*
26	fork	โครง	*khrohng*
27	front wheel	ล้อหน้า	*láw nâa*
28	seat	อานนั่ง	*aan nâng*

Do I need a (special) license for that?

chán tâwng mii bai anúyâat (phísèht) rúe plào

ฉันต้องมีใบอนุญาต(พิเศษ) หรือเปล่า

I'd like to rent the...for...

chán yàak châo...naan...

ฉันอยากเช่า...นาน...

a day

nùeng wan

...หนึ่งวัน...

two days

sǎwng wan

...สองวัน...

How much is that per day/week?

wan lá/aathít lá thâorài

วันละ/อาทิตย์ละ เท่าไหร่

How much is the deposit?

khâa mátcam thâorài

ค่ามัดจำเท่าไร

Could I have a receipt for the deposit?

khǎw bai sèt khâa mátcam dûai dâi mái

ขอใบเสร็จค่ามัดจำด้วยได้ไหม

How much is the surcharge per kilometer?

khâa pràp kilohmét lá thâorài

ค่าปรับกิโลเมตรละเท่าไหร่

Does that include petrol?

ruam námman dûai rúe plào

รวมน้ำมันด้วยหรือเปล่า

Does that include insurance?

ruam prakan dûai rúe plào

รวมประกันด้วยหรือเปล่า

What time can I pick the...up?

maa ráp...dâi mûearài

มารับ...ได้เมื่อไหร่

When does the...have to be back?

tâwng sòng...khuehn mûearài

ต้องส่ง...คืนเมื่อไหร่

What sort of fuel does it take?

chái námman arai

ใช้น้ำมันอะไร

6 Arrival and Departure

6. Arrival and Departure

6.1 General

● **Bus tickets** are purchased on buses, whether private or public routes, from either the driver or the conductor who shouts out *pâi* or *pai* to the driver, depending upon whether the bus is to stop or to go. Thai train tickets must be purchased from stations. Be sure to state single or return, and try to travel first or second class.

Buses, taxis and tuktuks (*túk túk*) (three-wheeled motorized taxis) are the preferred mode of travel around town, with bicycles, mopeds or motorcycles available for hire in the provinces. Many major sois (lanes) in Bangkok have motorcycles ready to take pillion passengers into the smaller sois for 15 to 40 baht (depending on the journey). If you'd prefer to travel on the river, you can hire a long-tailed boat (*ruea hǎang yao*) for a fast ride, or take a ferry boat for a cheap and easy way to cross the Chaopraya river (*mâehnáam câo phráyaa*).

In Bangkok, skytrain tickets are available from ticket vending machines at stations en route. Tickets must be purchased for the particular zone to zone travel, but can be bought for several trips, and on a weekly or monthly basis as well.

Announcements

รถไฟไป…จะเสียเวลา(ราว)…นาที *rót-fai pai…cà sǐa wehlaa (raw)…naathii*	The train to…has been delayed by (about)…minutes
รถไฟไป…กำลังเข้าชานชาลาที่… *rót-fai pai…kamlang khâo chaan-chaalaa thîi…*	The train to…is now arriving at platform…
รถไฟจาก…กำลังเข้าชานชาลาที่… *rót-fai càak…kamlang khâo chaan-chaalaa thîi…*	The train from…is now arriving at platform…

รถไฟไป...จะออกจากชานชาลาที่...
rót-fai pai…cà àwk càak
chaan-chaalaa thîi…

The train to…will leave from platform…

วันนี้รถไฟไป...จะออกจากชานชาลาที่...
wan-níi rót-fai pai…cà àwk càak
chaan-chaalaa thîi…

Today the train to…will leave from platform…

สถานีต่อไปคือ...
sathǎan-ii tàw pai khueh…

The next station is…

Where does this train/ skytrain go to?	*rót fai/rót fai lawi fáa níi pai nǎi* รถไฟ/รถไฟลอยฟ้า นี้ไปไหน
Does this boat go to…?	*ruea lam níi pai…rúe plào* เรือลำนี้ไป...หรือเปล่า
Can I take this bus to…?	*chán khûen rót meh khan níi pai…dâi mái* ฉันขึ้นรถเมล์คันนี้ไป...ได้ไหม
Does this train stop at…?	*rót fai níi càwt thîi…rúe plào* รถไฟนี้จอดที่...หรือเปล่า
Does this bus stop at…?	*rót meh khan níi càwt thîi…rúe plào* รถเมล์คันนี้จอดที่...หรือเปล่า
Is this seat taken/free/ reserved?	*thîi níi mii khon nâng/wâang/cawng wái rúe plào* ที่นี้มีคน นั่ง/ว่าง/จองไว้ หรือเปล่า
I've reserved…	*chán jhong…* ฉันจอง...
Could you tell me where I have to get off for... ?	*chûai bàwk dûai ná khá/khráp wâa pai…tâwng long thîi nǎi* ช่วยบอกด้วยนะคะ/ ครับว่าไป...ต้องลงที่ไหน
Could you let me know when we get to…?	*thǔeng…láeo chûai bàwk dûai ná khá/khráp* ถึง...แล้วช่วยบอกด้วยนะคะ/ครับ
Could you stop at the next stop, please?	*chûai jhod pâi nâa dûai ná khá/khráp* ช่วยจอดป้ายหน้าด้วยนะคะ/ครับ

Where are we?	*rao thŭeng năi láeo*
	เราถึงไหนแล้ว
Do I have to get off here?	*chán tâwng long thîi nîi châi mái*
	ฉันต้องลงที่นี่ใช่ไหม
Have we already passed…?	*rao phàan…láeo rúe yang*
	เราผ่าน...แล้วหรือยัง
How long have I been asleep?	*chán làp pai naan thâorài*
	ฉันหลับไปนานเท่าไหร่
How long does the train stop here?	*rót fai jhod thîi nîi naan thâorài*
	รถไฟจอดที่นี่นานเท่าไหร่
Can I come back on the same ticket?	*chán chái tŭa kào klàp maa dâi mái*
	ฉันใช้ตั๋วเก่ากลับมาได้ไหม
Can I change on this ticket?	*chán chái tŭa níi plìan rót dài mái*
	ฉันใช้ตั๋วนี้เปลี่ยนรถได้ไหม
How long is this ticket valid for?	*tŭa níi chái dâi naan thâorài*
	ตั๋วนี้ใช้ได้นานเท่าไหร่
How much is the extra fare for the high speed train?	*rót fai dùan tâwng sĭa khâa doisăan phôehm ìik thâorài*
	รถไฟด่วนต้องเสียค่าโดยสารเพิ่มอีกเท่าไหร่

6.2 Customs

● **In Thailand,** it is advisable to carry some form of identification such as your passport with you. Thailand is famous for producing false IDs, so a passport is more acceptable. You'll need it when changing money.

Border documents: valid passport. No visa is required if staying for 30 days or less. A straightforward way to "stay longer" in Thailand is to leave the Thai kingdom, and re-enter it. You go to the border, e.g. Hat Yai on the Thai-Malaysian or Nong Khai on the Thai-Lao border, and have your passport stamped "out"; then you re-enter with it stamped "in," and can stay for up to another 30 days. Longer periods (up to six months) require a visa that can be stamped with a limited number of entries into Thailand.

Such visas must be obtained from the Thai embassy or consulate in your city before leaving. Charges apply.

Import and export specifications

Foreign currency: there are no restrictions on the import of currency into Thailand (amounts over US$20,000 must be declared). While cash is handy, travelers' cheques are recommended for safety and security. The Customs Hall has red (*châwng sĭi daehng*) and green (*châwng sĭi khĭao*) channels for "goods to declare" and "nothing to declare" respectively. Thai Customs can be difficult if you do not act responsibly, and fines of four times assessed value are charged when restricted goods are found. Thai Customs allow the import without duty on:

– Alcohol: 1 liter of spirits, liquor or wine
– Tobacco: 200 cigarettes or 250 grams of cigars or tobacco

You must be aged 18 or over to import alcohol and tobacco. The above restrictions apply to all alcohol and tobacco purchased in duty-free shops. Personal items of up to 10,000 baht in total value are not likely to attract duty.

On leaving the kingdom there are limits on the export of Thai currency. The amount of 50,000 baht or more in Thai currency must be reported on departure. For those travelling to the Lao PDR, Myanmar, Cambodia, Malaysia and Vietnam are permitted to take out Thai currency not exceeding 500,000 baht.

พาสปอร์ต (หนังสือเดินทาง) ค่ะ/ครับ *khăw passport (năngsŭeh doehn-thaang)* *khâ/khráp*	Your passport, please
ขอใบขับขี่ค่ะ/ครับ *khăw bai-khàp-khìi khâ/khráp*	Your driving license, please
ขอวีซ่าค่ะ/ครับ *khăw duu wii-sâa khâ/khráp*	May I see your visa, please
คุณจะไปไหน *khun cà pai năi*	Where are you going?

คุณคิดจะอยู่นานเท่าไหร่ *khun khít jàh yùu naan thâo-rai*	How long are you planning to stay?
คุณมีอะไรจะแจ้งไหม *khun mii arai cà câeng mái*	Do you have anything to declare?
เปิดนี่หน่อยค่ะ/ครับ *pòet níi nòi khâ/khráp*	Open this, please

My children are entered on this passport	*lûuk lûuk chái nǎngsǔeh doehn thaang níi* ลูกๆ ใช้หนังสือเดินทางนี้
I'm traveling through	*chán doehn thaang phàan* ฉันเดินทางผ่าน
I'm going on vacation to…	*…chán pai thâwng thîao thîi…* ฉันไปท่องเที่ยวที่…
I'm on a business trip	*chán pai tham thurákìt* ฉันไปทำธุรกิจ
I don't know how long I'll be staying	*chán mâi sâap ca yùu naan thâorài* ฉันไม่ทราบจะอยู่นานเท่าไหร่
I'll be staying here for a weekend	*chán ca yùu thîi níi sák sào aathít nueng* ฉันจะอยู่สักเสาร์อาทิตย์หนึ่ง
I'll be staying here for a few days	*chán ca yùu thîi níi sák sǎwng sǎam wan* ฉันจะอยู่สักสองสามวัน
I'll be staying here a week	*chán ca yùu thîi níi sák aathít nueng* ฉันจะอยู่ที่นี่สักอาทิตย์หนึ่ง
I'll be staying here for two weeks	*chán ca yùu thîi níi sák sǎwng aathít* ฉันจะอยู่ที่นี่สักสองอาทิตย์
I've got nothing to declare	*chán mâi mii arai ja jhang* ฉันไม่มีอะไรจะแจ้ง
I have…	*…chán mii…* ฉันมี…
– a carton of cigarettes	*burìi nùeng khlong* บุหรี่หนึ่งกล่อง

– a bottle of...	*...nùeng khùat* ...หนึ่งขวด...
– some souvenirs	*khǎwng thîi ralúek* ของที่ระลึก
These are personal items	*nîi khǎwng chái sùan tua* นี่ของใช้ส่วนตัว
These are not new	*nîi mâi mài* นี่ไม่ใหม่
Here's the receipt	*nîi bai sèt* นี่ใบเสร็จ
This is for private use	*nîi sǎmràp chái sùan tua* นี่สำหรับใช้ส่วนตัว
How much import duty do I have to pay?	*chán tâwng sǐa phaasǐi khǎa khâo* *thâorài* ฉันต้องเสียภาษีขาเข้าเท่าไหร่
May I go now?	*chán pai dâi rúe yang* ฉันไปได้หรือยัง

6.3 Luggage

Porter!	*náwng* น้อง
Could you take this luggage to...?	*...chûai khǒn krapǎo nîi pai thîi...* ช่วยขนกระเป๋านี้ไปที่...ได้ไหม
How much do I owe you?	*tâwng cài thâorài* ต้องจ่ายเท่าไหร่
Where can I find a cart?	*ao rót khěn dâi thîi nǎi* เอารถเข็นได้ที่ไหน
Could you store this luggage for me?	*khun chûai kèp krapǎo níi hâi nàwi dâi* *mái* คุณช่วยเก็บกระเป๋านี้ให้หน่อยได้ไหม
Where are the luggage lockers?	*láwkkôeh kèp krapǎo yùu thîi nǎi* ล็อคเกอร์เก็บกระเป๋าอยู่ที่ไหน

I can't get the locker open	*chán pòeht láwkkôeh mâi dâi* ฉันเปิดล็อคเกอร์ไม่ได้
How much is it per item per day?	*chín lá thâorài tàw wan* ชิ้นละเท่าไหร่ต่อวัน
My suitcase is damaged	*krapǎo doehn thaang khǎwng chán chamrút* กระเป๋าเดินทางของฉันชำรุด
There's one item/bag/ suitcase missing	*mii khǎwng/krapǎo/krapǎo doehn thaang hǎi an nueng* มี ของ/กระเป๋า/กระเป๋าเดินทาง หายอันหนึ่ง
This is not mybag/ suitcase	*nîi mâi châi krapǎo/krapǎo doehn thaang khǎwng chán* นี่ไม่ใช่ กระเป๋า/กระเป๋าเดินทาง ของฉัน

6.4 Questions to passengers

Ticket types

ตั๋วชั้นหนึ่งหรือชั้นสอง *tǔa chán nùeng rǔe chán sǎwng*	First or second class?
เที่ยวเดียวหรือไปกลับ *thîao diao rǔe pai klàp*	Single or return?
สูบบุหรี่หรือไม่สูบบุหรี่ *sùup burìi rǔe mâi sùup burìi*	Smoking or nonsmoking?
นั่งใกล้หน้าต่างไหม *nâng klâi nâa-tàang mái*	Window seat?
ข้างหน้าหรือข้างหลัง *khâang-nâa rǔe khâang-lǎng*	Front or back (of the train)?
ที่นั่งหรือตู้นอน *thîi-nâng rǔe tûu-nawn*	Seat or berth/cabin?

ชั้นบน/กลางหรือล่าง
chán-bon/klaang rǔe lâang

Top, middle or bottom?

ชั้นประหยัดหรือชั้นหนึ่ง
chán prayàt rǔe chán nùeng

Economy or First Class?

เดี่ยวหรือคู่
dìao rǔe khûu

Single or double?

เดินทางกี่คน
doehn-thaang kìi khon

How many people are traveling?

Destination

คุณจะเดินทางไปไหน
khun jàh doehn-thaang pai nǎi

Where are you traveling?

คุณจะไปเมื่อไหร่
khun jàh pai mûea-rai

When are you leaving?

...ออกตอน...
...àwk tawn...

(Your train/bus)...leaves at...

คุณต้องเปลี่ยนที่...
khun tâwng plìan thîi...

You have to change at...

คุณต้องลงที่...
khun tâwng long thîi...

You have to get off at...

คุณต้องไปทาง
khun tâwng pai thaang...

You have to go via...

ออกเดินทางวันที่...
àwk doehn-thaang wan-thîi...

The outward journey is on (day/date)...

เดินทางกลับวันที่...
doehn-thaang klàp wan-thîi...

The return journey is on (day/date)...

ท่านต้องขึ้นเครื่องก่อน...
นาฬิกา
*khun tâwng khûen khrûeng
kàwn...nalikaa*

You have to be on board (the plane)
by...(time)

Inside the vehicle

ขอดูตั๋วค่ะ/ครับ *khǎw tǔa khâ/khráp*	Tickets, please
ขอดูตั๋วจองค่ะ/ครับ *khǎw tǔa cawng khâ/khráp*	Your reservation, please
ขอดูพาสปอร์ต (หนังสือเดินทาง) ค่ะ/ครับ *khǎw duu passport (nǎngsǔeh doehn-thaang) khâ/khráp*	Your passport, please
คุณนั่งผิดที่ *khun nâng phìt thîi*	You're in the wrong seat
คุณทำผิดแล้ว คุณอยู่ผิด… *khun tham phìt láeo/khun yùu phìt*	You have made a mistake/ You are in the wrong…
ที่นี้จองแล้ว *thîi níi cawng láeo*	This seat is reserved
คุณต้องจ่ายเพิ่ม *khun tâwng jaai phôem*	You'll have to pay extra
…มาช้า…นาที *…maa cháa…naathii*	The (train/bus)…has been delayed by…minutes

6.5 Tickets

Where can I…?	*chán cà…dâi thîi nǎi* ฉันจะ…ได้ที่ไหน
– buy a ticket?	*súeh tǔa* ซื้อตั๋ว
– reserve a seat?	*jhong thîi nâng* จองที่นั่ง
– reserve a flight?	*jhong thîao bin* จองเที่ยวบิน

Could I have…for…, please?	*khǎw súeh…pai…khá/khráp* ขอซื้อ…ไป…ค่ะ/ครับ
– A single to…please	*thîao diao pai…nùeng bai khá/khráp* เที่ยวเดียวไป…หนึ่งใบค่ะ/ครับ
– A return ticket, please	*tǔa pai klàp nùeng bai khá/khráp* ตั๋วไปกลับหนึ่งใบค่ะ/ครับ
first class	*chán nùeng* ชั้นหนึ่ง
second class	*chán sǎwng* ชั้นสอง
economy class	*chán prayàt* ชั้นประหยัด
I'd like to reserve a seat/berth/cabin	*chán yàak cawng <u>thîi nâng</u>/<u>thîi nawn</u>/<u>tûu nawn</u>* ฉันอยากจอง ที่นั่ง/ที่นอน/ตู้นอน
I'd like to reserve a top/middle/bottom berth in the sleeping car	*chán yàak cawng thîi nawn <u>chán bon</u>/<u>chán klaang</u>/<u>chán lâang</u> nai rót nawn* ฉันอยากจองที่นอน ชั้นบน/ชั้นกลาง/ชั้นล่าง ในรถนอน
smoking/nonsmoking	*sùup burìi/mâi sùup burìi* สูบบุหรี่/ไม่สูบบุหรี่
by the window	*khâang nâatàang* ข้างหน้าต่าง
single/double	*dìao/khûu* เดี่ยว/คู่
at the front/back	*khâng nâa/khâng lǎng* ข้างหน้า/ข้างหลัง
There are…of us	*rao mii…khon* เรามี…คน
We have a car	*rao mii rót khan nùeng* เรามีรถคันหนึ่ง
We have a trailer	*rao mii rót phûang khan nùeng* เรามีรถพ่วงคันหนึ่ง

We have…bicycles	*rao mii càkrayaan…khan* เรามีจักรยาน…คัน
Do you have a…?	*mii…mái khá/khráp* มี…ไหมคะ/ครับ
– travel card for 10 trips?	*tǔa doehn thaang sǎmràp sìp thîao* ตั๋วเดินทางสำหรับสิบเที่ยว
– weekly travel card?	*tǔa doehn thaang sǎmràp nùeng sàpdaa* ตั๋วเดินทางสำหรับหนึ่งสัปดาห์
– monthly season ticket?	*tǔa duean* ตั๋วเดือน
Where's…?	*…yùu thîi nǎi* …อยู่ที่ไหน
Where's the information desk?	*tó khâw muun nák thiao thawng yùu thîi nǎi* โต๊ะข้อมูลนักท่องเที่ยวอยู่ที่ไหน

6.6 Information

Where can I find a schedule?	*duu taaraang wehlaa dâi thîi nǎi khá/khráp* ดูตารางเวลาได้ที่ไหนคะ/ครับ
Where's the…desk?	*tó…yùu thîi nǎi* โต๊ะ…อยู่ที่ไหน
Do you have a city map with the bus/skytrain routes on it?	*mii phaehn thîi nai mueang thîi bàwk sǎi rót meh/rót BTS dûai mái khá/khráp* มีแผนที่ในเมืองที่บอกสาย รถเมล์/รถไฟลอยฟ้า ด้วยไหมคะ/ครับ
Do you have a schedule?	*mii taaraang wehlaa mái khá/khráp* มีตารางเวลาไหมคะ/ครับ
Will I get my money back?	*chán ca dâi ngoen khuehn mái* ฉันจะได้เงินคืนไหม

I'd like to confirm/cancel/ change my reservation for/trip to…	*chán yàak yeun yan/yók lôehk/plìan tǔa sǎmrawng pai/kaan doehn thaang pai…* ฉันอยาก ยืนยัน/ยกเลิก/เปลี่ยนตั๋ว สำรองไป/การเดินทางไป…
I'd like to go to…	*chán yàak pai…* ฉันอยากไป…
What is the quickest way get there?	*thaang nǎi ca pai thǔeng thîi nân reo to thîisùt* ทางไหนจะไปถึงที่นั่นเร็วที่สุด
How much is a single/ return to…?	*tǔa thîao diao/pai klàp pai…thâorài* ตั๋ว เที่ยวเดียว/ไปกลับ ไป…เท่าไหร่
Do I have to pay extra?	*chán tâwng jhai phôehm mái* ฉันต้องจ่ายเพิ่มไหม
Can I break my journey with this ticket?	*tǔa níi chái wáe klaang thaang dâi mái* ตั๋วนี้ใช้แวะกลางทางได้ไหม
How much luggage am I allowed?	*chán ao krapǎo pai dâi thâorài* ฉันเอากระเป๋าไปได้เท่าไหร่
Is this a direct train?	*rót fai níi pai trong rúe plào* รถไฟนี้ไปตรงหรือเปล่า
Do I have to change?	*tâwng pai plìan ìik rúe plào* ต้องไปเปลี่ยนอีกหรือเปล่า
Where?	*thîi nǎi* ที่ไหน
Does the plane stop anywhere?	*khrûeang níi long thîi nǎi ìik mái* เครื่องนี้ลงที่ไหนอีกไหม
Will there be any stopovers?	*mii phák kháang khuehn thîi nǎi mái* มีพักค้างคืนที่ไหนไหม
Does the boat stop at any ports on the way?	*ruea níi càwt thâa ùehn taam thaang ìik mái* เรือนี้จอดท่าอื่นตามทางอีกไหม
Does the train/bus stop at…?	*rót fai/rót meh càwt thîi…mái* รถไฟ/รถเมล์ จอดที่…ไหม

Where do I get off?	*chán tâwng long thîi nǎi* ฉันต้องลงที่ไหน
Is there a connection to…?	*mii arai tàw pai…mái* มีอะไรต่อไป…ไหม
How long do I have to wait?	*chán tâwng raw naan thâorài* ฉันต้องรอนานเท่าไหร่
When does…leave?	*…àwk kìi mohng* …ออกกี่โมง
What time does the first/ next/last…leave?	*…thîao râehk/tàw pai/sùt thái àwk kìi mohng khá/khráp* …เที่ยวแรก/ต่อไป/สุดท้าย ออกกี่โมงคะ/ครับ
How long does…take?	*chái wehlaa thâorài* …ใช้เวลาเท่าไหร่
What time does…arrive in…?	*…maa thǔeng…kìi mohng* …มาถึง…กี่โมง
Where does the…to… leave from?	*…pai…àwk càak nǎi* …ไป…ออกจากไหน
Is this the train/bus (from)…to…?	*nîi rót fai/rót meh (càak)…pai…châi mái* นี่ รถไฟ/รถเมล์ (จาก)…ไป…ใช้ไหม

6.7 Airplanes

● **On arrival** at a Thai airport (*thâa aakàatsayaan*), you will find the following signs:

เช็คอิน *chék in* check-in	โรงแรมสนามบิน *rohng-raehm sanǎam-bin* airport hotel	การจองตั๋วผ่านเครือ ข่ายการสื่อสาร *kaan cawng tǔa phàan khruea-khàai kaan sùeh-sǎan* eBooking/eReservation
ต่างประเทศ *tàang prathêht* international	บัตรผ่านขึ้นเครื่องบิน *bàt phàan khûen khrûeng-bin* boarding pass	

ภายในประเทศ
phai nai prathêht
domestic (flight)

ขาเข้า
khǎa khâw
arrivals

ขาออก
khǎa àwk
departures

ศุลกากร
sula-kaa-kawn
Customs

รับกระเป๋าเดินทาง
thîi ráp krapǎo doehn thaang
baggage claim

เครื่องตรวจสแกน
khrûeng trùat sa-kaen
scanner

เครื่องกระตุ้นกล้ามเนื้อหัวใจ
khrûeng-kra-tûn klâam-núea hǔa-jai
pacemaker

ห้องนั่งเล่นอินเตอร์เนต
hâwng nâng-lên internet
Internet lounge

เครื่องมือตรวจคลื่นแม่เหล็ก
khrûeng mueh trùat khlûen mâe-lèk
metal detector

หน่วยรักษาความปลอดภัยสนามบิน
nùai raksǎa khwaam plàwt-phai sanǎam-bin
airport security

 Trains

● **In addition** to flying or taking an air-conditioned coach/bus for longer journeys you may wish to travel by train. When you purchase a ticket state whether you want a one-way or return fare. The lines are built north to Chiang Mai via Phitsanulok; north-east to Nong Khai (and Laos); west to Kanchanaburi and Nam Tok; east to Aranyaprathet (and Cambodia); and south to Hat Yai (then on to Malaysia and Singapore if you like the Orient Express!) The sprinter service, e.g. to Chiang Mai, is quite comfortable, but other trains can be an experience to say the least—third class carriages are just "open," and some passengers ride wherever there's a handhold. Many Thais prefer air-conditioned coach travel to go upcountry but, like train travel, watch your belongings!

6.9 **Taxis**

● **There are plenty** of taxis in Bangkok, as well as in major towns. In Bangkok metered taxi fares are quite reasonable. There are taxi queues at both airports in Bangkok, Suwannaphum and Don Muang. They are also to be found at major train and bus stations. Otherwise hail a taxi from the roadside. Use the meter for every trip, unless you bargain on a day's hire to see the sights (expect over 2000 baht, but less upcountry). There is a surcharge for taxis using expressways as there are entry tolls to the often above ground structures. The cab might have to leave one expressway to go up onto another, costing an additional toll—to save time, believe me! Tolls vary from 20 to 100 baht each time.

ให้เช่า	ไม่ว่าง	ป้ายจอดแท็กซี่
hâi châw	*mâi wâang*	*pâi jhod tháeksîi*
for hire	occupied	taxi stand

Taxi!	*taxi* แท็กซี่
Could you get me a taxi, please?	*chûai rîak taxi hâi nòi dâi mái khá/ khráp* ช่วยเรียกแท็กซี่ให้หน่อยได้ไหมคะ/ ครับ
Where can I find a taxi around here?	*thǎeo níi hǎa taxi dâi thîi nǎi khá/khráp* แถวนี้หาแท็กซี่ได้ที่ไหนคะ/ครับ
Could you take me to…, please?	*chûai pai sòng thîi…ná khá/khráp* ช่วยไปส่งที่…นะคะ/ครับ
Could you take me to this address, please	*pai taam thîi yùu níi ná khá/khráp* ไปตามที่อยู่นี้นะคะ/ครับ
– to the…hotel, please	*pai rohng raehm…ná khá/khráp* ไปโรงแรม…นะคะ/ครับ
– to the town/city center, please	*pai jai klaang mueang/krung ná khá/ khráp* ไป ใจกลางเมือง/กรุง นะคะ/ครับ
– to the station, please	*pai sathǎanii ná khá/khráp* ไปสถานีนะคะ/ครับ
– to the airport, please	*pai sanǎam bin ná khá/khráp* ไปสนามบินนะคะ/ครับ
How much is the trip to…?	*pai…thâorài* ไป…เท่าไหร่

How far is it to…?	*pai…klai thâorài*
	ไป…ไกลเท่าไหร่
Could you turn on the meter, please?	*pòeht mítôeh dûai ná khá/khráp*
	เปิดมิเตอร์ด้วยนะคะ/ครับ
I'm in a hurry	*chán rîip*
	ฉันรีบ
Could you speed up/slow down a little?	*khàp <u>reo</u>/<u>cháa long</u> nòi dâi mái khá/khráp*
	ขับ เร็ว/ช้าลง หน่อยได้ไหมคะ/ครับ
Could you take a different route?	*pai thaang ùehn dâi mái khá/khráp*
	ไปทางอื่นได้ไหมคะ/ครับ
I'd like to get out here, please.	*khăw long thîi níi khá/khráp*
	ขอลงที่นี่ค่ะ/ครับ
Go…	*pai*
	ไป…
You have to go left/right/straight on here	*tâwng líao sái/líao khwǎa/trong pai thîi níi*
	ต้อง เลี้ยวซ้าย/เลี้ยวขวา/ตรงไป ที่นี่
Go straight ahead	*trong pai*
	ตรงไป
Turn left	*líao sái*
	เลี้ยวซ้าย
Turn right	*líao khwǎa*
	เลี้ยวขวา
This is it/We're here	*níi làe/thǔeng láeo*
	นี่แหละ/ถึงแล้ว
Could you wait a minute for me, please?	*raw sák khrûu dâi mái khá/khráp*
	รอสักครู่ได้ไหมคะ/ครับ

7 A Place to Stay

7. A Place to Stay

7.1 General

● **There is a great variety** of overnight accommodation in Thailand. Prices vary from the inexpensive backpacker-style to the very expensive, but luxurious Oriental Hotel.

In Bangkok there are guest houses charging a few hundred baht a night to hotels that charge up to several thousand baht. If staying in a guesthouse, there's no necessity to make reservations, but the better places will require it. For hotels, there generally are vacancies, but if there's not one in your price range, an expensive upgrade may be called for. It's much better to make a hotel booking as part of a package, even if you may not use the associated tour(s), as turning up at a three- to four-star hotel counter to ask for a room can be expensive. One- or two-star hotels allow you to make arrangements more easily and, of course, more cheaply, but inexpensive rooms often mean less security.

Upcountry resorts and towns usually have both hotel-style and bungalow/guesthouse-style accommodation. Camping is not yet popular in the lowlands, but is becoming more accepted when mountain trekking. Try to seek permission from the landowner before you camp—your guide should help. The greatest problem a backpacker faces is being robbed of small but precious possessions. Speaking some Thai is a strong advantage, especially if you need to report a loss or an offense to the local police.

My name is…	*phŏm/dichán chûeh…* ผม/ดิฉันชื่อ…
I've made a reservation by email	*phŏm/dichán jhong wái thaang email láeo* ผม/ดิฉันจองไว้ทางอีเมล์แล้ว
How much is it per night/week/month?	*khuehn/aathít/duean lá thâorài* คืน/อาทิตย์/เดือน ละเท่าไหร่
We'll be staying at least…nights/weeks	*rao ca phák yàang nòi…khuehn/aathít* เราจะพักอย่างน้อย…คืน/อาทิตย์

คุณจะพักนานเท่าไหร่ *khun cà phàk naan thâo-rai*	How long will you be staying?
ช่วยกรอกฟอร์มนี้นะคะ/ครับ *chûai kràwk fawm níi ná khá/khráp*	Fill out this form, please
ขอดูพาสปอรัต (หนังสือเดินทาง) หน่อย *khǎw duu passport (nǎngsǔeh doehn-thaang) nòi*	Could I see your passport?
คุณต้องวางมัดจำ *khun tâwng waang mát-cam*	I'll need a deposit
คุณต้องจ่ายล่วงหน้า *khun tâwng jàai lûang nâa*	You'll have to pay in advance

We don't know yet	*rao yang mâi sâap* เรายังไม่ทราบ
Do you allow pets (cats/dogs)?	*mii sàt líang (maeo/sunák) dâi mái khá/khráp* มีสัตว์เลี้ยง(แมว/สุนัข)ได้ไหมคะ/ครับ
What time does the gate/door open/close?	*pratuu/pratuu yài pòeht/pìt kìi mohng* ประตู/ประตูใหญ่ เปิด/ปิด กี่โมง
Could you get me a taxi, please?	*rîak tháeksîi hâi nòi dâi mái khá/khráp* เรียกแท็กซี่ให้หน่อยได้ไหมคะ/ครับ
Is there any mail for me?	*mii jod mái thǔeng phǒm/dichán mái khá/khráp* มีจดหมายถึงผม/ดิฉันไหมคะ/ครับ

7.2 Hotels/apartments/holiday rentals

Do you have a single/ double room available?	*mii hâwng dìao/khûu wâang rúe plào* มี ห้องเดี่ยว/คู่ว่าง หรือเปล่า
per person/per room	*tàw khon/tàw hâwng* ต่อคน/ต่อห้อง

Does that include breakfast/lunch/dinner?
ruam aahăan cháo/aahăan klaang wan/aahăan yen rúe plào
รวม อาหารเช้า/อาหารกลางวัน/อาหารเย็น หรือเปล่า

Could we have two adjoining rooms?
rao khăw hâwng tìt kan dâi mái
เราขอห้องติดกันได้ไหม

with/without toilet/bath/shower
mii/hâwng náam/thîi àap náam
มี/ห้องน้ำ/ที่อาบน้ำ

facing the street
tìt thanŏn
ติดถนน

at the back
yùu khâng lăng
อยู่ข้างหลัง

with/without sea view
mii/mâi mii wiu thaleh
มี/ไม่มี วิวทะเล

มีห้องน้ำกับห้องอาบน้ำในตัวไหม
mii hông nâm kup hông arb nam nai taui mai?
There is a toilet and shower on the same floor/in the room

ทางนี้ค่ะ/ครับ
thaang níi khâ/khráp
This way, please

ห้องคุณอยู่ชั้น...เบอร์...
hâwng khun yùu chán...ber...
Your room is on the...floor, number...

Is there...in the hotel?
mii...nai rohng raehm rúe plào
มี...ในโรงแรมหรือเปล่า

Is there an elevator in the hotel?
mii bandai lûean nai rohng raehm rúe plào
มีบันไดเลื่อนในโรงแรมหรือเปล่า

Do you have room service?
mii room service rúe plào
มีรูมเซอร์วิชหรือเปล่า

A Place to Stay

7

115

Could I see the room?

khǎw duu hâwng nòi dâi mái
ขอดูห้องหน่อยได้ไหม

I'll take this room

phǒm/dichán ca ao hâwng níi
ผม/ดิฉันจะเอาห้องนี้

We don't like this one

rao mâi châwp hâwng níi
เราไม่ชอบห้องนี้

Do you have a larger/
less expensive room?

khun mii hâwng <u>yài kwàa</u>/<u>thùuk kwàa</u> mái
คุณมีห้อง ใหญ่กว่า/ถูกกว่า ไหม

Could you put in a cot?

khǎw tiang dèk nòi dâi mái
ขอเตียงเด็กหน่อยได้ไหม

What time's breakfast?

aahǎan cháo kìi mohng khá/khráp
อาหารเช้ากี่โมงคะ/ครับ

Where's the dining room?

hâwng aahǎan yùu thîi nǎi
ห้องอาหารอยู่ที่ไหน

Can I have breakfast in
my room?

thaan aahǎan cháo thîi hâwng dâi mái
ทานอาหารเช้าที่ห้องได้ไหม

Where's the emergency
exit/fire escape?

<u>thaang àwk chùk chǒehn</u>/<u>thaang nǐi fai</u> yùu thîi nǎi
ทางออกฉุกเฉิน/ทางหนีไฟ อยู่ที่ไหน

Where can I park my
car (safely)?

jhod rót thîi nǎi (plàwt phai) dâi
จอดรถที่ไหน (ปลอดภัย) ได้

The key to room..., please

khǎw kunjae hâwng…khá/khráp
ขอกุญแจห้อง…ค่ะ/ครับ

Could you put this in
the safe, please?

chûai ao sài nai séhf dâi mái khá/khráp
ช่วยเอาใส่ในเซฟได้ไหมคะ/ครับ

Could you wake me
at…tomorrow?

chûai plùk tawn…phrûng níi dâi mái khá/khráp
ช่วยปลุกตอน…พรุ่งนี้ได้ไหมคะ/ครับ

Could you find a
babysitter for me?

chûai hǎa khon líang dèk hâi nòi dâi mái khá/khráp
ช่วยหาคนเลี้ยงเด็กให้หน่อยได้ไหมคะ/ครับ

Could I have an extra blanket?	*khǎw phâa hòm phôehm dâi mái khá/ khráp* ขอผ้าห่มเพิ่มได้ไหมคะ/ครับ
What days do the cleaners come in?	*khon tham khwaam sà-àat maa wan nǎi* คนทำความสะอาดมาวันไหน
When are the sheets/ towels/dish towels changed?	*plìan phâa puu/phâa chét tua/phâa chét caan mûearài* เปลี่ยน ผ้าปู/ผ้าเช็ดตัว/ผ้าเช็ดจาน เมื่อไหร่

7.3 Complaints

While westerners (*faràng*) might complain over both large and small matters, Thais would rather say little or nothing at all. The point is partly one of face, but it is also Thai custom to praise the good and ignore the bad. Complain if you must, but try to be more accommodating than you might otherwise be at home. Such will not only help your relationship with Thais now, but will also assist those wishing to follow after you. The Thais will respect you as a *farang*, and you will enjoy your stay even more.

We can't sleep for the noise	*rao nawn mâi làp phráw sǐang dang* เรานอนไม่หลับเพราะเสียงดัง
Could you turn the radio down, please?	*chûai rìi wítthayú nòi dâi mái khá/khráp* ช่วยหรี่วิทยุหน่อยได้ไหมคะ/ครับ
We're out of toilet paper	*kradàat chamrá mòt* กระดาษชำระหมด
There aren't any…/there's not enough…	*mâi mii…/mii…mâi phaw* ไม่มี…/มี…ไม่พอ
The bed linen's dirty	*phâa puu tiang sòkkapròk* ผ้าปูเตียงสกปรก
The room hasn't been cleaned.	*hâwng yang mâi dâi tham khwaam sà-àat* ห้องยังไม่ได้ทำความสะอาด

The kitchen is not clean	*khrua mâi sà-àat* ครัวไม่สะอาด
The kitchen utensils are dirty	*khrûeang khrua sòkkapròk* เครื่องครัวสกปรก
The heater's not working	*khrûeang tham khwaam ráwn mâi tham ngaan* เครื่องทำความร้อนไม่ทำงาน
There's no (hot) water/ electricity	*mâi mii náam (ráwn)/fai fáa* ไม่มี น้ำ(ร้อน)/ไฟฟ้า
…doesn't work/is broken	*mâi tham ngaan/sĭa* ไม่ทำงาน/เสีย
Could you have that seen to?	*chûai hâi khrai duu dâi mái* ช่วยให้ใครดูได้ไหม
Could I have another room/site?	*khăw ìik hâwng/hàehng dâi mái* ขออีก ห้อง/แห่ง ได้ไหม
The bed creaks terribly	*tiang mii sĭang yâeh mâak* เตียงมีเสียงแย่มาก
The bed sags	*thîi nawn yúp* ที่นอนยุบ
Could I have a board under the mattress?	*khăw mái kradaan waang tâi thîi nawn dâi mái* ขอไม้กระดานวางใต้ที่นอนได้ไหม
It's too noisy	*sĭang dang mâak pai* เสียงดังมากไป
There are a lot of insects/ bugs	*mii malaehng yóe yáe* มีแมลงเยอะแยะ
There are a lot of cockroaches here	*mii malaehng sàap yóe yáe thîi níi* มีแมลงสาบเยอะแยะที่นี่
This place is full of mosquitoes	*thîi níi yung chum mâak* ที่นี่ยุงชุมมาก

7.4 Departure

See also 8.2 Settling the bill

I'm leaving tomorrow	*phŏm/dichán ca àwk phrûng níi* ผม/ดิฉัน จะออกพรุ่งนี้
Could I pay my bill, please?	*khăw cài ngoen nòi khá/khráp* ขอจ่ายเงินหน่อยค่ะ/ครับ
What time should we check out?	*khuan check out tawn kìi mohng* ควรเช็คออกตอนกี่โมง
Could I have my deposit/ passport back, please?	*khăw <u>ngoen mát jum/nangsŭeh doehn thaang</u> khuehn dâi mái khá/khráp* ขอ เงินมัดจำ/หนังสือเดินทาง คืนได้ไหมคะ/ครับ
We're in a big hurry	*rao kamlang rîip mâak* เรากำลังรีบมาก
Could you forward my mail to this address?	*khun chûai sòng còtmǎi pai thîi thîi yùu níi dâi mái khá/khráp* คุณช่วยส่งจดหมายไปที่ที่อยู่นี้ได้ ไหมคะ/ครับ
Could we leave our luggage here until we leave?	*rao fàak krapǎo wái thîi níi con kwàa rao ca pai dâi mái khá/khráp* เราฝากกระเป๋าไว้ที่นี่จนกว่าเราจะ ไปได้ไหมคะ/ครับ
Thanks for your hospitality	*khàwp khun nai khwaam jai dii khǎwng khun khá/khráp* ขอบคุณในความใจดีของคุณค่ะ/ครับ

7.5 Camping

See the diagram on page 123.

คุณเลือกที่ของคุณได้
khun lûeak thîi khǎwng khun dâi

You can pick your own site

จะจัดที่ไว้ให้ *ja jad thîi wái hâi*	You'll be allocated a site
นี่หมายเลขที่ของคุณ *nîi măai-lêhk thîi khăwng khun*	This is your site number
ให้แน่นที่รถของคุณนะคะ/ครับ *tìt hâi nâen thîi rót khăwng khun khá/khráp*	Please stick this firmly to your car
บัตรนี้ต้องไม่ทำหาย *bàt níi tâwng mâi tham hăai*	You must not lose this card

Where's the manager?	*phûu jad kaan yùu thîi năi* ผู้จัดการอยู่ที่ไหน
Are we allowed to camp here?	*rao tâng kháehm thîi nîi dâi mái* เราตั้งแคมป์ที่นี่ได้ไหม
There are…of us and we have…tents	*rao mii…khon láe mii…tén* เรามี…คนและมี…เต็นท์
Can we pick our own site?	*rao lûeak thîi khăwng rao dâi mái* เราเลือกที่ของเราได้ไหม
Do you have a quiet spot for us?	*mii thîi ngîap ngîap hâi rao mái* มีที่เงียบๆให้เราไหม
Do you have any other sites available?	*mii thîi ùehn wâang ìik mái* มีที่อื่นว่างอีกไหม
It's too windy/sunny/shady here	*thîi nîi <u>lom raehng</u>/<u>dàeht ráwn</u>/<u>rôm mâak</u> pai* ที่นี่ ลมแรง/แดดร้อน/ร่มมาก ไป
It's too crowded here	*thîi nîi aeh àt koehn pai* ที่นี่แออัดเกินไป
The ground's too hard/uneven	*<u>din khăeng</u>/<u>khrùkhrà</u> pai* ดินแข็ง/ขรุขระ ไป
Do you have a level spot for the camper/trailer/folding trailer?	*mii thîi càwt rót rîap ríap sămràp <u>rót kháehm</u>/<u>rót lâak</u>/<u>rót lâak pháp</u> mái* มีที่จอดรถเรียบ ๆสำหรับ รถแคมป์/ รถลาก/รถลากพับ ไหม

Could we have adjoining sites?	*khǎw rao yùu thîi tìt kan dâi mái* ขอเราอยู่ที่ติดกันได้ไหม
Can we park the car next to the tent?	*rao càwt rót khâang tén dâi mái* เราจอดรถข้างเต็นท์ได้ไหม
How much is it per person/tent/trailer/car?	*khon/tén/rót lâak/rót la thâorài* คน/เต็นท์/รถลาก/รถ ละเท่าไหร่
Do you have chalets for hire?	*mii bâan lék lék hâi châo mái* มีบ้านเล็ก ๆให้เช่าไหม
Are there any...?	*mii...mái* มี...ไหม
– hot/cold showers?	*thîi àap náam ráwn/yen* ที่อาบน้ำ ร้อน/เย็น
– washing machines?	*khrûeang sák phâa* เครื่องซักผ้า
Is there a...on the site?	*mii...thîi nân mái* มี...ที่นั่นไหม
Is there somewhere for children to play?	*mii thîi hâi dèk lên mái* มีที่ให้เด็กเล่นไหม
Are there covered cooking facilities on the site?	*mii tham aahǎan nai rôm thîi nân mai* มีที่ทำอาหารในร่มที่นั่นไหม
Are we allowed to barbecue here?	*rao tham bar be cue thîi nîi dâi mái* เราทำบาบิคิวที่นี่ได้ไหม
Are there any power outlets?	*mii plák fai mái* มีปลั๊กไฟไหม
Is there drinking water?	*mii náam dùehm mái* มีน้ำดื่มไหม
When's the garbage collected?	*kèp khayà mûearài* เก็บขยะเมื่อไหร่
Do you sell gas bottles (butane gas/propane gas)?	*khun khǎi thǎng káeht/káehs (káeht buuthehn/káeht phrohphehn) rúe plào* คุณขายถังแก๊ซ (แก๊ซบูเทน/แก๊ซโพรเพน) หรือเปล่า

Camping equipment
(The diagram shows the numbered parts)

	luggage space	ที่เก็บกระเป๋า	*thîi kèp krapǎ*
	can opener	ที่เปิดกระป๋อง	*thîi pòeht krapǎwng*
	butane gas	ก๊าซบูเทน	*káat/káas buuthehn*
	bottle	ขวด	*khùat*
1	pannier, tool bag	กระเป๋าใส่ของ	*krapǎo sài khǎwng*
2	gas cooker	เตาแก๊ซ	*tao káeht/káehs*
3	groundsheet	ผ้าใบปูพื้น	*phâa bai puu phúehn*
	hammer	ฆ้อน	*kháwn*
	hammock	เปล	*pleh*
4	gas can	ถังแก๊ซ	*thǎng káeht/káehs*
	campfire	แคมป์ไฟ	*kháehm fai*
5	folding chair	เก้าอี้พับ	*kâo-îi pháp*
6	insulated picnic box	ตะกร้าปิคนิคบุนวม	*takrâa píkník bùnuam*
	ice pack	ห่อน้ำแข็ง	*hàw nám khǎeng*
	compass	เข็มทิศ	*khěm thít*
	corkscrew	ที่เปิดจุก	*thîi pòeht jùk*
7	airbed	เตียงลม	*tiang lom*
8	airbed pump	ที่ปั๊มเตียงลม	*thîi pám tiang lom*
9	awning	ผ้าใบกันแดด	*phâa bai kan dàeht*
10	sleeping bag	ถุงนอน	*thǔng nawn*
11	saucepan	หม้อ	*mâw*
12	handle (pan)	หูหม้อ	*hǔu mâw*
	primus/gas stove	เตาแก๊ซใช้ถัง	*tao káeht/káehs chái thǎng*
	lighter	ที่จุดบุหรี่, ไฟแช็ค	*thîi cùt burìi, fai cháek*
13	backpack	กระเป๋าสะพาย	*krapǎo saphai*
14	guy rope	เชือกขึงเต็นท์	*chûeak khǔeng tén*
15	storm lantern	ตะเกียงเจ้าพายุ	*takiang câo phaayú*
	camp bed	เตียงแคมป์	*tiang kháehm*
	table	โต๊ะ	*tó*
16	tent	เต็นท์	*tén*
17	tent peg	หมุดเต็นท์	*mùt tén*
18	tent pole	เสาเต็นท์	*sǎo tén*
	thermos	กระติก	*kratìk*

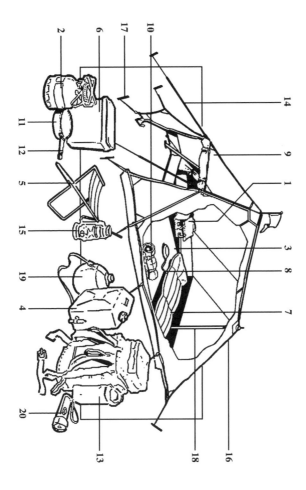

19	water bottle	ขวดน้ำ	*khùat náam*
	clothes pin	ไม้หนีบ	*mái nìip*
	clothes line	ราวตากผ้า	*rao tàak phâa*
	windbreak	ที่กั้นลม	*thîi kân lom*
20	flashlight	ไฟฉาย	*fai chăi*
	penknife	มีดพก	*mîit phók*

8 Money Matters

8. Money Matters

● **In general**, banks are open to the public Monday to Friday from 8:30 am to 3:30 pm, but it is possible to find an exchange office (*thîi lâek ngoen*) open in the towns and tourist centers after these hours. Rates vary among both banks and money changers. Make sure you ask about commission before handing over any money. Proof of identity such as a passport is usually required to exchange currency. Credit cards are widely accepted in Thailand; however, smaller stores will sometimes add three to five per cent of the bill to cover transaction costs. When purchasing by credit/debit card, try to keep the card in your view at all times.

8.1 Banks

Where can I find a bank/ an ATM machine around here?	*thǎeo níi mii thanaakhaan/tûu a-thii-em thîi nǎi khá/khráp* แถวนี้มี ธนาคาร/ตู้เอทีเอ็ม ที่ไหนคะ/ครับ
Where can I cash this traveler's check/giro check?	*phǒm/dichán lâehk chék doehn thaang/ cairoh chék dâi thîi nǎi* ผม/ดิฉันแลก เช็คเดินทาง/ไจโรเช็ค ได้ที่ไหน
Can I cash this...here?	*phǒm/dichán lâehk ngoen...thîi nîi dâi mái* ผม/ดิฉันแลกเงิน...ที่นี่ได้ไหม
Can I withdraw money on my credit card here?	*phǒm/dichán thǎwn ngoen càak bàt khrehdìt thîi nîi dâi mái* ผม/ดิฉันถอนเงินจากบัตรเครดิตที่นี่ได้ไหม
I'd like to withdraw cash	*phǒm/dichán yàak cà thǎwn ngoen sòt* ผม/ดิฉัน อยากจะถอนเงินสค
What's the minimum/ maximum amount?	*nòi thîi sùt/mâak thîi sùt thâorài* น้อยที่สุด/มากที่สุด เท่าไหร่

Can I take out less than that?	*phǒm/dichán ao àwk nòi kwàa nán dâi mái*
	ผม/ดิฉันเอาออกน้อยกว่านั้นได้ไหม
I had some money cabled here	*phǒm/dichán sòng ngoen maa thîi nîi thaang khehbôen*
	ผม/ดิฉันส่งเงินมาที่นี่ทางเคเบิล
Has it arrived yet?	*maa thǔeng rúe yang*
	มาถึงหรือยัง
These are the details of my bank in the U.S.	*nîi pen rai lá-iat khǎwng thanaakhaan phǒm/dichán nai amehríkaa*
	นี่เป็นรายละเอียดของธนาคารผม/ ดิฉันในอเมริกา
This is the number of my bank/giro account	*nîi lêhk thîi <u>banchii thanaakhaan</u>/ <u>banchii cairoh</u>*
	นี่เลขที่ บัญชีธนาคาร/บัญชีไจโร
I'd like to change some money	*yàak lâehk ngoen nòi*
	อยากแลกเงินหน่อย
– pounds into…	*ngoen pawn pen…*
	เงินปอนด์เป็น…
– dollars into…	*ngoen rǐan pen…*
	เงินเหรียญเป็น…
What's the exchange rate?	*àtraa lâehk plìan thâorài*
	อัตราแลกเปลี่ยนเท่าไหร่
Could you give me some small change with it?	*khǎw báeng lék lék dûai ná khá/khráp*
	ขอแบ๊งเล็ก ๆ ด้วยนะคะ/ครับ
This is not right	*nîi mâi thùuk*
	นี่ไม่ถูก

เซ็นที่นี่
sen thîi nîi

กรอกที่นี่หน่อย
kràwk thîi nîi nòi

Sign here, please

Fill this out, please

ขอดูหนังสือเดินทางหน่อย	Could I see your passport, please?
khǎw duu nǎngsǔeh doehn-thaang nòi	
ขอดูบัตรประจำตัวหน่อย	Could I see your identity card, please?
khǎw duu bàt pracam tua nòi	
ขอดูบัตรเครดิตการ์ดหน่อย	Could I see your credit card, please?
kôh doo budd credit card noi	

8.2 Settling the bill

Could you put it on my bill?	*sài nai bin phǒm/dichán dâi mái* ใส่ในบิลผม/ดิฉันได้ไหม
Is the tip(s) included?	*ruam thíp rúe yang* รวมทิปหรือยัง
Can I pay by…?	*jhài dûai…dâi mái* จ่ายด้วย…ได้ไหม
Can I pay by credit card?	*jhài dûai bàt khrehdìt dâi mái* จ่ายด้วยบัตรเครดิตได้ไหม
Can I pay by traveler's check?	*jhài dûai tǔa doehn thaang dâi mái* จ่ายด้วยตั๋วเดินทางได้ไหม
Can I pay with foreign currency?	*jhài ngoen tàang prathêht dâi mái* จ่ายเงินต่างประเทศได้ไหม
You've given me too much/ you haven't given me enough change	*khun hâi mâak pai/khun thawn hâi mâi khróp* คุณให้มากไป/คุณทอนให้ไม่ครบ
Could you check this again, please?	*chék ìik thii dâi mái* เช็คอีกทีได้ไหม
Could I have a receipt, please?	*khǎw bai sèt dûai ná* ขอใบเสร็จด้วยนะ
I don't have enough oney on me	*phǒm/dichán mâi mii ngoen tìt tua phaw* ผม/ดิฉันไม่มีเงินติดตัวพอ

| This is for you | *hâi khun*
ให้คุณ |
| Keep the change | *mâi tâwng thawn*
ไม่ต้องทอน |

เราไม่รับบัตรเครดิต/เช็คเดินทาง/ เงินต่างประเทศ *rao mâi ráp bàt khredìt/chék doehn-thaang/ngoen tàang phrathêht*	We don't accept credit cards/ traveler's checks/ foreign currency
ขอดูบัตรเอทีเอ็ม/บัตรเดบิต ของคุณได้ไหม *khǎw duu bàt a-thii-em/bàt debìt khǎwng khun dâi mái*	Can I see your ATM/cash card?
กรุณากดรหัสส่วนตัว *karunaa kòt rahàt sùan tua*	Please enter your PIN number

9 Mail, Phone and Internet

9. Mail, Phone and Internet

9.1 Mail

● **Bangkok's Central Post Office** (*praisanii klaang*) is open Monday to Friday from 8 am to 6 pm and on weekends, and public holidays from 9 am to 1 pm. Other major post offices and upcountry branches hold similar hours, but close at 4:30 pm. Besides post offices, stamps (*sataehm*) can be purchased at smaller post office agencies and often at hotel receptions and shops selling postcards. Some stamps are particularly pretty and make good but cheap souvenirs. The cost of sending a letter depends on its size and weight; the cost of sending an airmail letter also depends on the zone it is being sent to. The Thai postal service is quite efficient, deliveries in the city are usually twice a day, and at least once a day upcountry, including Sundays. You will find the parcel service (air, SAL [sea-air-land] or surface) to be an effective way of sending items home when your baggage is overweight. The usual customs declaration applies.

แสตมป์ *sa–taem* stamp(s)	แฟกซ์ *fáek* fax	ตั๋วเงิน *tǔa ngoen* money orders
พัสดุ *phátsadù* parcel(s)	ตู้รับไปรษณีย์ *tûu ráp praisanii* post office box	ต่างประเทศ *tàang prathêht* international

Where is…?	*yùu thîi nǎi* …อยู่ที่ไหน…
– the nearest post office?	*praisanii thîi klâi thîisùt* ไปรษณีย์ที่ใกล้ที่สุด
– the main post office	*praisanii klaang* ไปรษณีย์กลาง
– the nearest mail box?	*tûu praisanii thîi klâi thîisùt* ตู้ไปรษณีย์ที่ใกล้ที่สุด

Which counter should I go to…?	*khuan pai khaotôeh năi* ควรไปเคาน์เตอร์ไหน
Which counter should I go to to send a fax?	*sòng fáek(s) khuan pai khaotôeh năi* ส่งแฟกซ์ควรไปเคาน์เตอร์ไหน
Which counter should I go to to change money?	*lâehk ngoen khuan pai khaotôeh năi* แลกเงินควรไปเคาน์เตอร์ไหน
Which counter should I go to to change giro checks?	*lâehk cairoh khuan pai khaotôeh năi* แลกไจโรเช็คควรไปเคาน์เตอร์ไหน
Which counter should I go to to wire a money order?	*súeh tŭa lâehk ngoen khuan pai khaotôeh năi* ซื้อตั๋วแลกเงินควรไปเคาน์เตอร์ไหน
Which counter should I go to for general delivery?	*sòng khǎwng thûa pai khuan pai khaotôeh năi* ส่งของทั่วไปควรไปเคาน์เตอร์ไหน
Is there any mail for me?	*mii còtmăi thǔeng phǒm/dichán mái* มีจดหมายถึงผม/ดิฉันไหม
My name's…	*phǒm/dichán chûeh…* ผม/ดิฉันชื่อ…

Stamps

What's the postage for a…to…?	*sòng…pai…khâa sòng thâorài* ส่ง…ไป…ค่าส่งเท่าไร
Are there enough stamps on it?	*tìt sataehm phaw mái* ติดแสตมป์พอไหม
I'd like [quantity] [value] stamps	*phǒm/dichán yàak súeh sataehm… duang* ผม/ดิฉันอยากซื้อแสตมป…ดวง
I'd like to send this…	*phǒm/dichán yàak sòng…* ผม/ดิฉันอยากส่ง…
– express	*dùan* ด่วน
– by air mail	*meh(l) aakàat* เมล์อากาศ

| – by registered mail | *long thabian*
ลงทะเบียน |
| Please give me a customs declaration sticker | *khăw bai câehng sămràp súnlakaakawn nòi*
ขอใบแจ้งสำหรับศุลกากรหน่อย |

Fax

I'd like to send a fax to…	*phŏm/dichán yàak sòng fáek(s) pai…* ผม/ดิฉันอยากส่ง โทรเลข/แฟกซ์ ไป…
Shall I fill out the form myself?	*phŏm/dichán tâwng kràwk khâw khwaam ehng rúe plào* ผม/ดิฉันต้องกรอกข้อความเองหรือเปล่า
Can I make photocopies/ send a fax here?	*phŏm/dichán àt sămnao/sòng fáek(s) thîi nîi dâi mái* ผม/ดิฉัน อัดสำเนา/ส่งแฟกซ์ ที่นี่ได้ไหม
Can I scan this picture/ photo here?	*khăw sa-kaen rûup níi dâi mái khrâp/ khá* ขอสแกรูปนี้ได้ไหมครับ/คะ
How much is it per page?	*nâa lá thâorài* หน้าละเท่าไร

9.2 Telephone

See also 1.9 Telephone alphabet

● **Direct international calls** can be made from blue public telephones showing the international phone symbol. The booths require use of a phone card available from many stores and smaller shops, as well as newspaper stands, and vending machines in Thai Telecom offices. Phone cards have various values ranging from 20 to 100 baht. Dial 001 to get out of Thailand, then the relevant country code (USA: 1; UK: 44; Australia: 61), city code and number. If you call using a THAICARD, dial 1544 for international access. To make a collect call from a public telephone, dial 100 to access the operator. Many operators speak English, but speak slowly, clearly and politely for the best service. A 24-hour call center is available on 02 614 1000. When phoning someone in Thailand, you will hear single long tones, but if engaged shorter, quicker tones. Thailand also supports the 900 MHz Digital GSM and 1800 MHz Digital PCN mobile phone networks for international roaming.

May I use your phone, please?	*khǎw chái thohrasàp nòi dâi mái khá/ khráp* ขอใช้โทรศัพท์หน่อยได้ไหมคะ/ครับ
Do you have a (city/region)…phone directory?	*mii samùt thohrasàp (nai mueang/nai khèht) mái* มีสมุดโทรศัพท์(ในเมือง/ในเขต)ไหม
Where can I get a phone card?	*phǒm/dichán súeh bàt thohrasàp dâi thîi nǎi* ผม/ดิฉันซื้อบัตรโทรศัพท์ได้ที่ไหน
Could you give me…	*phǒm/dichán khǎw…* ผม/ดิฉันขอ…
– the number for international directory assistance?	*mǎi lêhk sàwp thǎam mǎi lêhk naanaa châat* หมายเลขสอบถามหมายเลขนานาชาติ
– the number of room…?	*mǎi lêhk thohrasàp hâwng…* หมายเลขโทรศัพท์ห้อง…
– the international access code?	*rahàt khâo naanaa châat* รหัสเข้านานาชาติ
– the country code for…?	*rahàt prathêht…* รหัสประเทศ…
– the area code for…?	*rahàt khèht khǎwng…* รหัสเขตของ…
– the number of [subscriber]…?	*mǎi lêhk khǎwng [phûu chái sǎi]…* หมายเลขของ[ผู้ใช้สาย]…

Could you check if this number's correct?	*chûai chék nòi dâi mái wâa măi láhk níi thùuk rúe plào* ช่วยเช็คหน่อยได้ไหมว่าหมายเลขนี้ถูกหรือเปล่า
Can I dial international direct?	*phŏm/dichán mŭn trong àwk nâwk prathêht dâi mái* ผม/ดิฉันหมุนตรงออกนอกประเทศได้ไหม
Do I have to go through the switchboard?	*phŏm/dichán tâwng thoh phàan klaang rúe plào* ผม/ดิฉันต้องโทร.ผ่านกลางหรือเปล่า
Do I have to dial '0' first?	*phŏm/dichán tâwng mŭn sŭun kàwn rúe plào* ผม/ดิฉันต้องหมุนศูนย์ก่อนหรือเปล่า
Do I have to reserve my calls?	*phŏm/dichán tâwng jhong rúe plào* ผม/ดิฉันต้องจองหรือเปล่า
Could you dial this number for me, please?	*chûai mŭn boeh níi hâi nòi dâi mái khá/khráp* ช่วยหมุนเบอร์นี้ให้หน่อยได้ไหมคะ/ครับ
Could you put me through to…/extension…, please?	*chûai tàw boeh…/tàw…hâi nòi dâi mái khá/khráp* ช่วยต่อเบอร์…/ต่อ…ให้หน่อยได้ไหมคะ/ครับ
I'd like to place a collect call to...	*phŏm/dichán yàak thoh kèp ngoen plai thaang thŭeng…* ผม/ดิฉันอยากโทร.เก็บเงินปลายทางถึง…
What's the charge per minute?	*khít naathii lá thâorài* คิดนาทีละเท่าไร
Can I use my cell (mobile) phone here?	*phŏm/dichán chái thoorasàp mueh tŭeh thîi nîi dâi mái khráp/khá* ผม/ดิฉัน ใช้โทรศัพท์มือถือที่นี่ได้ไหมครับ/คะ

Have there been any calls for me?	*mii thohrasàp thǔeng phǒm/dichán mái* มีโทรศัพท์ถึงผม/ดิฉันไหม
Do you have a smartphone?	*khun mii sa-mart fone mái khráp/khá* คุณมีสมาร์ทโฟนไหมครับ/คะ
I've lost my SIM card	*phǒm/dichán tham sim-káad hǎi khráp/khá* ผม/ดิฉัน ทำซิมการ์ดหายครับ/คะ
I'd like to buy a SIM card	*phǒm/dichán yàak cà súeh sim-káad mài khráp/khá* ผม/ดิฉัน อยากจะซื้อซิมการ์ดใหม่ครับ/คะ
The (mobile) signal is weak	*thǎeo níi mâi mii khlûen* แถวนี้ไม่มีคลื่น

The conversation

Hello, this is…	*sawàt dii khá/khráp, nîi…* สวัสดีค่ะ/ครับ นี่…
Who is this, please?	*nân khrai khá/khráp* นั่นใครคะ/ครับ
Is this…?	*nân…châi mái* นั่น…ใช่ไหม
I'm sorry, I've dialed the wrong number	*khǎw thôht khá/khráp, phǒm/dichán thoh phìt* ขอโทษค่ะ/ครับ โทร.ผิด
I can't hear you	*phǒm/dichán mâi dâi-yin khá/khráp* ผม/ดิฉันไม่ได้ยินค่ะ/ครับ
I'd like to speak to...	*khǎw phûut kàp...nòi khá/khráp* ขอพูดกับ...หน่อยค่ะ/ครับ
Is there anybody who speaks English?	*mii khrai phûut phaasǎa angkrìt bâang mái* มีใครพูดภาษาอังกฤษบ้างไหม
Extension..., please	*tàw...khá/khráp* ต่อ...ค่ะ/ครับ

มีโทรศัพท์ถึงคุณ *mii thorasàp thǔeng khun*	There's a phone call for you
คุณต้องหมุนศูนย์ก่อน *khun tâwng mǔn sǔun kàwn*	You have to dial '0' first
สักครู่ค่ะ/ครับ *sàk khrûu khâ/khráp*	One moment, please
ไม่มีคนรับ *mâi mii khon ráp*	There's no answer
สายไม่ว่าง *sǎai mâi wâang*	The line's busy
จะถือสายรอไหม *cà thěu sǎai raw*	Do you want to hold?
ต่อให้แล้ว *taw hâi láeo*	Connecting you
คุณโทร.ผิด *khun thoo phìt*	You've got the wrong number
ตอนนี้เขาไม่อยู่ *tawn níi kháo mâi yùu*	He's/she's not here right now
เขาจะกลับตอน… *kháo cà klàp tawn…*	He'll/she'll be back (time/ time of day)
นี่เป็นเครื่องรับฝากข้อความของ… *nîi pen khrûeng ráp fàak khâw khwaam khǎwng…*	This is the answering machine of…

Could you ask him/her to call me back?	*chûai bàwk kháo hâi thoh klàp dâi mái khá/khráp* ช่วยบอกเขาให้โทร.กลับได้ไหมคะ/ ครับ
My name's…	*phǒm/dichán chûeh…* ผม/ดิฉันชื่อ
My number's…	*boeh phǒm/dichán…* เบอร์ผม/ดิฉัน…

Could you tell him/her I called?	*chûai bàwk kháo wâa phǒm/dichán thoh maa*	
	ช่วยบอกเขาว่าผม/ดิฉันโทร.มา	
I'll call him/her back tomorrow	*phǒm/dichán ca thoh maa mài phrûng níi*	
	ผม/ดิฉันจะโทร.มาใหม่พรุ่งนี้	

9.3 Internet/email

อินเตอร์เน็ต *internet* Internet	อีเมล์ *ii-mei* email	รหัส *rahàt* password
ร้านอินเตอร์เน็ต *ráan internet* cybercafe	เอสเอ็มเอส *SMS* texting/sms	เว็บไซต์ *web-sai* website
แทบเล็ต พีซี *tháeb-lét phii sii* tablet PC	ชื่อผู้ใช้ *chûe phûu chái* username	อีบุ๊ค *ii-búk* e-book
เบราว์เซอร์ *brao-ser* browser	ดอท *dot* dot	บล็อก *bláwk* blog
เครื่องมือช่วยค้นหา *khrûeng-mueh chûai khón hǎa* search engine	เครื่องชาร์ท *khrûeng cháat* charger	เฟสบุ๊ค *Faes-búk* Facebook
แอป/แอปลิเคชั่น *áep/áep-li-khay-chân* app/application	หน้าแรก *nâa râek* log-in-page	ทวิทเตอร์ *ta-wít-er* Twitter
ปลั๊กไฟที่มีหลายเต้ารับ *plúk fai thîi mii lǎi tâw ráp* adaptor	ไวรัส *wai-rút* virus	ทวิท *ta-wîit* tweet
ซอฟท์แวร์ *sawf-wae* software	แฮ็กเกอร์ *hác-ker* hacker	วายฟาย *wai-fai* Wifi
	โน๊ตบุ๊ค *nóo-t-búk* laptop	

Did you receive my (e)mail? (male speaking)	*khun dâi ráp còt-măi khăwng phŏm rūe plàw khráp* คุณได้รับจดหายของผมหรือเปล่าครับ
I'd like to send an email	*phŏm/dichăn yàak cà sòng ii-mei khráp/khá* ผม/ดิฉัน อยากจะส่งอีเมล์ ครับ/คะ
Is there a cyber café (Internet café) around here?	*thăeo níi mii ráan internet rŭe plàw khráp/khá* แถวนี้มีร้านอินเตอร์เน็ตหรือเปล่าครับ/คะ
Is there Wifi around here?	*thăeo níi mii wifi rŭe plàw khráp/khá* แถวนี้มีวายฟายหรือเปล่าครับ/คะ
Do you have a Wifi connection here?	*thîi nîi tàw wai-fai dâi rŭe plàw khráp/khá* ทีนีต่อวายฟายได้หรือเปล่าครับ/คะ
Do you do Facebook?	*khun lên Facebook mái khráp/khá* คุณเล่นเฟสบุ๊คไหมครับ/คะ
Can we become friends on Facebook?	*raw pen phûen kan thîi Faes-búk dâi mái* เราเป็นเพื่อนกันที่เฟสบุ๊คได้ไหม
What's your Facebook ID?	*Faes-búk khun chûe arai* เฟสบุ๊คคุณชื่ออะไร
Can you upload your photos to Facebook?	*khun sài rûup khăwng khun thîi Faes-búk dâi mái* คุณใสรูปของคุณที่เฟสบุ๊คได้ไหม
Do you use Twitter?	*khun dâi chái ta-wít-er rŭe plàw* คุณได้ใช้ทวิทเตอร์หรือเปล่า
Do you tweet?	*khun lên ta-wîit mái* คุณเล่นทวิทไหม
What is your twitter handle?	*chûe lên ta-wít-er khăwng khun chûe arai* ชื่อเล่นทวิทเตอร์ของคุณชื่ออะไร
What is your blog address?	*thîi yùu bláwk khăwng khun chûe arai* ที่อยู่บล็อกของคุณชื่ออะไร

English	Thai (romanized / script)
My smartphone/iPhone is not working	*sa-mart fone/ai-fone khǎwng phǒm/dichǎn sǐa* สมาร์ทโฟน/ไอโฟนของผม/ดิฉัน เสีย
Please text me/send me an SMS	*karunaa sòng khâw-khwaam/sòng es-em-es hǎa phǒm/dichǎn* กรุณาส่งข้อความ/ส่งเอสเอ็มเอสหา ผม/ดิฉัน
I'll send you a text message	*phǒm/dichǎn cà sòng khâw-khwaam thǔeng khun* ผม/ดิฉัน จะส่งข้อความถึงคุณ
The phone connection is not good, it keeps dropping out	*thorasàp sanyaan mâi dii sǐang khàat-khàat hǎi-hǎi* โทรศัพท์สัญญาณไม่ดี เสียงขาดๆ หายๆ
I can't get on the Internet (Net)	*phǒm/dichǎn mâi sǎamâat tàw internet dâi* ผม/ดิฉันไม่สามารถต่ออินเตอร์เน็ตได้
You can find it on Google	*khun sǎamâat khón-hǎa man thîi koo-koel* คุณสามารถค้นหามันที่กูเกิล
Do I need a password to get onto the Internet?	*phǒm tâwng mii rahàt rǔe plàw thǔeng cà tàw internet dâi* ผมต้องมีรหัสหรือเปล่าถึงจะ ต่ออินเตอร์เน็ตได้

10 Shopping

● **Larger shops** are generally open every day from 10 am to 10 pm. The smaller shops may open and close earlier, but there are no specific opening and closing times for them; their times of business will depend on the goods and services they sell. For example, a noodle shop or café will open at 6 or 7 am to serve breakfast, and may close after dinner in the evening. A hairdresser's will open at 10 am in a shopping center, but possibly 9 am or earlier on the street. Closing time may depend on the last client going home.

As well as the established shops, you'll find street stalls, markets, night bazaars and those selling wares from a small blanket laid out on the ground. There's nothing to say that quality will be better or worse from any of these shops. Like the Chinese in Bangkok, Thais aim to trade for turnover—although they may not be as fervent at it. And when you shop in other than the larger fixed-price stores, always be prepared to bargain.

ร้านตัดผม
ráan tàt phǒm
barber

ร้านขายของชำ
ráan khǎai khǎwng cham
grocery shop

ร้านขายรองเท้า
ráan khǎai ráwng-tháo
shoe/footwear shop

ร้านซักผ้า/ซักแห้งหยอดเหรียญ
ráan sák phâa yàwt rǐan/sák hâeng
coin-operated laundry/dry cleaner

ร้านตัดรองเท้า
ráan tàt ráwng-tháo
shoe repair shop

ร้านซ่อมมอเตอร์ไซค์และจักรยาน
ráan sâwm mo-toer-sai láe càkrayaan
motorbike and bicycle repairs

ร้านเครื่องเขียน
ráan khrûeng khǐan
stationery shop

ร้านขายของมือสอง
ráan khǎai khǎwng mueh sǎwng
second-hand shop

ร้านขายไวน์
ráan khǎai wai
wine/bottle shop

ร้านขายเสื้อผ้า
ráan khǎai sûea-phâa
clothing shop

ร้านขายยา
ráan khǎai yaa
pharmacy, chemist

ร้านขายเนื้อ
ráan khǎai núea
butcher's shop

ร้านหนังสือ
ráan nǎngsǔeh
bookshop

ร้านก๋วยเตี๋ยว
ráan kǔai tǐao
noodle shop

ร้านขายดอกไม้
ráan khǎai dàwk-mái
florist

ร้านเบเกอรี่
ráan bakery
bakery

ร้านขายผัก
ráan khǎai phàk
greengrocer

ร้านขายไอศครีม
ráan khǎai ais-khriim
ice cream shop

ร้านขายอัญมณี
ráan khǎai an-monii
jeweler

ห้างสรรพสินค้า
hang sapha-sǐn-kháa
department store

ร้านเสริมสวย
ráan sǒem sǔai
beauty salon

ร้านขายผ้า
ráan khǎai phâa
haberdashery

ร้านขายเครื่องอุปกรณ์ แคมป์
ráan khǎai khrûeng ùp-pakawn khaemping
camping supplies shop

ร้านขายเครื่องใช้ในบ้าน
ráan khǎai khrûeng chai nai bâan
household goods store

ร้านผลไม้และผัก
ráan phǒnlamái láe phàk
fruit and vegetable shop

ร้านขายขนมหวาน/เค้ก
ráan khǎai khanǒm wǎan/khék
confectioner's/cake shop

ร้านขายสมุนไพร
ráan khǎai samǔn-phrai
herbalist's shop/herbalist

ที่ขายหนังสือพิมพ์
thîi khǎai nǎngsǔeh-phim
newsstand

ร้านขายกล้องถ่ายรูป
ráan khǎai klâwng thàai rûup
camera shop

ร้านขายเครื่องกีฬา
ráan khǎai khrûeng kiilaa
sporting goods store

ร้านขายเครื่องนอน
ráan khǎai khrûeng nawn
household linen shop

ร้านเพลง
ráan phleng (sii dii, dii wii dii, em-phi-sǎam)
music shop (CDs, DVDs, MP3s, etc)

ร้านขายเครื่องไฟฟ้า
ráan khǎai khrûeng fai-fáa
household appliances (white goods)

ร้านหนังสือการ์ตูน
ráan nǎngsǔeh kaa-tun
comic/animé shop

ตลาด
talàat
market

ร้านนาฬิกา
ráan naalikaa
watches and clocks

ร้านขายทอง
ráan khǎai thawng
goldsmith/gold shop

ร้านขายแว่นตา
ráan khǎai wâen-taa
optician/optometrist

ร้านนวด
ráan nûat
massage shop

สถานอาบอบนวด
àab àwp nûat
massage parlor

ร้านขายขนสัตว์
ráan khǎai khǒn sàt
furrier

ร้านขายปลา
ráan khǎai plaa
fishmonger

ร้านขายไก่
ráan khǎai kài
poultry shop

ซูเปอร์มาเก็ต
su-poer-maa-kèt
supermarket

ร้านขายบุหรี่
ráan khǎai burìi
tobacconist

ร้านขายต้นไม้
ráan khǎai tôn-mái
nursery (plants)

ร้านขายเครื่องดนตรี
ráan khǎai khrûeng don-trii
musical instrument shop

ร้านขายเครื่องหนัง
ráan khǎai khrûeng nǎng
leather goods shop

ร้านขายของเล่นเด็ก
ráan khǎai khǎwng lên dèk
toy shop

ร้านขายเครื่องดื่ม
ráan khǎai khrûeng-dùehm
shop selling refreshments

ร้านรับซักผ้า/ซักแห้ง
ráan ráp sák phâa/sák hâeng
laundry/dry cleaners

ร้านคอมพิวเตอร์
ráan khawm-phiw-toer
computer (hardware) shop

ร้านขายซอฟแวร์คอมพิวเตอร์
ráan khǎai sawf-wae khawm-phiw-toer
computer (software) shop

ร้านเฟอร์นิเจอร์
ráan foe-nít-coe (fer-nit-jer)
furniture shop

ร้านขายของขวัญ
ráan khǎai khǎwng khwǎn
gift shop

ร้านขายของที่ระลึก
ráan khǎai khǎwng thîi ra-luk
souvenir shop

คลีนิคแพทย์
khliník phâet
clinic (in shopping centre/mall)

ร้านขายน้ำหอม
ráan khǎai náam-hǎwm
perfumery

ร้านอนิเมะ/เกมส์
ráan ani-meh/kem
anime/game store

ร้านขายเนยแข็ง
ráan khǎai noei-khǎeng
delicatessen

ร้านเครื่องไฟฟ้า
ráan khrûeng fai-fáa
electronics shop

ร้านหนังสือมือสอง
ráan nǎngsǔeh mueh sǎwng
used bookstore

10.1 Shopping conversations

Where can I get…?
phǒm/dichán súeh…dâi thîi nǎi
ผม/ดิฉันซื้อ…ได้ที่ไหน

When does this shop open?
ráan níi pòeht kìi mohng
ร้านนี้เปิดกี่โมง

Could you tell me where the…department is?
sâap mái khráp/khá wâa phanàehk… yùu thîi nái
ทราบไหมครับ/คะ
ว่าแผนก…อยู่ที่ไหน

Could you help me, please?
chuâi nàwi dâi mái khráp/khá
ช่วยหน่อยได้ไหมครับ/คะ

Do you sell English/ American newspapers?
khun mii nangsǔeh phim angkrìt/ amehrikan khǎi rúe plào
คุณมีหนังสือพิมพ์อังกฤษ/อเมริกั
นขายหรือเปล่า

I'm looking for…
phǒm/dichán kamlang hǎa…
ผม/ดิฉันกำลังหา…

มีใครเสริฟคุณหรือยัง *mii khrai soef khun rǔe yang*	Are you being served?

No, I'd like…
mâi mii khráp/khá, phǒm/dichán yàak dâi…
ไม่มีครับ/ค่ะ ผม/ดิฉันอยากได้…

I'm just looking, if that's all right	*phǒm/dichán duu chǒei chǒei ná khráp/khá* ผม/ดิฉันดูเฉย ๆนะครับ/คะ
I don't need a bag	*phǒm/dichán mâi tâwng kaan thǔng phlas-tìk khráp/khá* ผม/ดิฉัน ไม่ต้องการถุงพลาสติกครับ/ค่ะ
Can I have a receipt?	*khǎw bai set dûai khráp/khá* ขอใบเสร็จด้วยครับ/ค่ะ

(ต้องการ) อะไรอีกไหมครับ/คะ   (Would you like) anything else?
(tâwng-kaan) arai iik mái khráp/khá

Yes, I'd also like…	*tâwngkaan…dûai* ต้องการ…ด้วย
No, thank you. That's all	*mâi khráp/khá, khàwp khun; thâo nán la* ไม่ครับ/ค่ะ ขอบคุณ เท่านั้นละ
Could you show me…?	*khǎw duu…nòi khráp/khá* ขอดู…หน่อยครับ/ค่ะ
I'd prefer…	*phǒm/dichán châwp…mâak kwàa* ผม/ดิฉันชอบ…มากกว่า
This is not what I'm looking for	*nîi mâi châi thîi phǒm/dichán tâwngkaan* นี่ไม่ใช่ที่ผม/ดิฉันต้องการ
Thank you, I'll keep looking	*khàwp khun khráp/khá, phǒm/dichán ca hǎa tàw pai* ขอบคุณครับ/ค่ะ ผม/ดิฉันจะหาต่อไป
Do you have something…?	*khun mii arai thîi…mái* คุณมีอะไรที่…ไหม
– less expensive?	*thùuk kwàa níi* ถูกกว่านี้
– something smaller?	*lék kwàa níi* เล็กกว่านี้

– something larger?	*yài kwàa níi* ใหญ่กว่านี้
I'll take this one	*phŏm/dichán ca ao an níi* ผม/ดิฉันจะเอาอันนี้
Does it come with instructions?	*mii wíthii chái yùu dûai rúe plào* มีวิธีใช้อยู่ด้วยหรือเปล่า
It's too expensive	*phaehng pai* แพงไป
I'll give you…	*phŏm/dichán hâi…* ผม/ดิฉันให้…
Could you keep this for me?	*kèp níi wái hai phŏm/dichán dâi mái* เก็บนี้ไว้ให้ผม/ดิฉันได้ไหม
I'll come back for it later	*phŏm/dichán ca klàp maa ao thii lăng* ผม/ดิฉันจะกลับมาเอาทีหลัง
Could you gift wrap it, please?	*chûai hàw khăwng khwăn hâi nòi dâi mái khráp/khá* ช่วยห่อของขวัญให้หน่อยได้ไหมครับ/ คะ
Do you have a bag for me, please?	*khun mii thŭng mái khráp/khá* คุณมีถุงไหมครับ/คะ

เสียใจนะครับ/คะ เราไม่มี *sĭa-cai ná khráp/khá rao mâi mii*	I'm sorry, we don't have that
เสียใจนะครับ/คะ ขายหมดแล้ว *sĭa-cai ná khráp/khá khăai mòt láeo*	I'm sorry, we're sold out
เสียใจนะครับ/คะ มันจะไม่มาจน… *sĭa-cai ná khráp/khá man cà mâi maa con…*	I'm sorry, it won't come back in until…
กรุณาจ่ายที่เคาน์เตอร์เก็บตัง *karunaa càai thîi khawn-toer kèp tang*	Please pay at the cash register

10.2 Food

I'd like a hundred grams of…, please	*phǒm/dichán ao nùeng khìit khráp/khâ* ผม/ดิฉัน เอาหนึ่งขีดครับ/ค่ะ
I'd like half a kilo/five hundred grams of…	*phǒm/dichán ao…<u>khrûeng kiloh</u>/<u>hâa</u>* *<u>ráwi kram</u> khráp/khá* ผม/ดิฉันเอา…ครึ่งกิโล/ห้าร้อยกรัม ครับ/ค่ะ
I'd like a kilo of…	*phǒm/dichán ao…nùeng kiloh khráp/ khá* ผม/ดิฉันเอา…หนึ่งกิโลครับ/ค่ะ
Could you…it for me, please?	*chûa…hâi nòi dâi mái khráp/khá* ช่วย…ให้หน่อยได้ไหมครับ/คะ
– slice it/cut it up for me, please?	*chûai <u>hàn</u>/<u>tàt</u> hâi nòi khráp/khá* ช่วย หั่น/ตัด ให้หน่อยครับ/ค่ะ
– grate it for me, please?	*soi hâi nòi khráp/khá* ซอยให้หน่อยครับ/ค่ะ
Can I order it?	*sàng maa dâi mái khráp/khá* สั่งมาได้ไหมครับ/คะ
I'll pick it up tomorrow at…	*phǒm/dichán ca pai ao phrûng níi thîi…* ผม/ดิฉันจะไปเอาพรุ่งนี้ที่…
Can you eat/drink this?	*<u>kin</u>/<u>dùehm</u> nîi dai mái* กิน/ดื่ม นี้ได้ไหม
What's in it?	*arai yùu khâng nai* อะไรอยู่ข้างใน

10.3 Clothing and shoes

I saw something in the window	*phǒm/dichán hěn arai baang yàang nai nâatàang* ผม/ดิฉันเห็นอะไรบางอย่างในหน้าต่าง
Shall I point it out?	*ca hâi chíi hâi duu mái* จะให้ชี้ให้ดูไหม

I'd like something to go with this	*yàak dâi arai thîi khâo kàp nîi* อยากได้อะไรที่เข้ากับนี่
Do you have shoes to match this?	*mii rawng tháo thîi khâo chút kàp nîi mái* มีรองเท้าที่เข้าชุดกับนี้ไหม
I'm a size…in the US	*phǒm/dichán khanàat…khǎwng amehríkaa* ผม/ดิฉันขนาด…ของอเมริกา
I'm a size…in Australia	*phǒm/dichán khanàat…khǎwng áws(a)trehlia* ผม/ดิฉันขนาด…ของออสเตรเลีย
Can I try this on?	*khǎw lawng dâi mái* ขอลองได้ไหม
Where's the fitting room?	*hâwng lawng sûea yùu thîi nái* ห้องลองเสื้ออยู่ที่ไหน
It doesn't suit me	*mâi màw kàp phǒm/dichán* ไม่เหมาะกับผม/ดิฉัน
This is the right size	*khanàat níi thùuk tâwng* ขนาดนี้ถูกต้อง
It doesn't look good on me	*phǒm/dichán sài láeo duu mâi dii* ผม/ดิฉันใส่แล้วดูไม่ดี
Do you have this/these in…[size]?	*khun mii yàang níi khanàat…mái* คุณมีอย่างนี้ขนาด…ไหม
Do you have this/these in…[color]?	*khun mii yàang níi sǐi…mái* คุณมีอย่างนี้สี…ไหม
The heel's too high/low	*sôn sǔung pai/tîa pai* ส้น สูงไป/เตี้ยไป
Is this real leather/ genuine hide?	*nîi nǎng tháeh rúe plào* นี่หนังแท้หรือเปล่า
I'm looking for a…for a…-year-old child	*phǒm/dichán kamlang hǎa…sǎmràp dèk…khùap* ผม/ดิฉันกำลังหา…สำหรับเด็ก…ขวบ
I'd like a…	*phǒm/dichán yàak dâi…* ผม/ดิฉันอยากได้…

– silk	*phâa măi thai*
	ผ้าไหมไทย
– cotton	*phâa fâi*
	ผ้าฝ้าย
– woolen	*phâa khŏn sàt*
	ผ้าขนสัตว์
– linen	*phâa línin*
	ผ้าลินิน
What temperature can I wash it at?	*khuan sák nai unhàphuum thâorài*
	ควรซักในอุณหภูมิเท่าไร
Will it shrink in the wash?	*sák láeo ca hòt mái*
	ซักแล้วจะหดไหม

ซักมือ	ซักแห้ง	อย่ารีด
sák mueh	*sák hâeng*	*yàa rîit*
Hand wash	Dry clean	Do not iron
ซักเครื่องได้	อย่าปั่นแห้ง	วางราบ
sák khrûeng dâi	*yahh phun hange*	*waang râap*
Machine washable	Do not spin dry	Lay flat

At the shoe repair shop/stall

Could you mend these shoes?	*chûai sâwm rawng tháo níi dâi mái*
	ช่วยซ่อมรองเท้านี้ได้ไหม
Could you resole/reheel these shoes?	*chûai sài phúehn/sôn rawng tháo níi mài dâi mái*
	ช่วยใส่ พื้น/ส้น รองเท้านี้ใหม่ได้ไหม
When will they be ready?	*ca sèt mûearài*
	จะเสร็จเมื่อไร
I'd like…, please	*phŏm/dichán yàak dâi…khráp/khá*
	ผม/ดิฉันอยากได้…ครับ/ค่ะ
– a can of shoe polish	*yaa khàt rawng tháo nùeng krapăwng*
	ยาขัดรองเท้าหนึ่งกระป๋อง

– a pair of shoelaces | *chûeak phùuk rawng tháo nùeng khûu*
เชือกผูกรองเท้าหนึ่งคู่

10.4 Cameras

เอสแอลอาร์
es-el-aa
single-lens-reflex
  camera (SLR)

วีดีโอ
wii-dii-oo
video

กล้องดิจิตอล
klâwng di-cìt-toel
digital camera

พิกเซล
phík-sun
pixel

ออพติคอล ซูม
off-tìk-khol suum
optical zoom

เอสดีการ์ด
es dii káad
SD card

กล้องวงจรปิด
klâwng wongcawn pìt
face recognition camera

การตัดต่อ-รูปภาพ
kaan tàt-taw rûup-phâap
photo-editing

Problems

Should I replace the batteries? | *khuan plàan baehttoehrîi mái*
ควรเปลี่ยนแบตเตอรี่ไหม

Could you have a look at my camera, please? | *chûai duu klâwng hâi nòi dâi mái khráp/khá*
ช่วยดูกล้องให้หน่อยได้ไหมครับ/คะ

It's not working | *man mâi tham ngaan*
มันไม่ทำงาน

The…is broken | *sĭa*
…เสีย…

The flash isn't working | *fláet mâi tham ngaan*
แฟลชไม่ทำงาน

Processing and prints

I'd like to have these pictures printed, please | *phŏm/dichán yàak àt rûup nòi khráp/khá*
ผม/ดิฉัน อยากอัดรูปหน่อยครับ/ค่ะ

I'd like…prints from each negative | *phŏm/dichán yàak dâi yàang lá…chút*
ผม/ดิฉันอยากได้อย่างละ…ชุด

glossy/matte	*man/dâan* มัน/ด้าน
6 x 9	*khanàat hòk khuun kao* ขนาดหกคูณเก้า
I'd like to order reprints of these photos	*phǒm/dichán yàak sàng àt rûup phûak níi ìik* ผม/ดิฉันอยากสั่งอัดรูปพวกนี้อีก
I'd like to have this photo enlarged	*phǒm/dichán yàak khayǎi rûup níi* ผม/ดิฉันอยากขยายรูปนี้
How much for printing?	*khâa àt thâorài* ค่าอัดเท่าไร
How much are the reprints?	*khâa àt phôehm thâorài* ค่าอัดเพิ่มเท่าไร
How much is it for enlargement?	*khâa khayǎi rûup thâorài* ค่าขยายรูปเท่าไร
When will they be ready?	*ca sèt mûearài* จะเสร็จเมื่อไร
Can you process onto CD?	*khun àt rûup khâo sii dii dâi mái* คุณอัดรูปเข้าซีดีได้ไหม
How much is it to process onto a CD?	*khâa àt rûup khâo sii dii thâorài* ค่าอัดรูปเข้าซีดีเท่าไหร่

10.5 At the hairdresser

Do I have to make an appointment?	*phǒm/dichán tâwng nát mái* ผม/ดิฉันต้องนัดไหม
Can I come in right now?	*phǒm/dichán maa tawn níi dâi mái* ผม/ดิฉันมาตอนนี้ได้ไหม
How long will I have to wait?	*phǒm/dichán tâwng raw naan thâorài* ผม/ดิฉันต้องรอนานเท่าไร
I'd like a shampoo/haircut	*phǒm/dichán yàak sà phǒm/tàt phǒm* ผม/ดิฉันอยาก สระผม/ตัดผม

I'd like a shampoo for oily/dry hair, please	*phǒm/dichán yàak dâi chaehmphuu sǎmràp phǒm man/phǒm hâehng khráp/khâ* ผม/ดิฉันอยากได้แชมพูสำหรับ ผมมัน/ผมแห้ง ครับ/ค่ะ
I'd like an anti-dandruff shampoo	*phǒm/dichán yàak dâi chaehmphuu kan rangkhaeh* ผม/ดิฉันอยากได้แชมพูกันรังแค
I'd like a color-rinse shampoo, please	*phǒm/dichán yàak dâi chaehmphuu láang sǐi khráp/khá* ผม/ดิฉันอยากได้แชมพูล้างสีครับ/ค่ะ
I'd like a shampoo with conditioner, please	*phǒm/dichán yàak dâi chaehmphuu thîi mii khawndichan-nôeh khráp/khá* ผม/ดิฉันอยากได้แชมพูที่มีคอนดิชันเนอร์ครับ/ค่ะ
I'd like highlights, please	*phǒm/dichán yàak dâi hailái(t) phǒm khráp/khá* ผม/ดิฉันอยากได้ไฮไลต์ผมครับ/ค่ะ
Do you have a color chart, please?	*khun mii phàen sǐi hâi lûeak mái* คุณมีแผ่นสีให้เลือกไหม
I'd like to keep the same color	*phǒm/dichán yàak kèp sǐi kào wai* ผม/ดิฉันอยากเก็บสีเก่าไว้
I'd like it darker/lighter	*phǒm/dichán yàak dâi sǐi khêm kwàa/àwn kwàa* ผม/ดิฉันอยากได้สี เข้มกว่า/อ่อนกว่า
I'd like/I don't want hairspray	*phǒm/dichán yàak chìit/mâi yàak chìit sapreh* ผม/ดิฉัน อยากฉีด/ไม่อยากฉีด สเปรย์
– gel	*sài cehl* ใส่เจล
– lotion	*sài lohchân* ใส่โลชั่น
I'd like short bangs (a short fringe)	*yàak dâi phǒm máa* อยากได้ผมม้า

Not too short at the back	*khâng lăng mâi sân mâak* ข้างหลังไม่สั้นมาก
Not too long	*mâi yao pai* ไม่ยาวไป
I'd like it curly/not too curly	*phŏm/dichán yàak hâi yìk/mâi yìk mâak* ผม/ดิฉันอยากให้ หยิก/ไม่หยิกมาก
It needs a little/a lot taken off	*tâwng ao àwk nít nòi/yóe yóe* ต้องเอาออก นิดหน่อย/เยอะๆ
I'd like a completely different style/ a different cut	*phŏm/dichán yàak plìan pen song mài/ tàt bàehp mài tháng mòt* ผม/ดิฉันอยาก เปลี่ยนเป็นทรงใหม่/ ตัดแบบใหม่ ทั้งหมด
I'd like it the same as in this photo	*phŏm/dichán yàak hâi mŭean nai rûup níi* ผม/ดิฉันอยากให้เหมือนในรูปนี้
– as that woman's	*mŭean khăwng phûu yĭng khon nán* เหมือนของผู้หญิงคนนั้น
Could you turn the drier up/down a bit?	*chûai rêng thîi pào phom/lót thîi pào phŏm nít nòi dâi mái* ช่วย เร่งที่เป่าผม/ลดที่เป่าผม นิดหน่อยได้ไหม
I'd like to thin my hair a bit	*phŏm/dichán yàak cà soi phŏm nít nùeng khráp/khá* ผม/ดิฉัน อยากจะซอยผมนิดหนึ่งครั บ/ค่ะ

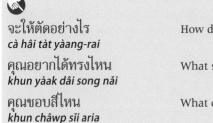

จะให้ตัดอย่างไร *cà hâi tàt yàang-rai*	How do you want it cut?
คุณอยากได้ทรงไหน *khun yàak dâi song năi*	What style did you have in mind?
คุณชอบสีไหน *khun châwp sĭi aria*	What color would you like?

อุณหภูมิพอดีไหม *un-aphuum phaw-dii mái*	Is the temperature all right for you?
คุณอยากอ่านอะไรไหม *khun yàak àan arai mái*	Would you like something to read?
คุณอยากดื่มอะไรไหม *khun yàak dùehm arai*	Would you like a drink?
คุณอยากได้อย่างนี้หรือ *khun yàak dâi yang níi rǔe*	Is this what you had in mind?

I'd like a facial	*yàak tham nâa* อยากทำหน้า
– a manicure	*yàak tham lép* ทำเล็บ
– a massage	*yàak nûat* นวด
Could you trim my…, please?	*chûai lem…hâi nòi khráp/khá* ช่วยเล็ม…ให้หน่อยครับ/ค่ะ
– bangs (fringe)	*phŏm máa* ผมม้า
– beard	*khrao* เครา
– mustache?	*nùat* หนวด
(male) I'd like a shave, please	*phŏm yàak kohn nùat/khrao khráp/khá* ผมอยากโกนหนวด/เคราครับ/ค่ะ
(male) I'd like a wet shave, please	*phŏm yàak kohn nùat bàehp sài khriim* ผมอยากโกนหนวดแบบใส่ครีม

11 Tourist Activities

11. Tourist Activities

11.1 Places of interest

● **Places of interest** to tourists in Thailand are many and varied. At the renowned Lumpini Boxing Stadium (*sanăam muai lumphí-nii*), for example, you can enjoy the excitement of Thai kick boxing (*muai thai*), and savor an authentic local experience in a colorful and often boisterous environment. The crocodile farm (*faam cawrákhêh*) at Samut Prakan (*samùt prakaan*) on the southeast fringe of Bangkok is most certainly worth the short trip, while the floating market (*talàat náam*) at Damnoen Saduak (*damnoehn sadùak*) in Ratchaburi* province, not far from the capital, will provide the visitor with a taste of another aspect of traditional Thai life.

Bangkok is famous for its frenetic, bustling nightlife, in particular the bars and discos of Patpong Road and its immediate environs; Soi 4 Sukhumvit Road, commonly known as "Soi Nana," and "Soi Cowboy" which runs between Soi 21 and Soi 23, parallel to Sukhumvit Road. The city is also well-known for its quiet, majestic temples: Wat Phra Kaeo—the Temple of the Emerald Buddha at the old Grand Palace; Wat Pho the Temple of the Reclining Buddha, and Wat Arun, the Temple of Dawn on the west bank of the Chaophraya River.

The best place to find out about what's on, and where, is the Tourism Authority of Thailand (TAT) whose web address is: http://www.tourismthailand.org/campaign/en/

In case you wish to make direct enquiries before your departure TAT have offices in many major cities around the world. Their head office is in the Le Concorde Building, 202 Ratchaphisek Road, Huai Khwang, Bangkok 10310, tel. (66)2 694 1222.

Of course, hotels, backpacker hostels and guesthouses all have information on places to visit, tours to take, and locations of

---

* Note: while generally written as Ratchaburi the word is actually pronounced *Rart-buri*.

shopping malls, souvenir shop, and supermarkets. Do be wary of touts, although they can be useful sources of information.

Where's the Tourist Information, please?	*nùai bawríkaan nák thâwng thîao yùu thîi nái khráp/khá* หน่วยบริการนักท่องเที่ยว อยู่ที่ไหนครับ/คะ
Do you have a city map?	*mii phǎehn thîi khǎwng mueang mái* มีแผนที่ของเมืองไหม
Where is the museum?	*phíphíthaphan yùu thîi nái khráp/khá* พิพิธภัณฑ์อยู่ที่ไหนครับ/คะ
Where can I find a church?	*bòht yùu thîi nái khráp/khá* โบสถ์อยู่ที่ไหนครับ/คะ
Could you give me some information about…?	*chûai bàwk phǒm/dichán kìao kàp… nòi dâi mái khráp/khá* ช่วยบอกผม/ดิฉันเกี่ยวกับ… หน่อยได้ไหมครับ/คะ
How much is that?	*nîi thâorài* นี่เท่าไร
What are the main places of interest?	*thîi nǎi nâa thîao bâang* ที่ไหนน่าเที่ยวบ้าง
Could you point them out on the map?	*chûai chíi nai phǎehn thîi hâi nòi dâi mái* ช่วยชี้ในแผนที่ให้หน่อยได้ไหม
What do you recommend?	*khun náe-nam arai dii* คุณแนะนำอะไรดี
We'll be here for a few hours	*rao ca yùu thîi nîi sák sǎwng sǎam chûamohng* เราจะอยู่ที่นี่สักสองสามชั่วโมง
We'll be here for a day	*rao ca yùu thîi nîi sák nùeng wan* เราจะอยู่ที่นี่สักหนึ่งวัน
We'll be here for a week	*rao ca yùu thîi nîi sák nùeng aathít* เราจะอยู่ที่นี่สักหนึ่งอาทิตย์
We're interested in…	*rao sǒnjai…* เราสนใจ…

Are there any boat trips?	*mii nâng ruea thîao mái* มีนั่งเรือเที่ยวไหม
Where can we board?	*rao long ruea thîi nǎi dâi* เราลงเรือที่ไหนได้
Are there any bus tours?	*mii nâng rót thîao mái* มีนั่งรถเที่ยวไหม
Where do we get on?	*khûn rót dâi thîi nǎi* ขึ้นรถได้ที่ไหน
Is there a guide who speaks English?	*mii kái thîi phûut phaasǎa angkrìt mái* มีไกด์ที่พูดภาษาอังกฤษไหม
What trips can we take around the area?	*rao ca pai thîao râwp râwp bawríwehn dâi yàangrai* เราจะไปเที่ยวรอบ ๆบริเวณได้อย่างไร
Are there any excursions?	*mii thátsaná sùeksǎa mái* มีทัศนศึกษาไหม
Where do they go?	*phûak nán pai mái* พวกนั้นไปไหน
We'd like to go to…	*rao yâak pai…* เราอยากไป…
How long is the excursion?	*thátsaná sùeksǎa naan thâorài* ทัศนศึกษานานเท่าไร
How long do we stay in…?	*rao phák thîi…naan thâorài* เราพักที่…นานเท่าไร
Are there any guided tours?	*mii thua thîi mii kái mái* มีทัวร์ที่มีไกด์ไหม
How much free time will we have there?	*thîi nân rao mii wehlaa wâang thâorài* ที่นั่นเรามีเวลาว่างเท่าไร
We want to have a walk around/to go on foot	*rao yàak pai doehn lên râwp râwp/ doehn pai* เราอยาก ไปเดินเล่นรอบๆ/เดินไป
Can we hire a guide?	*rao jâang kai dâi mái* เราจ้างไกด์ได้ไหม

Can we reserve a hillside hut?	*rao jhong krathâwm sǒn dâi mái* เราจองกระท่อมสนได้ไหม
What time does...open/close?	*...pòeht/pìt kìi mohng* ...เปิด/ปิดกี่โมง
What days is...open/closed?	*...pòeht/pìt wan nǎi* ...เปิด/ปิดวันไหน
What's the admission price?	*khâa khâo thâorài* ค่าเข้าเท่าไร
Is there a group discount?	*pai pen klùm mii raakhaa phísèht mái* ไปเป็นกลุ่มมีราคาพิเศษไหม
Is there a child discount?	*mii raakhaa dèk mái* มีราคาเด็กไหม
Is there a discount for senior citizens?	*mii raakhaa phûu sǔung aayú mái* มีราคาผู้สูงอายุไหม
Can I take (flash) photos/can I film here?	*thài rûup (chái fláet) dâi mái/thài widiioh dâi mái* ถ่ายรูป(ใช้แฟลช)ได้ไหม/ถ่ายวิดีโอได้ไหม
Do you have any postcards of...?	*mii pohtsakàat khǎwng...mái* มีโปสการ์ดของ...ไหม
Do you have an English...?	*mii...phaasǎa angkrìt mái* มี...ภาษาอังกฤษไหม
– catalog?	*kháettaalàwk* แค็ตตาล็อก
– program?	*prohkraehm* โปรแกรม
– brochure?	*phàehn pháp* แผ่นพับ

11.2 Going out

● **In Bangkok** one can relax by having a traditional Thai-style massage (*nûat bàehp thai phàehn bohraan*). One can also enjoy a memorable evening at one of the many restaurants that combine a Thai-style meal with Thai classical music and dances, or patronize the numerous cabaret shows in town. For a spectacular cultural show watch Siam Niramita which showcases Thai art and heritage performances with special effects. Those who prefer hot music can head for the many discos found in hotels and other entertainment malls.

Other options: take a slow river cruise (with dinner included) down the Chao Phraya and admire the beautiful night views of famous landmarks along the route. Or get a group of like-minded friends and have a roaring time at the karoake or go bowling—these are usually found in shopping malls. Feel like watching a movie? Thai and foreign movies are shown in cinemas—foreign films could be dubbed into Thai or left in the original language with Thai subtitles. English subtitles are usually provided for Thai films.

Do you have this week's/ month's entertainment guide?	*khun mii raikaan thiiwii khǎwng <u>aathít níi</u>/<u>duean níi</u> mái* คุณมีรายการทีวีของ อาทิตย์นี้/ เดือนนี้ ไหม
What's on tonight?	*khuehn níi mii arai* คืนนี้มีอะไร
We want to go to…	*rao yàak pai thîi…* เราอยากไปที่…
What's playing at the cinema?	*mii nǎng arai chǎi* มีหนังอะไรฉาย
What sort of film is that?	*nân pen nǎng praphêht nǎi* นั่นเป็นหนังประเภทไหน
– not suitable for people under 12/under 16	*mâi màw sǎmràp dèk aayú tàm <u>kwàa</u> <u>sìp sǎwng</u>/<u>tàm kwàa sìp hòk</u>* ไม่เหมาะสำหรับเด็กอายุ ต่ำกว่าสิบสอง/ต่ำกว่าสิบหก

– suitable for everyone	*màw sǎmràp thúk khon* เหมาะสำหรับทุกคน
– original version	*nǎng dâng doehm* หนังดั้งเดิม
– subtitled	*thîi mii ban yai* ที่มีบรรยาย
– dubbed	*phâak* พากย์
Is it a continuous showing?	*chǎi tàw nûeang rúe plào* ฉายต่อเนื่องหรือเปล่า
What's on at…?	*mii arai thîi…* มีอะไรที่…
– the theater?	*rohng lakhawn* โรงละคร
– the opera?	*rohng lakhawn ohpehrâa* โรงละครโอเปร่า
What's happening in the concert hall?	*mii arai thîi khawnsòeht hawn* มีอะไรที่คอนเสิร์ตฮอลล์
Where can I find a good disco around here?	*thǎeo níi mii dìtsakoh dii dii thîi nǎi* แถวนี้มีดิสโกดี ๆที่ไหน
Is it members only?	*chapháw samaachík thâo nán lǒeh* เฉพาะสมาชิกเท่านั้นหรือ
Where can I find a good nightclub around here?	*thǎeo níi mii nái(t) khláp dii dii thîi nǎi* แถวนี้มีไนท์คลับดีๆที่ไหน
Is it evening wear only?	*sài dâi chapháw chút raatrii thâo nán lǒeh* ใส่ได้เฉพาะชุดราตรีเท่านั้นหรือ
Should I/we dress up?	*phǒm/dichán/rao khuan tàehng tua dii rúe plào* ผม/ดิฉัน/เราควรแต่งตัวดีหรือเปล่า
What time does the show start?	*ngaan rôehm kìi mohng* งานเริ่มกี่โมง
When's the next soccer match?	*fútbawn khûu tàw pai mûearai* ฟุตบอลคู่ต่อไปเมื่อไร

Who's playing? *khrai lên*
ใครเล่น

11.3 Booking tickets

Could you reserve some
tickets for us?
rao khǎw cawng tǔa nòi dâi mái khráp/khá
เราขอจองตั๋วหน่อยได้ไหมครับ/ค่ะ

We'd like to book…seats/
a table for…
rao yàak cawng…thîi/tó sǎmràp…khon
เราอยากจอง…ที่/โต๊ะ สำหรับ...คน

…seats in the orchestra
in the main section
…thîi trong klaang nai awkhes(a)trâa
…ที่ตรงกลางในออเคสตรา

…seats in the circle
…thîi nai wong klom
…ที่ในวงกลม

a box for…
chán báwk sǎmràp…
ชั้นบอกซ์สำหรับ…คน

…front row seats/a table
for…at the front
*…thîi thǎeo nâa/tó sǎmràp…khon
thǎeo khâng nâa*
…ที่แถวหน้า/โต๊ะสำหรับ…
คนแถวข้างหน้า

…seats in the middle/
a table in the middle
…thîi trong klaang/tó trong klaang
…ที่ตรงกลาง/โต๊ะตรงกลาง

…back row seats/a table
at the back
…thîi nai thǎeo lǎng/tó thǎeo khâng lǎng
…ที่ในแถวหลัง/โต๊ะแถวข้างหลัง

Could I reserve…seats
for the…o'clock
performance?
*khǎw cawng…thîi sǎmràp râwp…
naalíkaa*
ขอจอง…ที่สำหรับรอบ…นาฬิกา

Are there any seats left
for tonight?
mii thîi lǔea bâang mái sǎmràp khuehn níi
มีที่เหลือบ้างไหมสำหรับคืนนี้

How much is a ticket?
tǔa bai lá thâorài
ตั๋วใบละเท่าไร

When can I pick up
the tickets?
ráp tǔa dâi mûearai
รับตั๋วได้เมื่อไร

I've got a reservation
phǒm/dichán jhong tǔa wái láeo
ผม/ดิฉันจองตั๋วไว้แล้ว

| My name's… | phŏm/dichán chûeh…
ผม/ดิฉันชื่อ… |

คุณอยากจองรอบไหน khun yàak cawng râwp năi	Which performance/show do you want to make a reservation for?
คุณอยากนั่งที่ไหน khun yàak nâng thîi năi	Where would you like to sit?
ตั๋วขายหมดแล้ว tŭa khăai mòt láeo	All the tickets are sold out
มีแต่ที่ยืนเท่านั้น mii tàe thîi yeun thâo-nán	It's standing room only
เหลือแต่ที่ในวงกลม lŭea tàe thîi nai wong klom	We've only got circle seats left
เหลือแต่ที่ชั้นบนในวงกลม lŭea tàe thîi chán bon nai wong klom	We've only got upper circle seats left
เหลือแต่ที่ในออเคสตรา lŭea tàe thîi nai aw-khestraa	We've only got orchestra seats left
เหลือแต่ที่แถวหน้า lŭea tàe thîi thăeo nâa	We've only got front row seats left
เหลือแต่ที่แถวหลัง lŭea tàe thîi thăeo lăng	We've only got seats left at the back
คุณต้องการกี่ที่ khun tâwng-kaan kìi thîi	How many seats would you like?

คุณจะต้องมารับตั๋วก่อน…
  นาฬิกา
khun cà tâwng maa ráp tŭa
  kàwn…naalikaa
	You'll have to pick up the tickets
	  before…o'clock

ขอตั๋วครับ/ค่ะ khăw tŭa khráp/khâ	Tickets, please
นี่ที่ของคุณ nîi thîi khăwng khun	This is your seat
คุณนั่งผิดที่ khun nâng phìt thîi	You're in the wrong seat

12 Sports Activities

12. Sports Activities

12.1 Sporting questions

การเดินป่า *kaan doehn pàa* hiking	โยคะ *yoo-khá* yoga
สปาน้ำแร่ *sa-paa náam râe* open-air bath	การเที่ยวไปเช้า-เย็นกลับ *kaan thîao pai cháw-yen klàp* one-day trip

Where can we…around here?	*rao…dâi thîi nǎi thǎeo níi* เรา…ได้ที่ไหนแถวนี้
Can I/we hire a…?	*phǒm/dichán/rao châo…dâi mái* ผม/ดิฉัน/เรา เช่า…ได้ไหม
Can I/we take…lessons?	*phǒm/dichán/rao rian…dâi mái* ผม/ดิฉัน/เราเรียน…ได้ไหม
– swimming	*wâi náam* ว่ายน้ำ
– diving	*dam náam* ดำน้ำ
– water skiing	*lên sakii náam* เล่นสกีน้ำ
– motor boating	*khàp ruea yon* ขับเรือยนต์
How much is that per hour/per day	*nân chûamohng lá/wan lá thâorài* นั่น ชั่วโมงละ/วันละ เท่าไหร่
How much is each one?	*an lá thâorài* อันละเท่าไหร่
Do you need a permit for that?	*tâwng mii bai anúyâat mái* ต้องมีใบอนุญาตไหม
Where can I get the permit?	*khǎw anúyâat dâi mái thîi nǎi* ขอใบอนุญาตได้ที่ไหน

| Where's a good place to go hiking? | *thîi năi mòh samràp kaan doehn pàa*
ที่ไหนเหมาะสำหรับการเดินป่า |

12.2 By the waterfront

Is it far (to walk) to the sea?	*(doehn) pai thŭeng thaleh klai mái* (เดิน) ไปถึงทะเลไกลไหม
Is there a...around here?	*thăeo níi mii...mái* แถวนี้มี...ไหม
– swimming pool	*sà wâi náam* สระว่ายน้ำ
– sandy beach	*hàat sai* หาดทราย
– mooring (place)/dock	*thîi càwt ruea* ที่จอดเรือ
Are there any rocks here?	*thîi nîi mii khòht hĭn mái* ที่นี่มีโขดหินไหม
When's high/low tide?	*náam khûen/náam long mûearai* น้ำขึ้น/น้ำลง เมื่อไร
What's the water temperature?	*unhàphuum náam thâorài* อุณหภูมิน้ำเท่าไหร่
Is it (very) deep here?	*thîi nîi náam lúek (mâak) mái* ที่นี่น้ำลึก(มาก)ไหม
Is it safe (for children) to swim here?	*plàwt phai (sămràp dèk) mái thîi ca wâi náam thîi nîi* ปลอดภัย(สำหรับเด็ก)ไหมที่จะ ว่ายน้ำที่นี่
Are there any currents?	*mii krasăeh náam mái* มีกระแสน้ำไหม
Are there any rapids/ waterfalls along this river?	*mâeh náam níi mii náam chîao/náam tòk mái* แม่น้ำนี้มี น้ำเชี่ยว/น้ำตก ไหม

What does that flag/ buoy mean?	*thong náam/lûuk bawn lawi náam* nán *măi khwaam wâa arai* ธงนั้น/ลูกบอลล์ลอยน้ำนั้นหมายควา มว่าอะไร
Is there a lifeguard on duty?	*mii nùai kûu phai pracam kaan rúe plao* มีหน่วยกู้ภัยประจำการหรือเปล่า
Are dogs allowed here?	*sunák khâo dâi mái* สุนัขเข้าได้ไหม
Is camping on the beach allowed?	*tâng khaehm bon hàat dâi mái* ตั้งแคมป์บนหาดได้ไหม
Can we light a fire?	*cùt fai dâi mái* จุดไฟได้ไหม

เขตตกปลา	มีใบอนุญาตเท่านั้น	งดว่ายน้ำ
khèt tòk plaa	*mii bai anu-yâat thâorai*	*ngót wâi-náam*
Fishing area	Permits only	No swimming
อันตราย	งดเล่นกระดานโต้คลื่น	งดตกปลา
antarai	*ngót lên kradaan tôo khlûen*	*ngót tòk plaa*
Danger	No surfing	No fishing

12.3 Seaside water/jet-skiing

Can I take water/jet ski lessons here?	*rian lên sakii/cét sakii thîi nîi dâi mái* เรียนเล่น สกีน้ำ/เจ็ทสกี ที่นี่ได้ไหม
For beginners/ intermediates	*sǎmràp rádàp rôehm tôn/rádàp paan klaang* สำหรับ ระดับเริ่มต้น/ระดับปานกลาง
How large are the groups?	*klùm yài khâeh nǎi* กลุ่มใหญ่แค่ไหน
What language are the classes in?	*chái phaasǎa arai* ใช้ภาษาอะไร

I'd like to hire a water/ jet ski, please	*phŏm/dichán yàak châo thîi lên sakii/ cét sakii nàwi* ผม/ดิฉันอยากเช่า ที่เล่นสกี/เจ็ทสกี หน่อย
Do I need any special clothing?	*phŏm/dichán tâwngkaan sûea phâa phíseht bâang mái* ผม/ดิฉันต้องการเสื้อผ้าพิเศษ บ้างไหม
Are there any beaches safe to water/jet ski around here?	*thăeho níi mii hàat plàwt phai sămràp lên sakii/cét sakii bâang mái* แถวนี้มีหาดที่ปลอดภัยสำหรับเล่น สกี/เจ็ทสกี บ้างไหม
Have the water/jet-skiing areas been signposted?	*bawríwehn lên sakii/cét sakii ca mii pâi tìt rúe plào* บริเวณเล่น สกี/เจ็ทสกี จะมีป้ายติดหรือเปล่า
Are the…open?	*…pòeht rúe plào* …เปิดหรือเปล่า
– water/jet ski hirings	*ráan châo thîi lên sakii/cét sakii* ร้านเช่า ที่เล่นสกี/เจ็ทสกี
– beach cafés	*ráan kaafaeh thîi hàat* ร้านกาแฟที่หาด
– beach chair hirings	*ráan châo kâo îi chai hàat* ร้านเช่าเก้าอี้ชายหาด
– fresh-water showers	*thîi châo àap náam cùeht* ที่เช่าอาบน้ำจืด

13 Health Matters

13. Health Matters

13.1 **Calling a doctor**

● **If you become ill**, there are hospitals in major towns and in shopping centers in Bangkok—most have a doctor on call. Clinics are used to treating such matters as diarrhea (*tháwng doehn*), STDs (*rôhk tìt tàw*) and tropical ailments. If you need emergency treatment, go to Casualty (*hâwng phûu pùai chùk chǒehn*) at the nearest hospital. Hospitals in Thailand are not free and can be quite expensive, so if you are insured at home, remember to have the desk clearly mark the sickness and treatment received on your receipt. A credit card may be needed as surety for any stay in hospital.

Could you call (get) a doctor quickly, please?	*chûai rîak mǎw dùan khráp/khá* ช่วยเรียกหมอด่วนครับ/ค่ะ
When does the doctor have office hours?	*khliinìk mǎw pòeht kìi mohng* คลินิกหมอเปิดกี่โมง
When can the doctor come?	*mǎw maa dâi kìi mohng* หมอมาได้กี่โมง
Could I make an appointment to see the doctor?	*khǎw nát mǎw dâi mái khráp/khá* ขอนัดหมอได้ไหมครับ/ค่ะ
I've got an appointment to see the doctor at…o'clock	*phǒm/dichán nát mǎw wái tawn… naalíkaa* ผม/ดิฉันนัดหมอไว้ตอน…นาฬิกา
Which doctor/pharmacy has night/weekend duty?	*ráan mǎw/khǎi yaa thîi nai pòeht tawn klaang khuehn/wan sǎo aathít* หมอ/ร้านขายยาที่ไหนเปิด ตอนกลางคืน/วันเสาร์อาทิตย์

13.2 **What's wrong?**

I don't feel well	*phǒm/dichán mâi khôi sabai* ผม/ดิฉันไม่ค่อยสบาย

I'm dizzy	*phǒm/dichán muen hǔa* ผม/ดิฉันมึนหัว
– ill	*pùai* ป่วย
I feel sick (nauseous)	*phǒm/dichán khlûehn sâi* ผม/ดิฉันคลื่นไส้
I've got a cold	*phǒm/dichán pen wàt* ผม/ดิฉันเป็นหวัด
It hurts here	*jèp thîi nîi* เจ็บที่นี่
I've been sick (vomited)	*phǒm/dichán ca aacian* ผม/ดิฉันจะอาเจียน
I've got...	*phǒm/dichán pen...* ผม/ดิฉันเป็น...
I'm running a temperature of...degrees	*phǒm/dichán unhàphuum khûen...* *ongsǎa* ผม/ดิฉันอุณหภูมิขึ้น...องศา
I've been...	*phǒm/dichán dohn...* ผม/ดิฉันโดน...
– stung by a wasp/bee	*tàw/phûeng tòi* ต่อ/ผึ้ง ต่อย
– stung by an insect	*malaehng tòi* แมลงต่อย
– stung by a jellyfish	*maehngkaphrun* แมงกะพรุน
– bitten by a dog	*mǎa kàt* หมากัด
– bitten by a snake	*nguu kàt* งูกัด
– bitten by something	*tua arai kàt* ตัวอะไรกัด
I've cut myself	*phǒm/dichán dohn mîit bàat* ผม/ดิฉันโดนมีดบาด

I've burned myself	*phǒm/dichán thùuk lûak* ผม/ดิฉันถูกลวก
I've scratched myself	*phǒm/dichán khùan tua ehng* ผม/ดิฉันข่วนตัวเอง
I've had a fall	*phǒm/dichán hòk lóm* ผม/ดิฉันหกล้ม
I've grazed my...	*phǒm/dichán tham…thalàwk* ผม/ดิฉันทำ…ถลอก
– knee	*hǔa khào* หัวเข่า
– elbow	*khâw sàwk* ข้อศอก
– leg	*khǎa* ขา
– arm	*khǎehn* แขน
I've sprained my ankle	*khâw tháo klét* ข้อเท้าเคล็ด
I'd like the morning-after pill	*yàak dâi yaa khum thîi thaan lâng wan rûam* อยากได้ยาคุมกำเนิดหลังร่วมเพศ

13.3 The consultation

มีปัญหาอะไร *mii panhǎa arai*	What seems to be the problem?
คุณเป็นมานานแล้วหรือยัง *khun pen maa naan láeo rǔe-yàang*	How long have you had these complaints?
เคยเป็นอย่างนี้มาก่อนหรือเปล่า *khoei pen yang níi maa kàwn rǔe-plàao*	Have you had this trouble before?

ตัวร้อนไหม กี่องศา *tua ráwn mái kìi ongsǎa*	Do you have a temperature? What is it?
ถอดเสื้อซิ *thâwt sûea sí*	Get undressed, please
ถอดถึงเอว *thâwt thǔeng eo*	Strip to the waist, please
คุณไปถอดที่นั่นได้ *khun pai thâwt sûea thîi nân dâi*	You can undress there
เอาแขนเสื้อข้างซ้าย/ข้างขวาขึ้นซิ *ao khǎen sûea khâang sáai/khâang khwǎa khûen sí*	Roll up your left/right sleeve, please
นอนที่นี่ซิ *nawn thîi nîi sí*	Lie down here, please
เจ็บไหม *jèp mái*	Does this hurt?
หายใจลึกๆ *hǎai-jai léuk-léuk*	Breathe deeply
อ้าปากซิ *âa pàak sí*	Open your mouth

Health Matters

13

Patients' medical history

I'm a diabetic	*phǒm/dichán pen bao wǎan* ผม/ดิฉันเป็นเบาหวาน
I have a heart condition	*phǒm/dichán pen rôhk hǔa cai* ผม/ดิฉันเป็นโรคหัวใจ
I'm asthmatic	*phǒm/dichán pen rôhk hàwp hǔeht* ผม/ดิฉันเป็นโรคหอบหืด
I'm allergic to…	*phǒm/dichán pháeh…* ผม/ดิฉันแพ้…
I'm…months pregnant	*dichán tháwng…duean* ดิฉันท้อง…เดือน

173

I'm on a diet	*phŏm/dichán lót khwaam ûan*
	ผม/ดิฉันลดความอ้วน
I'm on medication/the pill	*phŏm/dichán kamlang ráp kaan ráksǎa yùu/thaan yaa khum kamnòeht yùu*
	ผม/ดิฉันกำลัง รับการรักษาอยู่/ทา นยาคุมกำเนิดอยู่
I've had a heart attack once before	*phŏm/dichán khoei hǔa cai wai maa láeo khráng nùeng*
	ผม/ดิฉันเคยหัวใจวายมาแล้วครั้งหนึ่ง
I've had a(n)…operation	*phŏm/dichán khoei phàa tàt…*
	ผม/ดิฉันเคยผ่าตัด…
I've been ill recently	*mûea mâi naan maa níi phŏm/ dichán pùai*
	เมื่อไม่นานนี้ผม/ดิฉันป่วย
I've got a stomach ulcer	*phŏm/dichán pen rôhk krapháw*
	ผม/ดิฉันเป็นโรคกระเพาะ
I've got my period	*dichán mii prajum duean*
	ดิฉันมีประจำเดือน

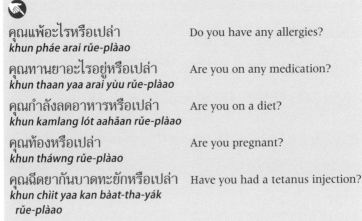

คุณแพ้อะไรหรือเปล่า	Do you have any allergies?
khun pháe arai rǔe-plàao	
คุณทานยาอะไรอยู่หรือเปล่า	Are you on any medication?
khun thaan yaa arai yùu rǔe-plàao	
คุณกำลังลดอาหารหรือเปล่า	Are you on a diet?
khun kamlang lót aahǎan rǔe-plàao	
คุณท้องหรือเปล่า	Are you pregnant?
khun tháwng rǔe-plàao	
คุณฉีดยากันบาดทะยักหรือเปล่า	Have you had a tetanus injection?
khun chìit yaa kan bàat-tha-yák rǔe-plàao	

The diagnosis

ไม่มีอะไรร้ายแรง
mâi mii arai ráai-raeng

It's nothing serious

...ของคุณหัก
...khǎwng khun hàk

Your...is broken

...ของคุณเคล็ด
...khǎwng khun khlét

You've got a sprained...

...ของคุณฉีกขาด
...khǎwng khun chìik khàat

You've got (a) torn...

คุณติดเชื้อ/มีการอักเสบ
khun tìt chúea/mii kaan àk-sèp

You've got an infection/some inflammation

คุณไส้ติ่งอักเสบ
khun sâi-tìng àk-sèp

You've got appendicitis

คุณเป็นโรคหลอดลมอักเสบ
khun pen rôhk làwt-lom àk-sèp

You've got bronchitis

คุณเป็นกามโรค
khun pen kaama-rôhk

You've got venereal disease

คุณเป็นไข้หวัดใหญ่
khun pen khâi-wàt yài

You've got the flu

คุณเป็นโรคหัวใจวาย
khun pen rôhk hǔa-cai waai

You've had a heart attack

คุณเป็นโรคไวรัสอักเสบ
khun pen rôhk wai-rus àk-sèp

You've got an (viral/bacterial) infection

คุณเป็นโรคปอดบวม
khun pen rôhk pàwt buam

You've got pneumonia

คุณเป็นแผลในกระเพาะอาหาร
khun pen phlǎe nai kra-phó aahǎan

You've got gastritis/an ulcer

คุณกล้ามเนื้อฉีก
khun klâam núea chìik

You've pulled a muscle

อักเสบในช่องคลอด
àk-sèp nai châwng-khlâwt

(You've got) a vaginal infection

อาหารเป็นพิษ *aahǎan pen phít*	(You've got) food poisoning
คุณเป็นลมแดด *khun pen lom dàet*	You've got sunstroke
คุณแพ้… *khun pháe…*	You're allergic to…
คุณท้อง *khun tháwng*	You're pregnant
ขอตรวจเลือด/ปัสสาวะ/อุจจาระ *khǎw trùat lûeat/pàtsǎawá/ùtcaará*	I'd like to have your blood/urine/ stool tested
ต้องเย็บ *tâwng yép*	It needs stitching
ผม/ดิฉันจะส่งคุณไปให้หมอเฉพ าะทาง/ส่งไปโรงพยาบาล *phǒm/dichán cà song khun pai hâi mǎw* *cha-phó/song pai rohng phayaabaan*	I'm referring you to a specialist/ sending you to hospital
ต้องไปเอกซเรย์ *tâwng pai ex-ray*	You'll need some x-rays taken
คุณจำเป็นต้องผ่าตัด *khun cam-pen tâwng phàa-tàt*	You'll need an operation
กรุณารอในห้องพักคนไข้นะครับ/ ค่ะ *karunaa raw nai hâwng phák* *khon-khâi ná khráp/khâ*	Could you wait in the waiting room, please?

Is it contagious?	*rôhk níi tìt tàw rúe plào* โรคนี้ติดต่อหรือเปล่า
How long do I have to stay…?	*tâwng yùu…naan thâorài* ต้องอยู่…นานเท่าไหร่
– in bed	*nawn phák nai tiang* นอนพักในเตียง
– in the hospital	*rohng phayaabaan* โรงพยาบาล

Do I have to go on a special diet?	*tâwng thaan aahăan phísèht mái* ต้องทานอาหารพิเศษไหม
Am I allowed to travel?	*doehn thaang dâi mái* เดินทางได้ไหม
Can I make another appointment?	*khăw nát mài ìik dâi mái* ขอนัดใหม่อีกได้ไหม
When do I have to come back?	*phŏm/dichán tâwng klàp maa ìik mûearai* ผม/ดิฉันต้องกลับมาอีกเมื่อไร
I'll come back tomorrow	*phŏm/dichán ca klàp maa ìik phrûeng níi* ผม/ดิฉันจะกลับมาอีกพรุ่งนี้
How do I take this medicine?	*yaa níi thaan yàangrai* ยานี้ทานอย่างไร

พรุ่งนี้/อีก...วันกลับมาใหม่นะครับ/คะ   Come back tomorrow/
phrûng-níi/ìik...wan klàp maa mài ná khráp/khá   in...days' time

13.4 Medications and prescriptions

How many pills/drops/injections/spoonfuls/tablets each time?	*khráng lá kìi <u>mét</u>/<u>yòt</u>/<u>khěm</u>/<u>cháwn</u>/<u>mét</u>* ครั้งละกี่ เม็ด/หยด/เข็ม/ช้อน/เม็ด
How many times a day?	*wan lá kìi khráng* วันละกี่ครั้ง
I've forgotten my medication	*phŏm/dichán luehm ao yaa maa* ผม/ดิฉันลืมเอายามา
At home I take...	*thîi bâan, phŏm/dichán thaan...* ที่บ้าน ผม/ดิฉันทาน...
Could you write a prescription for me?	*khăw bai sàng yaa nòi khráp/khá* ขอใบสั่งยาหน่อยครับ/ค่ะ

ผมสั่งยาแอนตี้ไบโอติก/ยานอนหลับ/
ยาแก้ปวด
phǒm sàng yaa aen-tîi bai otìk/
yaa nawn-làp/yaa kâe-pùat

I'm prescribing antibiotics/
a tranquilizer/pain killers

นอนพักมากๆ
nawn phák mâak-mâak

Have lots of rest

อยู่ในบ้าน
yùu nai bâan

Stay indoors

นอนในเตียง
nawn nai tiang

Stay in bed

ยา
yaa
medicine

ละลายในน้ำ
la-laai nai náam
dissolve in water

ก่อนอาหาร
kàwn aahǎan
before meals

ยาเม็ด
yaa-mét
tablets/pills

หลังอาหาร
lǎng aahǎan
after meals

วันละ...ครั้ง
wan lá...khráng
...times a day

ยานี้ลดสมรรถภาพในการขับขี่
yaa níi lót sǎmattaphâap nai
kaan-kàp-khìi
this medication impairs your
driving

กลืน (ทั้งหมด)
kluen (tháng mòt)
swallow (whole)

ช้อนโต๊ะ/ช้อนชา
cháwn tó/cháwn chaa
spoonful/teaspoonful

ทุก...ชั่วโมง
thúk ... chûa-moong
every (number of) ... hours

ยาทาภายนอก
yaa thaa phai nâwk
external use only

ทานยาในใบสั่งให้หมด
thaan yaa nai bai sàng hâi mòt
finish the prescription

ฉีดยา
chìit yaa
injection

หยด
yòt
drops

ยาทา
yaa thaa
ointment

ทา
thaa
rub on

...วัน
... wan
for...days

กิน
kin
take

13.5 At the dentist

Do you know a good dentist?	*khun rúujàk mǎw fan dii dii mái* คุณรู้จักหมอฟันดี ๆไหม
Could you make a dentist's appointment for me?	*chûai nát mǎw fan hâi nòi dâi mái* ช่วยนัดหมอฟันให้หน่อยได้ไหม
It's urgent	*dùan ná* ด่วนนะ
Can I come in today, please?	*phǒm/dichán khâo maa wan níi dâi mái khráp/khá* ผม/ดิฉันเข้ามาวันนี้ได้ไหมครับ/ค่ะ
I have (terrible) toothache	*phǒm/dichán pùat fan (mâak)* ผม/ดิฉันปวดฟัน (มาก)
I've got a broken tooth	*fan phǒm/dichán hàk* ฟันผม/ดิฉันหัก
Could you prescribe/give me a painkiller?	*chûai sàng/khǎw yaa kâeh pùat hâi nòi dâi mái khráp/khá* ช่วยสั่ง/ขอยาแก้ปวดให้หน่อยได้ไหมครับ/ค่ะ
My filling's come out	*thîi ùt fan lùt* ที่อุดฟันหลุด
I've got a broken crown	*thîi khrâwp fan hàk* ที่ครอบฟันหัก
I'd like/I don't want a local anaesthetic	*tâwngkaan/mâi tâwngkaan yaa chaa chapháw thîi* ต้องการ/ไม่ต้องการยาชาเฉพาะที่
Can you do a temporary repair?	*chûai sâwm chûa khrao dâi mái* ช่วยซ่อมชั่วคราวได้ไหม
I don't want this tooth pulled	*phǒm/dichán mâi tâwngkaan hâi thǎwn fan* ผม/ดิฉันไม่ต้องการให้ถอนฟัน
My denture is broken	*fan plawm phǒm/dichán hàk* ฟันปลอมผม/ดิฉันหัก

Can you fix it?	***khun sâwm dâi mái*** คุณซ่อมได้ไหม

ฟันไหนปวด
fan nǎi pùat

Which tooth hurts?

เหงือกเป็นหนอง
ngùeak pen nǎwng

You've got an abscess (literally,
"gums have pus")

ผม/ดิฉันต้องทำรากฟัน
phǒm/dichán tâwng tham râak fan

I'll have to do a root canal

ผม/ดิฉันจะใส่ยาชา
phǒm/dichán cà sài yaa-chaa

I'm giving you a local anaesthetic

ผม/ดิฉันต้องถอน/อุด/ตะไบฟันซี่นี้
phǒm/dichán tâwng <u>thǎwn</u>/<u>ùt</u>/
<u>tabai</u> fan sîi níi

I'll have to pull/fill/file this tooth

ผม/ดิฉันต้องกรอฟัน
phǒm/dichán tâwng kraw fan

I'll have to drill it

อ้าปากซิครับ/คะ
âa pàak sí khráp/khá

Open wide, please

หุบปากซิครับ/คะ
hùp pàak sí khráp/khá

Close your mouth, please

บ้วนปากซิครับ/คะ
bûan pàak sí khráp/khá

Rinse, please

ยังเจ็บอยู่หรือเปล่า
yang cèp yùu rǔe-plàao

Does it still hurt?

14 Emergencies

14. Emergencies

14.1 Asking for help

Help!	*chûai dûai!* ช่วยด้วย
Fire!	*fai mâi!* ไฟไหม้
Police!	*tamrùat!* ตำรวจ
Quick/Hurry!	*reo reo!* เร็วๆ
Danger!	*antarai!* อันตราย
Watch out!	*ra-wang!* ระวัง
Stop!	*yùt!* หยุด
Be careful!/You don't have to rush/hurry	*ra-wang/mâi tâwng rîip* ระวัง/ไม่ต้องรีบ
Get your hands off me!	*plòi phǒm/dichán!* ปล่อยผม/ดิฉัน
Let go!	*plòi ná!* ปล่อยนะ
Stop thief!	*khamoi khamoi!* ขโมย ขโมย
Could you help me, please?	*chûai phǒm/dichán nàwi dâi mái khráp/khá* ช่วยผม/ดิฉันหน่อยได้ไหมครับ/คะ
Where's the police station/ emergency exit/ fire escape?	*sathǎanii tamrùat/thaang àwk chùk chǒehn/bandai nǐi fai yùu thîi nǎi* สถานีตำรวจ/ทางออกฉุกเฉิน/บันไดหนีไฟอยู่ที่ไหน

Where's the nearest fire extinguisher?	*thîi dàp fai klâi thîisùt yùu thîi nǎi* ที่ดับไฟใกล้ที่สุดอยู่ที่ไหน
Call the fire department!	*rîak nùai dàp phloehng* เรียกหน่วยดับเพลิง
Call the police!	*rîak tamrùat!* เรียกตำรวจ
Call an ambulance!	*rîak rót phayaabaan* เรียกรถพยาบาล
Where's the nearest phone?	*thohrasàp klâi thîisùt yùu thîi nǎi* โทรศัพท์ใกล้ที่สุดอยู่ที่ไหน
Could I use your phone?	*khǎw chái thohrasàp khun dâi mái khráp/khá* ขอใช้โทรศัพท์คุณได้ไหมครับ/คะ
What's the emergency number?	*boeh câehng hèht chùk chǒehn boeh arai* เบอร์แจ้งเหตุฉุกเฉินเบอร์อะไร
What's the number for the police?	*boeh tamrùat boeh arai* เบอร์ตำรวจเบอร์อะไร

14.2 Lost items

I've lost my (digital) camera	*klâwng (di-cìt-toel) khǎwng phǒm/ dichán hǎi khráp/khá* กล้อง(ดิจิตอล)ของผม/ดิฉันหาย ครับ/คะ
I've lost my wallet/purse	*phǒm/dichán tham krapǎo sataang hǎi* ผม/ดิฉันทำกระเป๋าสตางค์หาย
I lost my…here yesterday	*phǒm/dichán tham…hǎi thîi níi mûeawaan níi* ผม/ดิฉันทำ…หายที่นี่เมื่อวานนี้
I left my…here	*phǒm/dichán luehm…wái thîi níi* ผม/ดิฉันลืม…ไว้ที่นี่
Did you find my…?	*khun hěn…phǒm/dichán mái* คุณเห็น…ผม/ดิฉันไหม

It was right here	*yùu trong nîi*
	อยู่ตรงนี้
It's very valuable	*mii khâa mâak*
	มีค่ามาก
Where's the lost and found office?	*phanàehk câehng khǎwng hǎi yùu thîi nǎi*
	แผนกแจ้งของหายอยู่ที่ไหน

14.3 Accidents

There's been an accident	*kòeht ùbatìhèht*
	เกิดอุบัติเหตุ
Someone's fallen into the water	*mii khon tòk náam*
	มีคนตกน้ำ
There's a fire	*mii fai mâi*
	ไฟไหม้
Is anyone hurt?	*mii khrai bàat cèp mái*
	มีใครบาดเจ็บไหม
[No]/someone has been injured	*[mâi] mii khrai bàat cèp*
	[ไม่] มีใครบาดเจ็บ
Someone's still trapped inside the car/train	*yang mii khon tìt yùu nai rót/rót fai*
	ยังมีคนติดอยู่ในรถ/รถไฟ
It's not too bad/much hurt	*mâi mâak/cèp thâorai*
	ไม่เลว
Don't worry	*mâi tâwng hùang*
	ไม่ต้องห่วง
Leave everything the way it is, please	*karunaa plòi wái yàang nán*
	กรุณาปล่อยไว้อย่างนั้น
I want to talk to the police first	*phǒm/dichán yàak phûut kàp tamrùat kàwn*
	ผม/ดิฉันอยากพูดกับตำรวจก่อน
I want to take a photo first	*phǒm/dichán yàak thài rûup kàwn*
	ผม/ดิฉันอยากถ่ายรูปก่อน

Here's my name and address	*nîi chûeh kàp thîi yùu khǎwng phǒm/ dichán* นี่ชื่อกับที่อยู่ของผม/ดิฉัน
May I have your name and address?	*khǎw chûeh kàp thîi yùu khǎwng khun nàwi khráp/khá* ขอชื่อกับที่อยู่ของคุณหน่อยครับ/ค่ะ
Could I see your identity card/your insurance papers?	*khǎw <u>duu bàt pracam tua/bai prakan</u> khǎwng khun dâi mái khráp/khá* ขอดู บัตรประจำตัว/ใบประกัน ของคุณได้ไหมครับ/คะ
Will you act as a witness?	*khun ca pen phayaan mái* คุณจะเป็นพยานไหม
I need this information for insurance purposes	*phǒm/dichán tâwngkaan khâwmuun nîi phûea prakan khǎwng phǒm/dichán* ผม/ดิฉันต้องการข้อมูลนี้เพื่อประกันของผม/ดิฉัน
Are you insured?	*khun mii prakan rúe plào* คุณมีประกันหรือเปล่า
Third party or all inclusive?	*bukkhon thîi sǎam rǔeh ruam mòt* บุคคลที่สามหรือรวมหมด
Could you sign here, please?	*sen chûeh thîi nîi khráp/khâ* เซ็นชื่อที่นี่ครับ/ค่ะ

14.4 Theft

I've been robbed	*phǒm/dichán thùuk plôn* ผม/ดิฉันถูกปล้น
My...has been stolen	*...khǎwng phǒm/dichán thùuk khamoi* ...ของผม/ดิฉันถูกขโมย
My car's been broken into	*rót phǒm/dichán thùuk ngát* รถผม/ดิฉันถูกงัด

14.5 Missing person

I've lost my child/ grandmother	*lûuk/khun yai khǎwng phǒm/dichán hǎi* ลูก/ยาย ของผม/ดิฉันหาย
Could you help me find him/her?	*chûai hǎa nàwi dâi mái khráp/khá* ช่วยหาหน่อยได้ไหมครับ/คะ
Have you seen a small child?	*khun hěn dèk lék lék mái* คุณเห็นเด็กเล็ก ๆไหม
He's/she's...years old	*aayú...khùap (pii)* อายุ...ขวบ (ปี)
He's/she's got...hair	*phǒm sǐi...* ผมสี...
short/long	*sân/yao* สั้น/ยาว
blond/red/brown/black/ gray	*sǐi thawng/daehng/námtaan/dam/thao* สี ทอง/แดง/น้ำตาล/ดำ/เทา
curly/straight/frizzy	*pen lawn/trong/yìk* เป็นลอน/ตรง/หยิก
...in a ponytail	*hǎang máa* หางม้า
...in braids	*thàk pia* ถักเปีย
...in a bun	*klâo muai* เกล้ามวย
He's/she's got blue/brown/ green eyes	*kháo taa sǐi fáa/námtaan/khǐao* เขาตาสี ฟ้า/น้ำตาล/เขียว
He's/she's wearing...	*kháo sài...* เขาใส่...
swimming trunks/ hiking boots	*chút àap náam/rawng tháo búut doehn thaang* ชุดอาบน้ำ/รองเท้าบู๊ทเดินทาง
with/without glasses	*sài/mâi sài wâen taa* ใส่/ไม่ใส่ แว่นตา

carrying/not carrying a bag	*hîu/mâi hîu thŭng* หิ้ว/ไม่หิ้ว ถุง
He/She is tall/short	*kháo sŭung/tîa* เขา สูง/เตี้ย
This is a photo of him/her	*nîi rûup kháo* นี่รูปเขา
He/she must be lost	*kháo khong lŏng thaang* เขาคงหลงทาง

14.6 The police

An arrest

ขอดูใบขับขี่ครับ/ค่ะ *khăw duu bai khàp-khìi khráp/khâ*	Your driver's license, please
คุณขับเร็วเกินอัตรา *khun khàp reo koen àt-traa*	You were speeding
คุณจอดที่นี่ไม่ได้ *khun càwt thîi-nîi mâi dâi*	You're not allowed to park here
คุณไม่ได้หยอดมิเตอร์ *khun mâi dâi yàwt mi-toer*	You haven't put money in the "Pay and display'/parking meter
ไฟรถคุณเสีย *fai rót khun sĭa*	Your lights aren't working
ถูกปรับ … บาท *thùuk pràp … bàat*	That's a … baht fine
คุณจะจ่ายเลยหรือเปล่า *khun cà càai loei rŭe-plàao*	Do you want to pay now?
คุณต้องจ่ายเดี๋ยวนี้ *khun tâwng càai dĭao-níi*	You'll have to pay now

I don't speak Thai	*phŏm/dichán phûut thai mâi dâi* ผม/ดิฉันพูดไทยไม่ได้

I didn't see the sign	*phǒm/dichán mâi hěn pâi (sǎnyaan)* ผม/ดิฉันไม่เห็นป้าย (สัญญาณ)
I don't understand what it says	*phǒm/dichán mâi khâo cai wâa bàwk wâa arai* ผม/ดิฉันไม่เข้าใจว่าบอกว่าอะไร
I was only doing… kilometers an hour	*phǒm/dichán khàp khâeh…kiloh tàw chûamohng* ผม/ดิฉันขับแค่...กิโลต่อชั่วโมง
I'll have my car checked	*phǒm/dichán ca ao rót pai trùat* ผม/ดิฉันจะเอารถไปตรวจ
I was blinded by oncoming lights	*phǒm/dichán mawng mâi hěn phráw fai rót sǔan maa man câa mâak* ผม/ดิฉันมองไม่เห็นเพราะไฟรถสวนมามันจ้ามาก

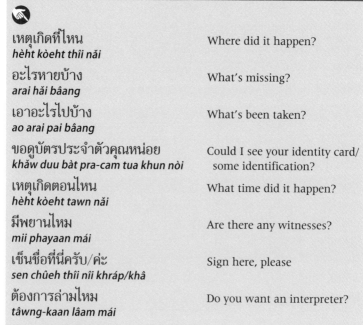

เหตุเกิดที่ไหน *hèht kòeht thîi nǎi*	Where did it happen?
อะไรหายบ้าง *arai hǎi bâang*	What's missing?
เอาอะไรไปบ้าง *ao arai pai bâang*	What's been taken?
ขอดูบัตรประจำตัวคุณหน่อย *khǎw duu bàt pra-cam tua khun nòi*	Could I see your identity card/ some identification?
เหตุเกิดตอนไหน *hèht kòeht tawn nǎi*	What time did it happen?
มีพยานไหม *mii phayaan mái*	Are there any witnesses?
เซ็นชื่อที่นี่ครับ/ค่ะ *sen chûeh thîi nîi khráp/khâ*	Sign here, please
ต้องการล่ามไหม *tâwng-kaan lâam mái*	Do you want an interpreter?

At the police station

I want to report a collision/missing person/ rape	*phǒm/dichán tâwngkaan câehng khwaam rót chon kan/khon hǎi/ khòm khǔehn* ผม/ดิฉันต้องการแจ้งความ รถชนกัน/คนหาย/ข่มขืน
Could you make a statement, please?	*chûai hâi kaan nòi khráp/khâ* ช่วยให้การหน่อยครับ/ค่ะ
Could I have a copy for the insurance?	*khǎw sǎmnao nùeng chabàp sǎmràp prakan ná khráp/khá* ขอสำเนาหนึ่งฉบับสำหรับประกั นนะครับ/คะ
I've lost everything	*khǎwng khǎwng phǒm/dichán hai mòt* ของของผม/ดิฉันหายหมด
I've no money left, I'm desperate	*phǒm/dichán mâi mii ngoen lǔea loei, yâeh cing cing* ผม/ดิฉันไม่มีเงินเหลือเลย แย่จริง ๆ
Could you lend me a little money?	*khǎw yuehm tang nòi dâi mái* ขอยืมตังหน่อยได้ไหม
I'd like an interpreter	*phǒm/dichán tâwngkaan lâam* ผม/ดิฉันต้องการล่าม
I'm innocent	*phǒm/dichán bawrísùt* ผม/ดิฉันบริสุทธิ์
I don't know anything about it	*phǒm/dichán mâi rúu rûeang arai loei* ผม/ดิฉันไม่รู้เรื่องอะไรเลย
I want to speak to someone from the Australian embassy	*phǒm/dichán tâwngkaan tìt tàw sathǎn thûut áwt(sa)trehlia* ผม/ดิฉันต้องการติดต่อ สถานทูตออสเตรเลีย
I want a lawyer who speaks...	*phǒm/dichán tâwngkaan thanaikhwaam thîi phûut phaasǎa...* ผม/ดิฉันต้องการทนายความที่พูด ภาษา...

15

English-Thai Word List

15. English-Thai Word List

A

about เกี่ยวกับ *kiao kàp*

above เหนือ *nŭea*

abroad ต่างประเทศ *tàang prathêht*

accident อุบัติเหตุ *ubatìhèht*

adaptor ตัวแปลงไฟฟ้า *tua plaehng fai fáa*

address ที่อยู่ *thîi yùu*

admission การเข้าชม *kaan khâo chom*

admission price ค่าผ่านประตู *khâa phàan pratuu*

adult ผู้ใหญ่ *phûu yài*

advice คำแนะนำ *kham náe-nam*

aeroplane เครื่องบิน *khrûeang bin*

after หลังจาก *lăng càak*

afternoon ตอนบ่าย *tawn bài*

aftershave น้ำยาหลังโกนหนวด *nám yaa lăng kohn nùat*

again อีก *ìik*

against ต่อต้าน *tàw tâan*

age อายุ *aayú*

AIDS โรคเอดส์ *rôhk ehd(s)*

air conditioning ปรับอากาศ *pràp aakàat*

airmail จดหมายอากาศ *còtmăi aakàat*

air mattress ที่นอนลม *thîi nawn lom*

airplane เครื่องบิน *khrûeang bin*

airport สนามบิน, ท่าอากาศยาน *sanăam bin, thâa aakàatsayaan*

airport security หน่วยรักษ าความปลอดภัยสนามบิน *nùai raksăa khwaam plàwt-phai sanăam-bin*

aisle seat ที่นั่งติดทางเดิน *thîi nâng tìt thaang doehn*

alarm เตือนภัย *tuean phai*

alarm clock นาฬิกาปลุก *naalíkaa plùk*

alcohol แอลกอฮอล *aehlkawhawn*

all day ทั้งวัน, ตลอดวัน *tháng wan, talàwt wan*

all the time ตลอดเวลา *talàwt wehlaa*

allergy แพ้ *pháe*

alone เดียว *diao*

altogether ทั้งหมด *tháng mòt*

always เสมอ *samŏeh*

ambulance รถพยาบาล *rót phayaabaan*

America อเมริกา *amehríkaa*

American คนอเมริกัน *khon amehríkan*

amount จำนวน *camnuan*

amusement park สวนสนุก *sŭan sanùk*

anaesthetic (local) ยาชา *yaa chaa*

anaesthetic (general) ยาสลบ *yaa salòp*

angry โกรธ *kròht*

animal สัตว์ *sàt*

ankle ข้อเท้า *khâw tháo*

answer คำตอบ *kham tàwp*

ant มด *mót*

antibiotics ยาปฏิชีวนะ (กิน) *yaa patìchiiwaná (kin)*

antifreeze ตัวกันไม่ให้แช่แข็ง *tua kan mâi hai châeh khăeng*

antique โบราณ *bohraan*

antiques ของโบราณ *khăwng bohraan*

antiseptic ยาปฏิชีวนะ (ทา) *yaa patìchiiwaná (thaa)*

anus ตูด *tùut*

apartment อพาร์ตเม้นท์ *apaatmén*

aperitif เครื่องดื่มเรียกน้ำย่อย *khrûeng dùehm rîak náam yôi*

apologies คำขออภัย *kham khăw aphai*

app แอป *áep*

apple แอปเปิ้ล *áeppôen*

apple juice น้ำแอปเปิ้ล *náam áeppôen*

application แอปพลิเคชัน *áep-li-khay-chân*

appointment นัด *nát*

April เมษายน *mehsǎayon*

architecture สถาปัตยกรรม *sathǎapàtayákam*

area เขต พื้นที่ *khèht, phúehn thîi*

area code รหัสพื้นที่ *rahàt phúehn thîi*

arm แขน *khǎehn*

arrange จัดการ *càtkaan*

arrive ถึง *thǔeng*

arrow ลูกศร *lûuk sǎwn*

art ศิลปะ *sǐnlapà*

art gallery ห้องศิลป์ *hâwng sǐnlapà*

artery เส้นเลือดแดง *sên lûeat daehng*

article บทความ *bòt khwaam*

artificial respiration
การช่วยให้เขาหายใจทางปาก *kaan chûai hâi hǎi cai thaang pàak*

ashtray ที่เขี่ยบุหรี่ *thîi khìa burìi*

ask ถาม *thǎam*

ask for ขอ *khǎw*

aspirin ยาแอสไพริน *yaa aehsphairin*

assault ทำร้ายร่างกาย *tham rái rânga kai*

assorted ชนิดต่างๆ *chanít tàang tàang*

at home ที่บ้าน *thîi bâan*

at night กลางคืน *klaang khuehn*

at the back ข้างหลัง *khâng lǎng*

at the front ข้างหน้า *khâng nâa*

at the latest ล่าสุด *lâa sùt*

ATM เอทีเอ็ม *a-thii-em*

aubergine มะเขือยาว *makhǔea yao*

August สิงหาคม *sǐnghǎakhom*

Australia ออสเตรเลีย *áws(a)trehlia*

Australian คนออสเตรเลีย *khon áws(a)trehlia*

automatic อัตโนมัติ *attànohmát*

autumn ฤดูใบไม้ร่วง *rúeduu bai mái rûang*

awake ตื่น *tùehn*

awning กันสาด *kansàat*

B

baby ทารก *thaarók*

baby food อาหารเด็กอ่อน *aahǎan dèk àwn*

babysitter คนเลี้ยงเด็ก *khon líang dèk*

back (rear) ข้างหลัง *khâng lǎng*

back (part of body) หลัง *lǎng*

backpack กระเป๋าสะพายหลัง *krapǎo saphai lǎng*

backpacker แบ็คแพ็คเคอร์ *báekpháek-khôeh*

bad (rotting) เสีย *sǐa*

bad (terrible) แย่ *yâeh*

bag ถุง, กระเป๋า *thǔng, krapǎo*

baggage claim ที่รับกระเป๋าเดินทาง *thîi ráp krapǎo doehn* thaang

baker คนขายขนมปัง *khon khǎi khanǒm pang*

balcony ระเบียง *rabiang*

ball ลูกบอลล์ *lûuk bawn*

ballpoint pen ปากกาหมึกแห้ง *pàakkaa mùek hâehng*

banana กล้วย *klûai*

bandage ผ้าพันแผล *phâa phan phlǎeh*

bandaids ที่ปิดแผล, แบนเดด *thîi pìt phlǎeh, baehndèt*

bangs, fringes ระบาย, ครุย *rabai, khrui*

bank (finance) ธนาคาร *thanaakhaan*

bank (river) ฝั่ง *fàng*

bar (café) บาร์ *baa*

barbecue บาร์บิคิว *baabìkhiu*

basketball บาสเก็ตบอลล์ *baasakèhtbawn*

bath อาบน้ำ *àap náam*

bathmat ที่เช็ดเท้า *thîi chét tháo*

bathrobe ผ้าคลุมอาบน้ำ *phâa khlum àap náam*

bathroom ห้องน้ำ *hâwng náam*

bath towel ผ้าเช็ดตัว *phâa chét tua*

battery แบ็ตเตอรี่, ถ่านไฟฉาย *baettoehrìi, thàan fai chǎi*

beach ชายหาด *chai hàat*

beans ถั่ว *thùa*

beautiful สวย *sǔai*

bed เตียง *tiang*

bedding เครื่องนอน *khrûeang nawn*

bee ผึ้ง *phûeng*

beef เนื้อวัว *núea wua*

beer เบียร์ *bia*

begin เริ่ม *rôehm*

behind ข้างหลัง *khâng lǎng*

belt เข็มขัด *khěm khàt*

berth ที่นอน (บนเรือหรือรถไฟ) *thîi nawn (bon ruea rǔeh rót fai)*

better (to get) ดีขึ้น *dii khûen*

bicycle รถจักรยาน *rót càkrayaan*

bikini ชุดว่ายน้ำ *chút wâi náam*

bill บิล *bin*

billiards บิลเลียดส์ *billîat*

birthday วันเกิด *wan kòeht*

biscuit บิสกิต *biskît*

bite กัด *kàt*

bitter ขม *khǒm*

black ดำ *dam*

black and white ขาวดำ *khǎo dam*

black eye ตาดำ *taa dam*

bland (taste) จืด *cùeht*

blanket ผ้าห่ม *phâa hòm*

bleach ฝ่าฝืน *fàa fǔehn*

bleed เลือดออก *lûeat àwk*

blind (on window) ที่กันแดด *thîi kan dàeht*

blind (can't see) ตาบอด *taa bàwt*

blister เม็ดพุพอง *mét phú phawng*

blog บล็อก *blàwk*

blond ผมทอง *phǒm thawng*

blood เลือด *lûeat*

blood pressure ความดันโลหิต *khwaam dan lohhìt*

bloody nose เลือดกำเดาออก *lûeat kamdao àwk*

blouse เสื้อ (ผู้หญิง) *sûea (phûu yǐng)*

blue สีฟ้า *sǐi fáa*

boarding pass บัตรผ่านขึ้นเดรื่องบิน *bàt phàan khûen khrûeng-bin*

boat เรือ *ruea*

body ตัว ร่างกาย *tua râang kai*

boiled ต้ม *tôm*

bone กระดูก *kradùuk*

book หนังสือ *nǎngsǔeh*

booked, reserved จองไว้ *cohng wái*

booking office ที่จองตั๋ว *thîi cawng tǔa*

bookshop ร้านหนังสือ *ráan nǎngsǔeh*

border ชายแดน *chai daehn*

bored เบื่อ *bùea*

boring น่าเบื่อ *nâa bùea*

born เกิด *kòeht*

borrow ยืม *yuehm*

botanic gardens สวนพฤกษชาติ *sǔan phrúekachâat*

both ทั้งคู่ *tháng khûu*

bottle ขวด *khùat*

bottle (wine) ขวดไวน์ *khùat wai(n)*

bottle (baby's) ขวดนม *khùat nom*

bottle-warmer ที่อุ่นขวดนม *thîi ùn khùat nom*

box กล่อง *klàwng*

box office ที่ขายตั๋ว *thîi khǎi tǔa*

boy เด็กชาย *dèk chai*

boyfriend เพื่อนชาย *phûean chai*

bra เสื้อชั้นใน *sûea chán nai*

bracelet สร้อยข้อมือ *sâwi khâw mueh*

braised ทา *thaa*

brake หยุด เบรค *yùt brèhk*

brake oil น้ำมันเบรค *námman brèhk*

bread ขนมปัง *khanǒm pang*

break พัก *phák*

breakfast อาหารเช้า *aahǎan cháo*

breast หน้าอก *nâa òk*

breast milk นมแม่ *nom mâeh*

bridge สะพาน *saphaan*

briefs กางเกงใน *kaangkehng nai*

bring เอามา, นำมา *ao maa, nam maa*

brochure แผ่นพับ *phàen pháp*

broken พัง, แตก *phang, tàehk*

bronze ทองสัมฤทธิ์ *thawng sǎmrít*

broth น้ำซุป *namsúp*

brother (elder) พี่ชาย *phîi chai*

brother (younger) น้องชาย *náwng chai*

brown น้ำตาล *nám taan*

browser เบราว์เซอร์ *braw-soer*

bruise รอยช้ำ *rawi chám*

brush แปรง *praehng*

bucket ถัง *thǎng*

buffet บุฟเฟ่ต์ *búffêh*

bugs แมลง *malaehng*

building ตึก *tùek*

bun ขนมปังก้อน *khanǒm pang kâwn*

burglary การขโมย *kaan khamoi*

burn (injury) แผลไหม้ *phlǎeh mâi*

burn (verb) ไหม้ *mâi*

burnt รอยไหม้ *rawi mâi*

bus รถเมล์ *rót meh*

bus station ชุมสายรถเมล์ *chum sǎi rót meh*

bus stop ป้ายรถเมล์ *pâi rót meh*

business card นามบัตร *naam bàt*

business class ชั้นนักธุรกิจ *chán nák thurákit*

business trip เดินทางไปธุรกิจ *doehn thaang pai thurákit*

busy (schedule) ยุ่ง *yûng*

busy (traffic) ติดขัด *tìt khàt*

butane แก๊สบูเทน *káeht buuthehn*

butcher คนขายเนื้อ *khon khǎi núea*

butter เนย *noei*

button กระดุม *kradum*

by airmail ทางอากาศ *thaang aakàat*

by phone ทางโทรศัพท์ *thaang thohrásàp*

C

cabbage กะหล่ำปลี *kalàmphlii*

cabin ห้อง *hâwng*

cake ขนมเค้ก *khanǒm khéhk*

call (phonecall) โทรศัพท์ *thohrásàp*

call (to phone) โทรศัพท์, โทร. *thohrásàp, thoh*

called เรียก *rîak*

camera กล้อง *klâwng*

camping ไปค่าย *pa khâi*

can opener ที่เปิดขวด *thîi pòeht khùat*

cancel ยกเลิก *yók lôehk*

candle เทียน *thian*

candy ลูกวาด, ท็อฟฟี่ *lûuk kwàat, tháwffíi*

car รถ *rót*

car documents คู่มือรถ *khûumueh rót*

car seat (child's) ที่นั่งเด็ก *thîi nâng dèk*

car trouble รถเสีย *rót sǐa*

cardigan เสื้อหนาว *sûea nǎo*

careful ระวัง *ra-wang*

carpet พรม *phrom*

carriage ตู้รถไฟ *tûu rót fai*

carrot แครอท *khaehràwt*

cartridge ตลับ *talàp*

cash เงินสด *ngoen sòt*

cash card บัตรเงินสด *bàt ngoen sòt*

cash desk ที่จ่ายเงิน *thîi cài ngoen*

cash machine ที่คิดเงิน *thîi khít ngoen*

casino บ่อนการพนัน *bàwn kaan phanan*

cassette เทปคาสเซ็ท *théhp kháasèt*

cat แมว *maeo*

catalog แค็ตตาล็อก *kháettaalàwk*

cauliflower ดอกกะหล่ำ *dàwk kalàm*

cause สาเหตุ *sǎahèht*

cave ถ้ำ *thâm*

CD ซีดี *sii dii*

CD-ROM ซีดีรอม *sii dii rawm*

celebrate ฉลอง *chalǎwng*

cell (or mobile) phone โทรศัพท์มือถือ/ โมบาย *thorasàp mue-thǔe/moo-bai*

cemetery ที่ฝังศพ *thîi fǎng sòp*

centimetre เซ็นติเมตร *sentìméht*

central heating เครื่องทำความร้อนกลาง *khrûeang tham khwaam ráwn klaang*

central locking เซ็นทรัลล็อคคิ้ง *sentrân láwkkhîng*

centre (middle) กลาง *klaang*

centre (of city) ศูนย์กลาง *sǔun klaang*

certificate ประกาศนียบัตร *prakàatsaniiyábàt*

chair เก้าอี้ *kâo-îi*

chambermaid คนทำความสะอาด *khon tham khwaam sà-àat*

champagne แชมเปญ *chaehmpehn*

change, swap เปลี่ยน *plìan*

change (money) เงินทอน *ngoen thawn*

change (trains) ต่อรถไฟ *tàw rót fai*

change the baby's diaper เปลี่ยนผ้าอ้อม *plìan paéom*

change the oil เปลี่ยนน้ำมันเครื่อง *plìan námman khrûeang*

charger เครื่องชาร์ท *khrûeng cháat*

charter flight เที่ยวบินพิเศษ *thîao bin phísèht*

chat คุย *khui*

checked luggage กระเป๋าที่ตรวจแล้ว *krapǎo thîi trùat láeo*

check, bill บิล *bin*

check (verb) ตรวจ *trùat*

check in เช็คอิน *chék in*

check out เช็คเอ๊าท์ *chék ao(t)*

cheers! โชคดี *chôhk dii*

cheese เนยแข็ง *noei khǎeng*

chef พ่อครัว *phâw khrua*

chess หมากรุก *màak rúk*

chewing gum หมากฝรั่ง *màak faràng*

chicken ไก่ *kài*

child เด็ก *dèk*

child's seat (in car) ที่นั่งเด็ก *thîi nâng dèk*

chilled (of body) เย็น *nǎo*

chilled (of foods) หนาว *yen*

chin คาง *khaang*

chocolate ช็อคโกแล็ต *cháwkkohláet*

choose เลือก *lûeak*

chopsticks ตะเกียบ *takìap*

church โบสถ์ *bòht*

church service พิธีในโบสถ์ *phíthii nai bòht*

cigar บุหรี่ซิการ์ *burìi siikaa*

cigarette บุหรี่ *burìi*

circle วงกลม *wong klom*

circus ละครสัตว์ *lakhawn sàt*

citizen ประชาชน *prachaachon*

city เมือง *mueang*

clean สะอาด *sa-àat*

clean (verb) ทำความสะอาด *tham khwaam sa-àat*

clearance (sale) ขายเลหลัง *khǎi lehlǎng*

clock นาฬิกา *naalíkaa*

closed ปิด *pìt*

closed off (road) ปิดถนน *pìt thanǒn*

clothes เสื้อผ้า *sûea phâa*

clothes hanger ที่แขวนเสื้อ *thîi khwǎen sûea*

clothes dryer ที่อบผ้า *thîi òp phâa*

clothing เสื้อผ้า *sûea phâa*

cloud computing คลาวด์ คอมพิวติ้ง *khlaw khawm-phiw-tîng*

clutch (car) คลัช *khlát*

coat (jacket) เสื้อแจ็คเก็ต *sûea cáekkèt*

coat (overcoat) เสื้อนอก *sûea nâwk*

cockroach แมลงสาบ *malaehng sàap*

cocoa โกโก้ *kohkôh*

coffee กาแฟ *kaafaeh*

cold (not hot) เย็น *yen*

cold, flu หวัด *wàt*

collar ปกเสื้อ *pòk sûea*

collarbone ไหปลาร้า *haiplaaráa*

colleague เพื่อนทำงาน *phûean tham ngaan*

collision การชน *kaan chon*

color สี *sǐi*

colored มีสี *mii sǐi*

comb หวี *wǐi*

come มา *maa*

come back กลับมา *klàp maa*

compartment ห้อง *hâwng*

complaint ร้องทุกข์ *ráwng thúk*

completely อย่างสมบูรณ์ *yàang sǒmbohn*

compliment คำชม *kham chom*

comprising ได้แก่ *dâi kàeh*

computer คอมพิวเตอร์ *khawm-phiw-toer*

computer game เกมส์ คอมพิวเตอร์ *kem khawm-phiw-toer*

concert คอนเสริต *khawnsòeht*

concert hall โรงฟังคอนเสริต *rohng fang khawnsòeht*

concierge คนเฝ้าประตู *khon fâo pratuu*

concussion ถูกกระทบอย่างแรง *thùuk krathóp yàang raehng*

condensed milk นมข้น *nom khôn*

condom ถุงยางอนามัย *thǔng yang anaamai*

confectionery ขนมหวาน *khanǒm wǎan*

congratulations! ขอแสดงความยินดีด้วย *khǎw sadaehng khwaam yindii dûai*

connection (transport) ต่อรถ *tàw rót*

constipation ท้องผูก *tháwng phùuk*

consulate กงสุล *kongsǔn*

consultation (by doctor) คำปรึกษา *kham prùeksǎa*

contact lens คอนแท็คเล็นซ์ *khawntháek len*

contagious ติดต่อ *tìt tàw*

contraceptive สิ่งคุมกำเนิด *sìng khum kamnòeht*

contraceptive pill ยาคุมกำเนิด *yaa khum kamnòeht*

cook (male) กุ๊ก, พ่อครัว *kúk, phâw khrua*

cook (female) กุ๊ก, แม่ครัว *kúk, mâeh khrua*

cook (verb) ทำอาหาร *tham aahǎan*

cookie คุ้กกี้ *khúkkîi*

copper ทองแดง *thawng daehng*

copy ก็อบปี้ *káwp-pîi*

copy document อัดสำเนา *àt sǎmnao*

copy tape อัดเทป *àt théhp*

corkscrew จุกไม้ก๊อก *cùkmáikáwk*

corner มุม *mum*

cornflower แป้งข้าวโพด *pâehng khâo phôht*

correct ถูก *thùuk*

correspond เขียนจดหมาย *khǐan còtmǎi*

corridor ทางเดินในตึก *thaang doehn nai tùek*

cosmetics เครื่องสำอางค์ *khrûeang sǎm-aang*

costume เครื่องแต่งตัว *khrûeang tàeng tua*

cot เตียงเด็ก *tiang dèk*

cotton ฝ้าย *fâai*

cotton wool สำลี *sǎmlii*

cough การไอ *kaan ai*

cough (verb) ไอ *ai*

cough syrup ยาแก้ไอ *yaa kâeh ai*

counter เคาน์เตอร์ *kháotôeh*

country (nation) ประเทศ *prathêht*

country (rural area) ชนบท, บ้านนอก *chonabòt, bâan nâwk*

country code รหัสประเทศ *rahàt prathêht*

courgette, zucchini ซูกินี *suukìnii*

course of treatment ระยะเวลารักษา *rayá wehlaa ráksǎa*

cousin ลูกพี่ลูกน้อง *lûuk phîi lûuk náwng*

crab ปู *puu*

cracker ขนมปังกรอบ *khanǒmpang kràwp*

cream ครีม *khriim*

credit card บัตรเครดิต *bàt khrehdìt*

crime อาชญากรรม *àatyaakam*

crockery เครื่องถ้วยชาม *khrûeang thûai chaam*

cross (road, river) ข้าม *khâam*

crossroad สี่แยก *sìiyâehk*

crutch ไม้ยันรักแร้ *mái yan rák ráeh*

cry ร้องไห้ *ráwng hâi*

cubic metre ลูกบาศก์เมตร *lûukbàat méht*

cucumber แตงกวา *taehng kwaa*

cuddly toy ของเล่นนุ่มๆ *khǎwng lên nûm nûm*

cuff ข้อมือเสื้อ *khâw mueh sûea*

cufflinks กระดุมข้อมือ *kradum khâw mueh*

cup ถ้วย *thûai*

curly หยิก *yìk*

current (electric) กระแสไฟฟ้า *krasǎeh fai fáa*

cursor เคอร์เซอร์ *khoer-soer*

curtains ม่าน *mâan*

cushion เบาะ *bàw*

custom ประเพณี *praphehnii*

customs ศุลกากร *sǔnlakaakawn*

cut (injury) บาด *bàat*

cut (verb) ตัด *tàt*

cutlery ช้อนส้อม *cháwn sâwm*

cybercafe ร้านอินเตอร์เน็ต *ráan internet*

cycling ขี่จักรยาน *khìi cakrayaan*

D

dairy products ผลิตภัณฑ์นม *phalìtaphan nom*

damage ความเสียหาย *khwaam sǐa hǎi*

dance เต้นรำ *tên ram*

dandruff ขี้รังแค *khîi rangkhaeh*

danger อันตราย *antarai*

dangerous น่าอันตราย *nâa antarai*

dark มืด *mûeht*

date วันที่ *wan thîi*

date of birth วันเกิด *wan kòeht*

daughter ลูกสาว *lûuk sǎo*

day วัน *wan*

day after tomorrow มะรืนนี้ *maruehn níi*

day before yesterday เมื่อวานซืน *mûea waansuehn*

dead ตาย *tai*

dead zone ที่ไม่มีสัญญาณ *thîi mâi mii sǎnyaan*

deaf หูหนวก *hǔu nùak*

decaffeinated กาแฟที่ไม่มีคาเฟอีน *kaafaeh thîi mâi mii khaafeh-in*

December ธันวาคม *thanwaakhom*

declare (customs) แจ้ง (ศุลกากร) *câeng (sǔnlakaakawan)*

delete ลบ *lóp*

deep ลึก *lúek*

deep freeze แช่แข็งจัด *châeh khǎeng càt*

deep-sea diving ดำน้ำทะเลลึก *dam náam thaleh lúek*

defecate ถ่าย *thài*

degrees องศา *ongsǎa*

delay ล่าช้า *lâa cháa*

delicious อร่อย *aròi*

dentist หมอฟัน *mǎw fan*

dentures ฟันปลอม *fan plawm*

deodorant ยาระงับกลิ่นตัว *yaa rangáp klìn tua*

department store ห้างสรรพสินค้า *hâang sapphasǐnkháa*

departure การออก *kaan àwk*

departure time เวลาออก *wehlaa àwk*

depilatory cream ครีมถอนขน *khriim thǎwn khǒn*

deposit (money in a bank) ฝาก (เงิน) *fàak (ngoen)*

deposit (for safekeeping) ฝากของ *fàak khǎwng*

desert ทะเลทราย *thaleh sai*

dessert ของหวาน *khǎwng wǎan*

destination จุดหมายปลายทาง *cùt mǎi plai thaang*

detergent ผงซักฟอก *phǒng sák fâwk*

develop (photo) ล้างรูป *láang rûup*

diabetic เบาหวาน *baw wǎan*

dial หมุน *mǔn*

diamond เพ็ชร *phét*

diaper ผ้าอ้อม *phâa âwm*

diarrhoea ท้องเสีย *tháwng sǐa*

dictionary พจนานุกรม *phótcanaanúkrom*

diesel oil น้ำมันดีเซล *námman diisên*

digital camera กล้องดิจิตอล *klâwng di-cit-toel*

diet จำกัดอาหาร *camkàt aahǎan*

difficulty ความลำบาก *khwaam lambàak*

dining car รถเสบียง *rót sabiang*

dining room ห้องอาหาร *hâwng aahǎan*

dinner อาหารเย็น *aahǎan yen*

direction ทิศทาง *thít thaang*

direct flight เที่ยวบินตรง *thîao bin trong*

directly โดยตรง *doi trong*

dirty สกปรก *sòkkapròk*

disabled พิการ *phíkaan*

disco ดิสโก้ *dískôh*

discount ลดราคา *lót raakhaa*

dish จาน *caan*

dish of the day อาหารพิเศษวันนี้ *aahǎan phísèht wan níi*

disinfectant ยาฆ่าเชื้อ *yaa khâa chúea*

distance ความไกล *khwaam klai*

distilled water น้ำกลั่น *náam klàn*

disturb รบกวน *rópkuan*

disturbance การรบกวน *kaan rópkuan*

dive ดำน้ำ *dam náam*

diving การดำน้ำ *kaan dam náam*

diving board กระดานกระโดด *kradaan kradòht*

diving gear เครื่องดำน้ำ *khrûeang dam náam*

divorced หย่าแล้ว *yàa láeho*

dizzy งง *ngong*

do ทำ *tham*

doctor หมอ *măw*

document copy สำเนา *sămnao*

dog หมา *măa*

do-it-yourself store ร้านของทำเอง *ráan kăwng tham ehng*

doll ตุ๊กตา *túkkataa*

domestic ภายในครัวเรือน *phai nai khrua ruean*

done (cooked) สุก *sùk*

do not disturb อย่ารบกวน *yàa rópkuan*

door ประตู *pratuu*

double สองเท่า *săwng thâo*

down ลง *long*

download ดาวน์โหลด *dawn-lòod*

drapes ม่าน *mâan*

draught ลม *lom*

dream (verb) ฝัน *făn*

dress แต่งตัว *tàeng tua*

dressing gown เสื้อคลุม *sûea khlum*

dressing table โต๊ะแต่งตัว *tó taehng tua*

drink (refreshment) เครื่องดื่ม *khrûeang dùehm*

drink (alcoholic) เครื่องดื่มเป็นเหล้า *khrûeang dùehm pen lâo*

drink (verb) ดื่ม *dùehm*

drinking water น้ำดื่ม *náam dùehm*

drive ขับ *khàp*

driver คนขับ *khon khàp*

driver's licence ใบขับขี่ *bai khàp khìi*

drugstore ร้านขายยา *ráan khăi yaa*

drunk เมา *mao*

dry แห้ง *hâehng*

dry (verb) ตากให้แห้ง *tàak hâi hâehng*

dry-clean ซักแห้ง *sák hâehng*

drycleaners ร้านซักแห้ง *ráan sák hâehng*

duck เป็ด *pèt*

during ระหว่าง *ra-wàang*

during the day ช่วงกลางวัน *chûang klaang wan*

duty (tax) ภาษี *phaasĭi*

duty-free goods สินค้าปลอดภาษี *sĭnkháa plàwt phaasĭi*

duty-free shop ร้านสินค้าปลอดภาษี *ráan sĭnkháa plàwt phaasĭi*

DVD ดีวีดี *dii wii dii*

E

e-book อีบุ๊ค *ii-búk*

e-booking (reservation) การจองตั๋วผ่านเครือข่ายการสื่อสาร *kaan cawng tŭa phàan khrue-khài kaan sùe-săan*

e-reader เครื่องอ่านหนังสืออีเล็กทรอนิกส์ *khrûeng-àan năngsŭe ii-lék-tron-ník*

e-ticket ตั๋วอีเล็กทรอนิกส์ *tŭa ii-lék-tron-ník*

ear หู *hŭu*

earache ปวดหู *pùat hŭu*

earbud หูฟัง *hŭu fang*

ear drops ยาหยอดหู *yaa yàwt hŭu*

early แต่เนิ่น ๆ *tàe nôehn nôehn*

earrings ตุ้มหู *tûm hŭu*

earth ดิน *din*

Earth โลก *lôhk*

earthenware เครื่องปั้นดินเผา *khruêang pân din phăo*

east ตะวันออก *ta-wan àwk*

easy ง่าย *ngâi*

eat กิน *kin*

Eau-de-cologne water น้ำหอม *num hom*

economy class ชั้นประหยัด *chán prayàt*

eczema โรคเอ็กซม่า *rôhk eksamâa*

eel ปลาไหล *plaa lăi*

egg ไข่ *khài*

eggplant มะเขือม่วง *makhŭea mûang*

electric ไฟฟ้า *fai fáa*

electricity ไฟฟ้า *fai fáa*

electronics อิเล็กทรอนิค *ilék thrawník*

elephant ช้าง *cháang*

elevator ลิฟต์ *líf*

email อีเมล์ *iimeh(l)/email*

email address ที่อยู่อีเมล์ *thîi yùu ii-mei*

embassy สถานทูต *sathăan thûut*

embroidery เย็บปักถักร้อย *yép pàk thàk ráwi*

emergency brake เบรคฉุกเฉิน *brèhk chùk chŏehn*

emergency exit ทางออกฉุกเฉิน *thaang àwk chùk chŏehn*

emergency phone โทรศัพท์ฉุกเฉิน *thohrasàp chùk chŏehn*

emery board ตะไบเล็บ *tabai lép*

empty ว่างเปล่า *wâang plào*

engaged (on the phone) พูดโทรศัพท์ *phûut thohrasàp*

engaged (to be married) หมั้น *mân*

England ประเทศอังกฤษ *prathêht angkrìt*

English ภาษาอังกฤษ *phaasăa angrìt*

enjoy สนุก *sanùk*

enquire สอบถาม *sàwp thăam*

envelope ซอง *sawng*

escalator บันไดเลื่อน *bandai lûean*

escort เพื่อนดูแล, เอสคอร์ท *phûean duu laeh, éskhàwt*

essential จำเป็น *campen*

evening ตอนเย็น *tawn yen*

evening wear ชุดกลางคืน *chút klaang khuehn*

event เหตุการณ์ *hèht kaan*

everything ทุกอย่าง *thúk yàang*

everywhere ทุกแห่ง *thúk hàeng*

examine ตรวจสอบ *trùat sàwp*

excavation การขุดแจาะ *kaan khùt càw*

excellent ยอดเยี่ยม *yâwt yîam*

exchange แลกเปลี่ยน *lâehk plìan*

exchange office ที่แลกเงิน *thîi lâehk ngoen*

excursion ทัศนศึกษา *thátsanásùeksăa*

exhibition นิทรรศการ *níthátsakaan*

exit ทางออก *thaang àwk*

expenses ค่าใช้จ่าย *khâa chái cài*

expensive แพง *phaehng*

explain อธิบาย *athíbai*

express ด่วน *dùan*

external ภายนอก *pai nâwk*

eye ตา *taa*

eye drops ยาหยอดตา *yaa yàwt taa*

eye specialist หมอตา *măw taa*

F

fabric ผ้า *phâa*

face หน้า *nâa*

Facebook เฟสบุ๊ค *Faes-búk*

factory โรงงาน *rohng ngaan*

fall (season) ฤดูใบไม้ร่วง *rúeduu bai mái rûang*

fall (verb) ตก *tòk*

family ครอบครัว *khrâwp khrua*

famous ดัง *dang*

fan (admirer) แฟน *faehn*

far away ไกลโพ้น *klai phón*

farm ฟาร์ม *faam*

farmer ชาวนา *chao naa*

fashion แฟชั่น *faehchân*

fast เร็ว *reo*

father พ่อ *phâw*

father-in-law พ่อตา *phâw taa*

fault ความผิด *khwaam phìt*

fax แฟกซ์ *fáek(s)*

February กุมภาพันธ์ *kumphaaphan*

feel รู้สึก *rúusùek*

feel like รู้สึกเหมือน *rúusùek mǔean*

fence รั้ว *rúa*

ferry เรือข้ามฟาก *ruea khâam fâak*

fever ไข้ *khâi*

fiancé, fiancée คู่หมั้น *khûu mân*

fill เติม *toehm*

filling (in food) ทำให้อิ่ม *tham hâi ìm*

filling (dental) อุดฟัน *ùt fan*

fill out (form) กรอก *kràwk*

film (photo) ฟิล์ม *fiim*

film (cinema) หนัง *nǎng*

filter เครื่องกรอง *khrûeang krawng*

filter cigarette ก้นกรอง *kôn krawng*

fine (good) ดี *dii*

fine (money) ค่าปรับ *khâa pràp*

finger นิ้ว *níu*

fire ไฟ *fai*

fire alarm สัญญาณไฟไหม้ *sǎnyaan fai mâi*

fire department สถานีดับเพลิง *sathǎanii dàp phloehng*

fire escape บันไดหนีไฟ *bandai nǐi fai*

fire extinguisher ที่ดับเพลิง *thîi dàp phloehng*

first แรก *râehk*

first aid ปฐมพยาบาล *pathǒm phayaabaan*

first class ชั้นหนึ่ง *chán nueng*

fish ปลา *plaa*

fish (verb) ตกปลา *tòk plaa*

fishing rod คันเบ็ด *khan bèt*

fitness club สโมสรออกกำลังกาย *samohsǎwn àwk kamlang kai*

fitness training การฝึกออกกำลังกาย *kaan fùek àwk kamlang kai*

fitting room ห้องลองเสื้อ *hâwng lawng sûea*

fix (puncture) แก้ *kâeh*

flag ธง *thong*

flash (camera) แฟลช *prai tai amp*

flashdrive แฟลชไดร์ฟ *flǎe-sh-drai*

flashlight ไฟฉาย *fai chǎi*

flatulence อาการท้องอืด *aakaan tháwng ùeht*

flavor รส *rót*

flavoring เครื่องปรุงรส *khrûeang prung rót*

flea หมัด *màt*

flea market ตลาดขายของเก่า *talàat khǎi khǎwng kào*

flight เที่ยวบิน *thîao bin*

flight number เที่ยวบินท *thîao bin thîi*

flood น้ำท่วม *náam thûam*

floor พื้น *phúehn*

flour แป้ง *pâehng*

flu ไข้หวัดใหญ่ *khâi wàt yài*

flush เปล่งปลั่ง *plèng plàng*

fly (insect) แมลงวัน *malaehngwan*

fly (verb) บิน *bin*

fog หมอก *màwk*

foggy หมอกจัด *màwk càt*

folklore นิทานพื้นบ้าน *níthaan phúehn bâan*

follow ตาม *taam*

food (groceries) กับข้าว *kàp khâo*

food (meal) อาหาร *aahǎan*

food court ที่ขายอาหาร *thîi khǎi aahǎan*

food poisoning อาหารเป็นพิษ *aahǎan pen phít*

foot เท้า *tháo*

foot brake ใช้เท้าเบรค *chái tháo brèhk*

forbidden ต้องห้าม *tâwng hâam*

forehead หน้าผาก *nâa phàak*

foreign ต่างประเทศ *tàang prathêht*

forget ลืม *luehm*

fork ส้อม *sâwm*

form รูปแบบ *rûup bàehp*

formal dress ชุดใหญ่ *chút yài*

forward (letter) ส่งจดหมาย *sòng còtmǎi*

fountain น้ำพุ *náam phú*

frame กรอบรูป *kràwp rûup*

free (no charge) ฟรี *frii*

free (unoccupied) ว่าง *wâang*

free time เวลาว่าง *wehlaa wâang*

freeze แช่แข็ง *châeh khǎeng*

french fries มันทอด *man thâwt*

fresh สด *sòt*

Friday วันศุกร์ *wan sùk*

fried (in pieces) ทอด *thâwt*

friend เพื่อน *phûean*

friendly เป็นกันเอง *pen kan ehng*

frightened ตกใจ *tòk cai*

fringe (hair) ผมม้า *phǒm máa*

frozen แช่แข็ง *châeh khǎeng*

fruit ผลไม้ *phǒnlamái*

fruit juice น้ำผลไม้ *náam phǒnlamái*

frying pan กะทะ *kàthá*

full เต็ม *tem*

fun สนุก *sanùk*

funeral งานศพ *ngaan sòp*

G

gallery ห้องแสดงภาพ *hâwng sadaehng phâap*

game เกม *kehm*

garage (car repair) อู่ซ่อมรถ *ùu sôm rót*

garbage ขยะ *khayà*

garlic กระเทียม *krathiam*

garden สวน *sǔan*

garment เสื้อผ้า *sûea phâa*

gas (for heating) แก๊ซ *káet*

gasoline น้ำมัน *námman*

gas station ปั๊มน้ำมัน *pám námman*

gate ประตู *pratuu*

gear (car) เกียร์ *kia*

gem เพชรพลอย *phét-phloi*

gender เพศ *phêht*

get off ลง *long*

get on ขึ้น *khûen*

gift ของขวัญ *khǎwng khwǎn*

ginger ขิง *khǐng*

girl เด็กผู้หญิง *dèk phûu yǐng*

girlfriend เพื่อนหญิง, แฟน *phûean yǐng, faehn*

given name ชื่อ *chûeh*

glass (material) กระจก *kracòk*

glass (for drinking) แก้ว *kâeo*

glasses, spectacles แว่นตา *wâen taa*

gliding การร่อน *kaan râwn*

glossy (photo) เป็นมัน *pen man*

gloves ถุงมือ *thǔng mueh*

glue กาว *kao*

gnat ริ้น เห็บ *rín hèp*

go ไป *pai*

go back กลับไป *klàp pai*

go out ออกไป *àwk pai*

gold ทอง *thawng*

golf กอล์ฟ *káwf*

golf course สนามกอล์ฟ *sanǎam káwf*

good afternoon สวัสดี *sawàt dii*

goodbye ลาก่อน *laa kàwn*

good evening สวัสดี *sawàt dii*

good morning สวัสดี *sawàt dii*

good night ราตรีสวัสดิ์ *sawàt dii, raatrii sawàt*

goose ห่าน *hàan*

gram กรัม *kram*

grandchild หลาน *lǎan*

granddaughter หลานสาว *lǎan sǎo*

grandfather (paternal) ปู่ *pùu*

grandfather (maternal) ตา *taa*

grandmother (paternal) ย่า *yâa*

grandmother (maternal) ยาย *yai*

grandparents ปู่ย่าตายาย *pùu yâa taa yai*

grandson หลานชาย *lǎan chai*

grape juice น้ำองุ่น *náam angùn*

grapes องุ่น *angùn*

grave หลุมศพ *lǔm sòp*

graze (injury) ถลอก *thalàwk*

greasy เปื้อนน้ำมัน *pûean námman*

green เขียว *khǐao*

greengrocer ร้านขายผักผลไม้ *ráan khǎi phàk phǒnlamái*

greeting การทักทาย *kaan thák thai*

grey สีเทา *sǐi thao*

grey-haired ผมขาว *phǒm khǎo*

grilled ปิ้ง *pîng*

grocer คนขายของชำ *khon khǎi khǎwng cham*

groceries กับข้าว *kàp khâo*

ground up จากต้น *càak tôn*

group กลุ่ม *klùm*

guest house เรือนรับรอง *ruean ráp rawng*

guide (book) คู่มือ *khûu mueh*

guide (person) ไกด์, มัคคุเทศก์ *kái, mákkhúthêht*

guided tour ทัศนาจรที่มีไกด์ *thátsanaacawn thîi mii kái*

guilty ความผิด *khwaam phìt*

gym โรงยิม *rohng yim*

gynecologist สูติแพทย์ *satìphâeht*

H

hair ผม *phǒm*

hairbrush แปรง *praehng*

haircut ตัดผม *tàt phǒm*

hairdresser ช่างทำผม *châang tàt phǒm*

hairdryer ที่เป่าผม *thîi pào phǒm*

hairspray สเปรย์ฉีดผม *sapreh chìit phǒm*

hairstyle ทรงผม *song phǒm*

half ครึ่ง *khrûeng*

half full ครึ่ง *khrûeng*

hammer ฆ้อน *kháwn*

hand มือ *mueh*

handbag กระเป๋าถือ *krapǎo thǔeh*

hand brake เบรคมือ *brèhk mueh*

handkerchief ผ้าเช็ดหน้า *phâa chét nâa*

hand luggage กระเป๋าหิ้ว *krapǎo hîu*

handmade ทำด้วยมือ *tham dûai mueh*

hand towel ผ้าเช็ดมือ *phâa chét mueh*

happy มีความสุข *mii khwaam sùk*

harbor ท่าเรือ *thâa ruea*

hard (firm) แข็ง *khǎeng*

hard (difficult) ยาก *yâak*

hardware ฮาร์ดแวร์ *háad-wae*

hardware store ร้านขายเครื่องก่อสร้าง *ráan khǎi khrûeang kàw sâang*

hat หมวก *mùak*

hay fever แพ้อากาศ *pháe aakàat*

head หัว *hǔa*

headache ปวดหัว *puàt hǔa*

headlights ไฟหน้า *fai nâa*

health food shop ร้านขายอาหารเพื่อสุขภาพ *ráan khǎi aahǎan phûea sùkhàphâap*

healthy สมบูรณ์, สุขภาพดี *sǒmbuun, sùkkhàphâap dii*

hear ได้ยิน *dâi-yin*

hearing aid เครื่องช่วยฟัง *khrûeang chûai fang*

heart หัวใจ *hǔa cai*

heart attack หัวใจวาย *hǔa cai wai*

heat ความร้อน *khwaam ráwn*

heater เครื่องทำความร้อน *khrûeang tham khwaam ráwn*

heavy หนัก *nàk*

heel (of foot) ส้นเท้า *sôn tháo*

heel (of shoe) ส้นรองเท้า *sôn rawng tháo*

hello ฮัลโลว์ *hal-lŏh*

help! ช่วยด้วย! *chûai dûai!*

help ช่วย *chûai*

helping (food) เสิร์ฟ *sòehf*

hem ตะเข็บ *takhèp*

herbal tea ชาสมุนไพร *chaa samŭn phrai*

herbs สมุนไพร *samŭn phrai*

here ที่นี่ *thîi nîi*

high สูง *sŭung*

high chair เก้าอี้เด็ก *kâo-îi dèk*

high tide น้ำขึ้นสุด *náam khûen sùt*

highway ทางหลวง *thaang lŭang*

hiking การเดินป่า *kaan doehn pàa*

hiking boots รองเท้าเดินป่า *rawng tháo doehn pàa*

hip สะโพก *saphôok*

hire เช่า *châo*

hitchhike โบกรถ *bòhk rót*

hobby งานอดิเรก *ngaan adirèhk*

holdup ปล้น, จี้ *plôn, cîi*

holiday (vacation) พักร้อน *phák ráwn*

holiday (festival) วันหยุดเทศกาล *wan yùt thêhtsakaan*

holiday (public) วันหยุดราชการ *wan yùt râatchakaan*

homesick คิดถึงบ้าน *khít thŭeng bâan*

honest สุจริต, ซื่อสัตย์ *sùcarit, sûehsàt*

honey น้ำผึ้ง *nám phûeng*

horizontal แนวราบ *naeo râap*

horrible น่าเกลียดมาก, แย่มาก *nâa klìat mâak, yâeh mâak*

horse ม้า *máa*

hospital โรงพยาบาล *rohng phayaabaan*

hospitality การรับรอง *kaan ráp rawng*

hot (warm) ร้อน *ráwn*

hot (sharp, spicy) เผ็ด *phèt*

hot spot จุดคลื่นสัญญาณถี่ *cùt khlûen sănyaan thìi*

hot spring น้ำพุร้อน *nám phú ráwn*

hot-water bottle กระเป๋าน้ำร้อน *krapăo nám ráwn*

hotel โรงแรม *rohng raehm*

hour ชั่วโมง *chûamohng*

house บ้าน *bâan*

houses of parliament รัฐสภา *ráthàsaphaa*

how? อย่างไร, ยังไง *yàangrai, yang-ngai*

how far? ไกลเท่าไร *klai thâorai*

how long (time)? นานเท่าไร *naan thâorai*

how many? เท่าไร, กี่อัน *thâorai, kìi an*

how much? เท่าไร *thâorai*

hundred grams ร้อยกรัม *ròi kram*

hungry หิว *hĭu*

hurry รีบ *rîip*

husband สามี *săamii*

hut กระท่อม *krathâwm*

hybrid car รถยนต์ไฮบริด *rót yon hai-brid*

I

ice cream ไอศครีม *aiskhriim, aitiim*

ice cubes น้ำแข็งก้อน *nám khăeng kâwn*

iced เย็น *yen*

ice-skating สเก็ตน้ำแข็ง *sakét nám khăeng*

idea ความคิด *khwaam khít*

identification (card) บัตรประจำตัว *bàt pracam tua*

identify ระบุ *rabù*

ignition key กุญแจติดเครื่อง *kuncaeh tìt khrûeang*

ill ป่วย *pùai*

illness ความเจ็บป่วย *khwaam cèp pùai*

imagine นึก, วาดภาพ *núek, wâat phâap*

immediately ทันที *than thii*

important สำคัญ *sǎmkhan*

import duty ภาษีขาเข้า *phaasǐi khǎa khâo*

impossible เป็นไปไม่ได้ *pen pai mâi dâai*

improve ปรับปรุง *pràp prung*

in ใน *nai*

in the evening ตอนเย็น *tawn yen*

in the morning ตอนเช้า *tawn cháo*

in-laws (female) สะใภ้ *sàphái*

in-laws (male) เขย *khǒei*

included รวมอยู่ *ruam yùu*

including รวม *ruam*

indicate บ่งชี้ *bòng chíi*

indicator (car) เข็มชี้ *khěm chíi*

indigestion การไม่ย่อย *kaan mâi yôi*

inexpensive ไม่แพง *mâi phaehng*

infection การติดเชื้อ *kaan tìt chûea*

infectious ติดเชื้อ *tìt chûea*

inflammation ไวไฟ *wai fai*

information ข้อมูล, ข่าวสาร *khâwmuun, khào sǎan*

information office สำนักงานให้ข้อมูล *sǎmnák ngaan hâi khâwmuun*

injection การฉีดยา *kaan chìit yaa*

injured บาดเจ็บ *bàat cèp*

inner tube ท่อใน *thâw nai*

innocent บริสุทธิ์ *bawrísùt*

insect แมลง *malaehng*

insect bite แมลงกัด *malaehng kàt*

insect repellant ยากันแมลง *yaa kan malaehng*

inside ข้างใน *khâng nai*

instructions คำแนะนำ *kham náènam*

insurance การประกัน *kaan prakan*

intermission พักครึ่งเวลา *phák khrûeng wehlaa*

internal ภายใน *phai nai*

international ต่างประเทศ *tàang prathêht*

Internet อินเตอร์เน็ต *internet*

Internet café อินเตอร์เน็ตคาเฟ่ *intoehnèt khaafêh*

interpreter ล่าม *lâam*

intersection สี่แยก *sìi yâehk*

introduce oneself แนะนำตัวเอง *náenam tua ehng*

invite เชิญ *choehn*

invoice ใบเรียกเก็บเงิน *bai rîak kèp ngoen*

iodine ไอโอดีน *ai-ohdiin*

iPhone ไอโฟน *ai-fone*

iPad ไอแพด *ai-pád*

Ireland ประเทศไอร์แลนด์ *prathêht ailaehn*

iron (metal) เหล็ก *lèk*

iron (for clothes) เตารีด *tao rîit*

iron (verb) รีด *rîit*

ironing board ที่รีดผ้า *thîi rîit phâa*

island เกาะ *kàw*

itch คัน *khan*

J

jack (for car) แม่แรง *mâe raehng*

jacket แจ๊คเก็ต *cáekkêt*

jackfruit ขนุน *khanǔn*

jam แยม *yaehm*

January มกราคม *mókkaraakhom*

jaw กราม *kraam*

jeans กางเกงยีนส์ *kaangkehng yiin*

jellyfish แมงกะพรุน *maengkàphrun*

jeweler ช่างทำเพชร *châang tham phét*

jewelery เพชรพลอย *phét phlawi*

job งาน *ngaan*

jog วิ่งออกกำลัง *wîng áwk kamlang*

joke ตลก *talòk*

journey การเดินทาง *kaan doehn thaang*

juice น้ำผลไม้ *nám phǒnlamái*

July กรกฎาคม *karákadaakhom*

June มิถุนายน *míthùnaayon*

K

kerosene น้ำมันก๊าด *námman káat*

key กุญแจ *kuncaeh*

key (on keyboard) แป้นพิมพ์ (แผงแป้นพิมพ์) *pâen phim (phǎeng pâen phim)*

kidney ไต *tai*

kilogram กิโลกรัม *kilohkram*

king พระมหากษัตริย์ *phrá-mahǎa-kasàt*

kiss จูบ *cùup*

kiss (verb) จูบ *cùup*

kitchen ครัว *khrua*

knee เข่า *khào*

knife มีด *mîit*

knit ถักนิตติ้ง *thàk níttîng*

know รู้ *rúu*

Korean (television) drama ละคร(ทีวี)เกาหลี *lakawn (thii-wii) kao-lǐi*

K-pop (Korean pop music) ป็อปเกาหลี *páwp kao-lǐi*

L

lace (fabric) ลูกไม้ *lûuk mái*

laces (for shoes) เชือกผูกรองเท้า *chûeak phùuk rawng tháo*

ladder บันได *bandai*

lake ทะเลสาบ *thaleh sàap*

lamb (mutton) เนื้อแกะ *núea kàe*

lamp ตะเกียง *takiang*

land (ground) พื้นดิน *phúehn din*

land (verb) ลง *long*

lane (of traffic) เลน *lehn*

language ภาษา *phaasǎa*

laptop computer โน้ตบุ๊ค *nó-t-búk*

large ใหญ่ *yài*

last (final) สุดท้าย *sùt thái*

last (endure) อยู่ได้นาน *yùu dâi naan*

last night เมื่อคืนนี้ *mûea khuehn níi*

last week อาทิตย์ที่แล้ว *aathít thîi láeo*

late สาย *sǎi*

later ทีหลัง *thii lǎng*

laugh หัวเราะ *hǔaráw*

launderette ร้านซักรีด *ráan sák rîit*

laundry soap น้ำยาซักผ้า *nám yaa sák phâa*

law กฎหมาย *kòtmǎi*

lawyer ทนายความ *thanai khwaam*

laxative ยาถ่าย *yaa thài*

leak รั่ว *rûa*

leather หนัง *nǎng*

leather goods สินค้าหนัง *sǐnkháa nǎng*

leave ออกจาก *àwk càak*

left (direction) ซ้าย *sái*

left behind ทิ้งไว้ *thíng wái*

leg ขา *khǎa*

leisure เวลาว่าง *wehlaa wâang*

lemon มะนาว *manao*

lend ให้ยืม *hâi yuehm*

lens (camera) เล็นส์ *len*

less น้อยกว่า *nòi kwàa*

lesson บทเรียน *bòt rian*

letter จดหมาย *còtmǎi*

lettuce ผักกาดแก้ว *phàkkàat kâeho*

level crossing ทางข้าม *thaang khâam rótfai*

library ห้องสมุด *hâwng samùt*

license ใบอนุญาต *bai anúyâat*

lie (not tell the truth) พูดเท็จ *phûut thét*

lie (falsehood) โกหก *kohhòk*

lie down นอนลง *nawn long*

lift (elevator) ลิฟต์ *líf*

light (lamp) ไฟ *fai*

light (not dark) สว่าง *sawàang*

light (not heavy) เบา *bao*

light bulb หลอดไฟ *làwt fai*

lighter ที่จุดบุหรี่ *fai cháek*

lightning ฟ้าผ่า *fáa phàa*

like (verb) ชอบ *châwp*

line เส้น *sên*

linen ลินิน *linin*

lining ซับใน *sáp nai*

liquor store ร้านเหล้า *ráan lâo*

liqueur เหล้า *lâo*

listen ฟัง *fang*

litre ลิตร *lít*

literature วรรณคดี *wannákhadii*

little (small) เล็ก *lék*

little (amount) น้อย *náwi*

live (alive) มีชีวิต *mii chiiwít*

live (verb) อยู่ *yùu*

liver ตับ *tàp*

lobster กุ้งใหญ่ *kûng yài*

local ท้องถิ่น *tháwng thìn*

lock ล็อค *láwk*

log off ล็อกออฟ *láwk awf*

log on ล็อกออน *láwk awn*

long (in length) ยาว *yao*

long-distance call โทร.ทางไกล *thoh thaang klai*

look at ดู *duu*

look for หา *hǎa*

look up ชมเชย *chom choei*

lose หาย *hǎi*

loss ความสูญเสีย *khwaam sǔun sǐa*

lost (missing) หายไป *hǎi pai*

lost (can't find way) หลงทาง *lǒng thaang*

lost and found office สำนักงานแจ้งของหาย *sǎmnákngaan câehng khǎwng hǎi*

lotion โลชั่น *lohchân*

loud ดัง *dang*

love ความรัก *khwaam rák*

love (verb) รัก *rák*

low ต่ำ *tàm*

low tide น้ำลงสุด *náam long sùt*

LPG แก๊สเหลว *káeht lěo*

luck โชค *chôhk*

luggage กระเป๋าเดินทาง *krapǎo doehn thaang*

luggage locker ที่เก็บสัมภาระ *thîi kèp sǎmphaará*

lumps (sugar) ก้อน *kâwn*

lunch อาหารกลางวัน *aahǎan klaang wan*

lungs ปอด *pàwt*

M

madam แหม่ม *màem*

magazine วารสาร *waarásǎan*

mail (letters) จดหมาย *còtmǎi*

mail (verb) ส่งจดหมาย *sòng còtmǎi*

main post office ไปรษณีย์กลาง *praisanii klaang*

main road ถนนใหญ่, ถนนหลวง *thanǒn yài, thanǒn lǔang*

make, create สร้าง *sâang*

make an appointment นัด *nát*

make love ทำรัก, รวมเพศ *tham rák, rûam phêht*

makeshift ใช้ชั่วคราว *chái chûa khrao*

makeup ที่แต่งหน้า *thîi tàeng nâa*

man ผู้ชาย *phûu chai*

manager ผู้จัดการ *phûu càt kaan*

mango มะม่วง *mamûang*

manicure การแต่งเล็บ *kaan tàeng lép*

many มาก *mâak*

map แผนที่ *phǎehn thîi*

marble หินอ่อน *hǐn àwn*

March มีนาคม *miinaakhom*

margarine เนยมาร์การีน *noei maakaariin*

marina ที่จอดเรือ *thîi càwt ruea*

marital status สถานะสมรส *sathǎana sǒmrót*

market ตลาด *talàat*

married แต่งงาน *tàeng ngaan*

Mass (go to) ไปรวมพิธีในโบสถ์ *(pai ruam) phíthii nai bòht*

massage นวด *nûat*

mat (on floor) เสื่อ *sùea*

mat (on table) ที่รอง *thîi rawng*

match เข้ากัน *khâo kan*

matches ไม้ขีด *mái khìit*

matte (photo) รูปถ่ายไม่มัน *rûup thài mâi man*

May พฤษภาคม *phrúetsaphaakhom*

maybe อาจจะ *àat ca*

mayonnaise มายองเนส *maayawngnêht*

mayor นายกเทศมนตรี *naayók-thêhtsamontrii*

meal มื้อ *múeh*

mean ใจแคบ *cai khâehp*

measure วัด *wát*

measuring jug ถ้วยตวง *thûai tuang*

measure out แบ่งวัด *bàeng wát*

meat เนื้อ *núea*

medication ยา *yaa*

medicine ยา *yaa*

meet พบ *phóp*

melon แตง *taehng*

member สมาชิก *samaachík*

member of parliament สมาชิกสภาผู้แทน *samaachík saphaa phûu thaehn*

membership card บัตรสมาชิก *bàt samaachík*

memory card เอสดีการ์ด *es-dii káad*

mend ซ่อมแซม *sâwm saehm*

menstruate มีประจำเดือน *mii pracam duean*

menstruation การมีประจำเดือน *kaan mii pracam duean*

menu เมนู, รายการอาหาร *mehnuu, raikaan aahǎan*

message ข้อความ *khâw khwaam*

metal เหล็ก *lèk*

meter (in taxi) มิเตอร์ *mítôeh*

metre เมตร *méht*

migraine ปวดหัวอย่างหนัก *pùat hǔa yàang nàk*

mild (taste) รสอ่อน *rót àwn*

milk นม *nom*

millimeter มิลลิเมตร *millíméht*

mineral water น้ำแร่ *nám râeh*

minute นาที *naathii*

mirror กระจก *kracòk*

miss (flight, train) ตกรถไฟ *tòk rót fai*

miss (loved one) คิดถึง *khít thǔeng*

missing หายไป *hǎi pai*

missing person คนหาย *khon hǎi*

mist หมอก *màwk*

misty มีหมอก *mii màwk*

mistake ความผิด *khwaam phìt*

mistaken เข้าใจผิด *khâocai phìt*

misunderstanding เข้าใจผิด *khâocai phìt*

mixed ผสม *phasǒm*

mobile phone โทรศัพท์มือถือ/โมบาย *thorasàp mue-thǔe/moo-bai* modern art ศิลปะสมัยใหม่ *sĭnlapà samăi mài*

moment เดี๋ยว *dĭao*

monastery วัด *wát*

Monday วันจันทร์ *wan can*

money เงิน *ngoen*

monkey ลิง *ling*

month เดือน *duean*

moon ดวงจันทร์ *duang can*

mope ซึมเศร้า *suem sâo*

mosquito ยุง *yung*

mosquito net มุ้งลวด *múng lûat*

motel โมเต็ล *mohten*

mother แม่ *mâeh*

mother-in-law แม่ยาย *mâeh yai*

motorbike มอเตอร์ไซค์ *mawtoehsai*

motorboat เรือยนต์ *ruea yon*

mountain ภูเขา *phuu khăw*

mountain climbing การปีนภูเขา *kaan piin phuu khăw*

mountain hut กระท่อมบนภูเขา *krathâwm bon phuu khăw*

mouse หนู *nŭu*

(computer) mouse เมาส์ (คอมพิวเตอร์) *mao (khawm-phiw-toer)*

mouth ปาก *pàak*

MP3 player เครื่องเล่นเอ็มพี3 *khrûeng lên em-phii-săam*

MSG ผงชูรส *phŏng chuu rót*

much มาก *mâak*

mud โคลน *khlohn*

muscle กล้ามเนื้อ *klâam núea*

muscle spasms กล้ามเนื้อกระตุก *klâam núea kratùk*

museum พิพิธภัณฑ์ *phíphítthaphan*

mushrooms เห็ด *hèt*

music ดนตรี *dontrii*

N

nail (metal) ตะปู *tapuu*

nail (finger) เล็บ *lép*

nail file ตะไบเล็บ *tabai lép*

nail scissors กรรไกรตัดเล็บ *kankrai tàt lép*

naked เปลือย *plueai*

nappy, diaper ผ้าอ้อม *phâa âwm*

nationality สัญชาติ *sănchâat*

natural ตามธรรมชาติ *taam thammachâat*

nature ธรรมชาติ *thammachâat*

nauseous คลื่นไส้ *khlûehn sâi*

near ใกล้ *klâi*

nearby (here) แถวนี้ *thăeo níi*

nearby (there) แถวนั้น *thăeo nán*

necessary จำเป็น *campen*

neck คอ *khaw*

necklace สร้อยคอ *sôi khaw*

necktie เน็คไท *nékthai*

needle เข็ม *khěm*

negative (photo) ฟิล์ม *fiim*

neighbour เพื่อนบ้าน *phûean bâan*

nephew หลานชาย *lăan chai*

never ไม่เคย *mâi khoei*

new ใหม่ *mài*

news ข่าว *khào*

newspaper หนังสือพิมพ์ *nangsŭe phim*

news stand ที่ขายหนังสือพิมพ์ *thîi khăi nangsŭeh phim*

next ต่อไป *tàw pai*

next to ถัดไป *thàt pai*

nice (pleasant) ดี ปลอดโปร่ง *dii, plàwt pròhng*

nice (person) ดี *dii*

niece หลานสาว *lăan săo*

night กลางคืน *klaang khuehn*

night duty เวรกลางคืน *wehn klaang khuehn*

nightclothes ชุดนอน *chút nawn*

nightclub ไนท์คลับ *nái(t) kláp*

nightdress ชุดนอน *chút nawn*

nipple (bottle) จุกนม *cùk nom*

no ไม่ *mâi*

no entry ห้ามเข้า *hâam khào*

no thank you ไม่เอา ขอบคุณ *mâi ao khàwp khun*

noise เสียง *sĭang*

non-smoking เขตปลอดบุหรี่ *khèet plàwt burìi*

nonstop (flight) บินตรง *bin trong*

noodles ก๋วยเตี๋ยว *kúai tĭao*

no-one ไม่มีใคร *mâi mii khrai*

normal ปกติ *pòkkatì*

north เหนือ *nŭea*

nose จมูก *camùuk*

nosebleed เลือดกำเดาออก *lûeat kamdao àwk*

nose drops ที่ฉีดจมูก *thîi chìit camùuk*

not ไม่ *mâi*

notebook สมุดบันทึก *samùt banthúk*

notebook computer คอมพิวเตอร์โน๊ตบุ๊ค *khawm-phiw-toer nóo-t-búk*

notepad สมุดฉีก *samùt chìik*

notepaper กระดาษจด *kradàat còt*

nothing ไม่มีอะไร *mâi mii arai*

November พฤศจิกายน *phrúetsacikaayon*

nowhere ไม่มีที่ไหน *mâi mii thîi năi*

number เบอร์, หมายเลข *boeh, măi lêhk*

number plate ป้ายทะเบียน *pâi thábian*

nurse พยาบาล *phaiaabaan*

nuts ถั่ว *thùa*

O

occupation อาชีพ *aachîip*

October ตุลาคม *tulaakhom*

off (gone bad) เสีย *sĭa*

off (turned off) ปิด *pìt*

offer เสนอให้ *sanŏeh hâi*

office ที่ทำงาน *thîi tham ngaan*

oil น้ำมันเครื่อง *námman khrûeang*

oil level ระดับน้ำมันเครื่อง *rádàp námman khrûeang*

ointment ขี้ผึ้งทา *khîi phûeng thaa*

okay ตกลง *tòk long*

old (of persons) แก่ *kàeh*

old (of things) เก่า *kào*

on, at ที่ *thîi*

on (turned on) เปิด *pòeht*

on board ขึ้น, อยู่บน *khûen, yùu bon*

oncoming car รถสวน *rót sŭan*

one-day trip การเที่ยวไปเช้า-เย็นกลับ *kaan thîao pai cháw-yen klàp*

one-way ticket ตั๋วเที่ยวเดียว *tŭa thîao diao*

one-way traffic รถเดินทางเดียว *rót doehn thaang diao*

onion หอมใหญ่ *hăwm yài*

on the left ทางซ้าย *thaang sái*

on the right ทางขวา *thaang kwăa*

on the way กำลังมา *kamlang maa*

online shopping ซื้อของผ่านทางอินเตอร์เน็ต *súeh khăwng phàan thaang internet*

open เปิด *pòeht*

open (verb) เปิด *pòeht*

operate (surgeon) ผ่าตัด *phàa tàt*

operator (telephone) โอเปอเรเตอร์ *ohpoehrehtôeh*

opposite ตรงข้าม *trong khâam*

optician คนตรวจตา *khon trùat taa*

orange (fruit) ส้ม *sôm*

orange (color) สีส้ม *sĭi sôm*

order (command) คำสั่ง *kham sàng*

order (written) ใบสั่ง *bai sàng*

order (verb) สั่ง *sàng*

other อื่นๆ *ùehn*

other side อีกข้าง *ìik khâang*

outside ข้างนอก *khâang nâwk*

overpass สะพานข้าม *saphaan khâam*

overseas ต่างประเทศ *tàang prathêht*

overtake แซง *saehng*

over there (yonder) ที่โน่น *thîi nôhn*

oyster หอยนางรม *hŏi naang rom*

P

pacemaker เครื่องกระตุ้นกล้ามเนื้อหัวใจ *khrûeng-kra-tûn klâam-núea hŭa-cai*

packed lunch ห่ออาหารกลางวัน *aahăan klaang wan hàw*

page หน้า *nâa*

pain เจ็บปวด *cèp pùat*

painkiller ยาแก้ปวด *yaa kâeh pùat*

paint สี *sĭi*

painting รูป *rûup*

pajamas ชุดนอน *chút nawn*

palace วัง *wang*

pan กะทะ *kàthá*

pane บานกระจก *baan kracòk*

panties กางเกงใน *kaangkehng nai*

pants กางเกง *kaangkehng*

pantyhose ถุงน่อง *thŭng nâwng*

papaya มะละกอ *malákaw*

paper กระดาษ *kradàat*

paraffin oil น้ำมันพาราฟิน *námman phaaraafin*

parasol ร่มกันแดด *rôm kan dàeht*

parcel พัสดุ *phátsadù*

pardon ขอโทษ *khăw thôht*

parents พ่อแม่ *phâw mâeh*

park, gardens สวน *sŭan*

park (verb) จอด *càwt*

parking garage โรงรถ *rohng rót*

parking space ที่จอดรถ *thîi càwt rót*

part (car-) อะไหล่ *alài*

partner (business) หุ้นส่วน *hûn sùan*

party งานปาร์ตี้ *ngaan paatîi*

passable (road) รถผ่านสองคันได้ *(thanŏn) rót phàan sǎwng khan dâi*

passenger ผู้โดยสาร *phûu doisăn*

passionfruit มะลเสาวรส *phol saowaroté*

passport หนังสือเดินทาง *nǎngsǔeh doehn thaang*

passport photo รูปถ่ายติดพาสปอร์ต *rûup thài tìt phaasapáwt*

password รหัส *rahàt*

patient คนไข้ *khon khâi*

pay จ่าย *cài*

pay the bill จ่ายบิล *cài bin*

peach พีช *phíit, phíich*

peanut ถั่วลิสง *thùa lísŏng*

pear แพร์ *phaeh*

pearl ไข่มุก *khài múk*

peas ถั่ว *thùa*

pedal ที่ถีบ *thîi thìip*

pedestrian crossing ทางม้าลาย *thaang máa lai*

pedicure การทำเล็บเท้า *kaan tham lép tháo*

pen ปากกา *pàakkaa*

pencil ดินสอ *dinsǎw*

penknife มีดพก *mîit phók*

penis ควย *khuai*

people คน *khon*

pepper (black) พริกไทย *phrík thai*

pepper (chilli) พริกหยวก *phrík yùak*

performance การทำงาน *kaan tham ngaan*

perfume น้ำหอม *nám hǎwm*

perhaps บางที *baang thii*

period (menstrual) ประจำเดือน *pracam duean*

permit ใบอนุญาต *bai anúyâat*

person คน *khon*

personal ส่วนตัว *sùan tua*

pet สัตว์เลี้ยง *sàt líang*

petrol น้ำมัน *námman*

petrol station ปั๊มน้ำมัน *pám námman*

pharmacy ร้านขายยา *ráan khăi yaa*

phone โทรศัพท์ *thohrásàp*

phone (verb) พูดโทรศัพท์ *phûut thohrásàp*

phone booth ตู้โทรศัพท์ *tûu thohrásàp*

phone card บัตรโทรศัพท์ *bàt thohrásàp*

phone directory สมุดโทรศัพท์ *samùt thohrásàp*

phone number หมายเลขโทรศัพท์ *măi lêhk thohrásàp*

photo รูปถ่าย *rûup thài*

photocopier เครื่องอัดสำเนา *khrûeang àt sămnao*

photocopy สำเนา *sămnao*

photocopy (verb) อัดสำเนา *àt sămnao*

photo-editing การตัดต่อ-รูปภาพ *kaan tàt-taw rûup-phâap*

phrasebook หนังสือคำศัพท์ *nangsŭeh khamsàp*

pick up (come to) มารับ *maa ráp*

pick up (go to) ไปรับ *pai ráp*

picnic ปิคนิค *píkník*

pill (contraceptive) ยาคุมกำเนิด *yaa khum kamnòeht*

pills, tablets ยาเม็ด *yaa mét*

pillow หมอน *măwn*

pillowcase ปลอกหมอน *plàwk măwn*

pin เข็มหมุด *khěm mùt*

PIN number รหัสส่วนตัว *rahàt sùan tua*

pineapple สับปะรด *sapparót*

pipe (plumbing) ท่อ *thâw*

pipe (smoking) ไปพ์, กล้อง *pái(p), klâwng*

pipe tobacco ยาสูบ *yaa sùup*

pity สงสาร *sŏngsăan*

place of interest สถานที่น่าเที่ยว *sathăan thîi nâa thîao*

plain (simple) ธรรมดา *thammadaa*

plain (not flavoured) เปล่า *plào*

plan (map) แผน *phăehn*

plan (intention) แผน *phăehn*

plane เครื่องบิน *khrûeang bin*

plant (factory) โรงงาน *rohngngaan*

plant (vegetation) ต้นไม้ *tôn mái*

plaster cast เฝือก *fùeak*

plastic พลาสติค *plaasatik, plaastìk*

plastic bag ถุงพลาสติค *thŭng plaasatik*

plate จาน *caan*

platform ชานชาลา *chaan chaalaa*

play (drama) ละคร *lakhawn*

play (verb) เล่น *lên*

play golf เล่นกอล์ฟ *lên káwf*

playground สนามเด็กเล่น *sanăam dèk lên*

playing cards ไพ่ *phâi*

play sports เล่นกีฬา *lên kiilaa*

play tennis เล่นเทนนิส *lên thehnít*

pleasant ดี *dii*

please ช่วย *chûai*

pleasure ความยินดี *khwaam yindii*

plug (electric) ปลั๊กไฟ *plák fai*

plum ลูกพลัม *lûuk phlam*

pocket กระเป๋า *krapăo*

pocketknife มีดพก *mîit phók*

point out ชี้ *chíi*

poisonous เป็นพิษ *pen phít*

police ตำรวจ *tamrùat*

police officer นายตำรวจ *nai tamrùat*

police station สถานีตำรวจ *sathăanii tamrùat*

pond สระน้ำ *sà-áam*

pony ม้าประเภทเล็ก *máa praphêht lék*

pop music ดนตรีป็อป *dontrii páwp*

population ประชากร *prachaachon*

pork หมู *mŭu*

port ท่าเรือ *thâa ruea*

porter (for bags) คนขนกระเป๋า *khon khŏn krapăo*

possible เป็นไปได้ *pen pai dâi*

post (verb) ส่ง *sòng*

postage ค่าส่งไปรษณีย์ *khâa sòng praisanii*

postbox ตู้ไปรษณีย์ *tûu praisanii*

postcard ไปรษณียบัตร *praisaniiyábàt*

postcode รหัสไปรษณีย์ *rahàt praisanii*

poste restante ที่เก็บพัสดุ *thîi kèp phátsadù*

post office ไปรษณีย์ *praisanii*

postpone เลื่อน *lûean*

potato มัน *man*

potato chips มันทอด *man thâwt*

poultry ไก่ *kài*

powdered milk นมผง *nom phŏng*

power outlet ที่เสียบปลั๊ก *thîi sìap plák*

prawn กุ้ง *kûng*

precious metal โลหะมีค่า *lohhà mii khâa*

precious stone พลอย *phlawi*

prefer ชอบมากกว่า *châwp mâak kwàa*

preference สิ่งที่ชอบมากกว่า *sìng thîi châwp mâak kwàa*

pregnant มีท้อง *mii tháwng*

prescription ใบสั่งยา *bai sàng yaa*

present (here) อยู่นี่ *yùu nîi*

present (gift) ของขวัญ *khăwng khwăn*

press กด *kòt*

pressure ความกดดัน *khwaam kòt dan*

price ราคา *raakhaa*

price list รายการราคา *raikaan raakhaa*

print (picture) ภาพพิมพ์ *phâap phim*

print (verb) พิมพ์ *phim*

probably อาจจะ *àat ca*

problem ปัญหา *panhăa*

profession อาชีพ *aachîip*

profit ผลกำไร *phŏn kamrai*

program โปรแกรม *prohkraehm*

pronounce ออกเสียง *àwk sĭang*

propane แก๊ซเชื้อเพลิง *káet chúea phloehng*

pudding พุดดิ้ง *phútdîng*

pull ดึง *dueng*

pull a muscle กล้ามเนื้อตึง *klâam núea tueng*

pulse ชีพจร *chîiphacawn*

pure บริสุทธิ์ *bawrísùt*

purify ทำให้บริสุทธิ์ *tham hâi bawrísùt*

purple สีม่วง *sĭi mûang*

purse (handbag) กระเป๋าถือ *krapăo thŭeh*

purse (for money) กระเป๋าสตางค์ *krapăo sataang*

push ผลัก *phlàk*

puzzle ปริศนา *pritsanăa*

pyjamas ชุดนอน *chút nawn*

Q

quarter เศษหนึ่งส่วนสี่ *sèht nùeng sùan sìi*

quarter of an hour สิบห้านาที *sìp hâa naathii*

queen ราชินี *râatchinii*

question คำถาม *kham thăam*

quick เร็ว *reo*

quiet เงียบ *ngîap*

R

radio วิทยุ *wítthayú*

railroad, railway ทางรถไฟ *thaang rót fai*

rain ฝน *fŏn*

rain (verb) ฝนตก *fŏn tòk*

raincoat เสื้อฝน *sûea fŏn*

rape ข่มขืน *khòm khŭen*

rapid รวดเร็ว *rûat reo*

rapids น้ำเชี่ยว *náam chîao*

rash ผื่นคัน *phùen khan*

rat หนู *nŭu*

raw ดิบ *dìp*

razor blade ใบมีดโกน *bai mîit kohn*

read อ่าน *àan*

ready พร้อม *phráwm*

really จริงๆ *cing cing*

reason เหตุผล *hèht phŏn*

receipt ใบเสร็จ *bai sèt*

reception desk แผนกต้อนรับ *phanàehk tâwn ráp*

recipe สูตรอาหาร *sùut aahăan*

reclining chair เก้าอี้ปรับได้ *kâo-îi pràp dâi*

recommend แนะนำ *náe-nam*

rectangle สี่เหลี่ยมผืนผ้า *sìi liam phúehn phâa*

red แดง *daehng*

red wine ไวน์แดง *wai(n) daehng*

reduction ส่วนลด *sùan lót*

refrigerator ตู้เย็น *tûu yen*

refund เบิกคืน *bòehk khuehn*

regards (closure) นับถือ *náp thŭeh*

region ภูมิภาค *phuumíphâak*

registered ลงทะเบียน *long thabian*

regular (unleaded) gasoline น้ำมันไร้สารตะกั่ว *náam-man rái săan ta-kùa*

relatives ญาติ *yâat*

reliable ไว้ใจได้ *wái cai dâi*

religion ศาสนา *sàatsanăa*

rent out ให้เช่า *hâi châo*

repair ซ่อม *sâwm*

repairs การซ่อม *kaan sâwm*

repeat ทำซ้ำ *tham sám*

report (police) แจ้ง *câehng*

reserve ถนอม, สำรอง *thanăwm, sămrawng*

responsible รับผิดชอบ *ráp phìt châwp*

rest พักผ่อน *phák phàwn*

restaurant ร้านอาหาร *ráan aahăan*

restroom ห้องพักผ่อน *hâwng phák phàwn*

result ผล *phŏn*

retired เกษียณ *kasĭan*

return ticket ตั๋วไปกลับ *tŭa pai klàp*

reverse (car) ถอยรถ *thăwi rót*

rheumatism โรคปวดในไขข้อ *rôhk pùat nai khăi khâw*

ribbon ริบบิ้น *ripbîn*

rice (cooked) ข้าวสวย *khâo sŭai*

rice (grain) ข้าวสาร *khâo săan*

ridiculous ไม่เข้าเรื่อง *mâi khâo rûeang*

riding (horseback) การขี่ม้า *kaan khìi máa*

right (side) ข้างขวา *khâng khwăa*

right (correct) ถูก *thùuk*

right of way มีสิทธิ์ไปก่อน *mii sìt pai kàwn*

rinse ล้างน้ำ *láang náam*

ripe สุก *sùk*

risk เสี่ยง *sìang*

river แม่น้ำ *mâeh náam*

road ถนน *thanŏn*

roadway ถนนหลวง *thanŏn lŭang*

roasted อบ *òp*

rock (stone) หิน *hĭn*

roll (bread) ขนมปัง *khanǒm pang*

roof หลังคา *lǎngkhaa*

roof rack ที่วางของบนหลังคารถ *thîi waang khǎwng bon lǎngkhaa rót*

room ห้อง *hâwng*

room number หมายเลขห้อง *mǎi lêhk hâwng*

room service บริการถึงห้อง *bawríkaan thǔeng hâwng*

rope เชือก *chûeak*

route เส้นทาง *sên thaang*

rowing boat เรือพาย *ruea phai*

rubber (material) ยาง *yaang*

rude ไม่สุภาพ *mâi suphâap*

ruins ของพัง *khǎwng phang*

run วิ่ง *wîng*

running shoes รองเท้าสำหรับวิ่ง *rawngtháo sǎmràp wîng*

S

sad เศร้า *sâo*

safe ปลอดภัย *plàwtphai*

safe (for cash) ตู้เซฟ *tûu séhf*

safety pin เข็มกลัด *khěm klàt*

sail (verb) ล่องเรือ *lâwng ruea*

sailing boat เรือใบ *ruea bai*

salad สลัด *salàt*

sale ขาย *khǎi*

sales clerk พนักงานขาย *phanákngaan khǎi*

salt เกลือ *kluea*

same เหมือนกัน *mǔeankan*

sandals รองเท้าแตะ *rawng tháo tàe*

sandy beach หาดทราย *hàat sai*

sanitary towel ผ้าอนามัย *phâa anaamai*

satisfied พอใจ *phaw cai*

Saturday วันเสาร์ *wan sǎo*

sauce ซอส, น้ำจิ้ม *sáws, nám cîm*

saucepan หม้อ *mâw*

sauna อบไอน้ำ *òp ai náam*

say พูด *phûut*

scald (injury) แผลน้ำร้อนลวก *phlǎeh nám ráwn lûak*

scales ที่ชั่งน้ำหนัก *thîi châng námnàk*

scanner เครื่องสแกน *khrûeng sa-kaen*

scarf (headscarf) ผ้าพันคอ *phâa phan khaw*

scarf (muffler) ผ้าพันคอหนา *phâa phan khaw nǎa*

scenic walk ที่เดินชมวิว *thîi doehn chom wiu*

school โรงเรียน *rohng rian*

scissors กรรไกร *kankrai*

Scotland สก็อตแลนด์ *sakàwtlaehn*

screen จอ *caw*

screw ตะปูควง *tapuu khuang*

screwdriver ไขควง *khǎi khuang*

scuba diving การดำน้ำใช้เครื่อง *kaan dam náam chái khrûeang*

sculpture รูปปั้น *rûup pân*

SD card เอสดีการ์ด *es-dii kàad*

sea ทะเล *thaleh*

seasick เมาเรือ *mao ruea*

seat ที่นั่ง *thîi nâng*

second (in line) ที่สอง *thîi sǎwng*

second (instant) วินาที *wínaathii*

second-hand มือสอง *mueh sǎwng*

security ความมั่นคงปลอดภัย *khawm mân-khong plàwt-phai*

sedative ยาระงับประสาท *yaa rangáp prasàat*

see เห็น *hěn*

send ส่ง *sòng*

sentence (words) ประโยค *prayòhk*

separate แยกกัน *yâek kan*

September กันยายน *kanyaayon*

serious จริงจัง *cing cang*

service บริการ *bawríkaan*

service station ปั๊มน้ำมัน *pám námman*
serviette ผ้าเช็ดมือ *phâa chét mueh*
sesame oil น้ำมันงา *námman ngaa*
sesame seeds งา *ngaa*
set ชุด *chút*
sew เย็บผ้า *yép phâa*
shade ร่มเงา *rôm ngao*
shallow ตื้น *tûehn*
shame ละอาย *lá-ai*
shampoo แชมพูสระผม *chaehmphuu sà phŏm*
shark ปลาฉลาม *plaa chalăam*
shave โกน *kohn*
shaver ที่โกน *thîi kohn*
shaving cream ครีมโกนหนวด *khriim kohn nùat*
sheet ผ้าปูที่นอน *phâa puu thîi nawn*
shirt เสื้อเชิ้ต *sûea chóeht*
shoe รองเท้า *rawng tháo*
shoe polish ยาขัดรองเท้า *yaa khàt rawng tháo*
shop, store ร้าน *ráan*
shop (verb) ไปซื้อของ *pai súeh khăwng*
shop assistant คนขาย *khon khăi*
shopping centre ศูนย์การค้า *sŭun kaan kháa*
shop window หน้าต่างโชว์สินค้า *nâatàang choh sĭn kháa*
short สั้น *sân*
short circuit วงจรสั้น *wongcawn sân*
shorts (short trousers) กางเกงขาสั้น *kaangkehng khăa sân*
shorts (underpants) กางเกงใน *kaangkehng nai*
shoulder บ่า *bàa*
show แสดง, โชว์ *sadaehng, choh*
shower อาบน้ำฝักบัว *àap náam fàk bua*
shrimp กุ้ง *kûng*

shutter (camera) ที่ปิดกั้นแสง *thîi pit kân săehng*
shutter (on window) บานหน้าต่าง *baan nâatàang*
sieve กระชอน *krachawn*
sightseeing ชมทิวทัศน์ *chom thiuthát*
sign (road) ป้ายสัญญาณ *pâi sănyaan*
sign (verb) เซ็น *sen*
signature ลายเซ็น *lai sen*
silence ความเงียบ *khwaam ngîap*
silk ไหม *măi*
silver เงิน *ngoen*
SIM card ซิมการ์ด *sim-káad*
simple ธรรมดา *thammadaa*
single (only one) เดียว *diao*
single (unmarried) โสด *sòht*
single ticket ตั๋วเที่ยวเดียว *tŭa thîao diao*
sir เซอร์ *soeh*
sister (older) พี่สาว *phîi săo*
sister (younger) น้องสาว *náwng săo*
sit (be sitting) นั่ง *nâng*
sit down นั่งลง *nâng long*
size ขนาด *khanàat*
skiing การเล่นสกี *kaan lên sakii*
skin ผิว *phĭu*
skirt กระโปรง *kraprohng*
Skype สไกป์ *sa-kai-p*
sleep หลับ *làp*
sleeping car ตู้นอน *tûu nawn*
sleeping pills ยานอนหลับ *yaa nawn làp*
sleeve แขนเสื้อ *khăehn sûea*
slip (underskirt) สลิป *salìp*
slippers รองเท้าแตะ *rawng tháo tàe*
slow ช้า *cháa*
slow train รถหวานเย็น *rót wăan yen*
small เล็ก *lék*
small change เศษสตางค์ *sèht staang*

smartphone สมาร์ทโฟน *sa-mart fone*

smell กลิ่น *klìn*

smoke (cigarette) สูบบุหรี่ *sùup burìi*

smoked พ่นควัน *phôn khwan*

smoke detector ที่ตรวจจับควัน *thîi trùat càp khwan*

snake งู *nguu*

snorkel ท่อหายใจนักประดาน้ำ *thâw hăi cai nák pradaa náam*

snow หิมะ *himá*

snow (verb) หิมะตก *himá tòk*

soap สบู่ *sabùu*

soap powder ผงซักฟอก *phŏng sák fâwk*

soccer ฟุตบอล *fút bawn*

soccer match รอบฟุตบอล *râwp fút bawn*

social networking เครือข่ายสังคม *khruea-khàai săngkhom*

socket (electric) ที่เสียบปลั๊ก *thîi sìap plák*

socks ถุงเท้า *thŭng tháo*

soft drink น้ำอัดลม *náam àt lom*

software ซอฟแวร์ *sawf-wae*

sole (of shoe) พื้นรองเท้า *phúehn rawng tháo*

someone บางคน *baang khon*

sometimes บางที *baang thii*

somewhere บางแห่ง *baang hàeng*

son ลูกชาย *lûuk chai*

soon เร็วๆนี้ *reo reo níi*

sore (ulcer) แผลมีหนอง *phlăeh mii năwng*

sore (painful) เจ็บ *cèp*

sore throat เจ็บคอ *cèp khaw*

sorry เสียใจ *sĭa jai*

soup ซุป *súp*

sour เปรี้ยว *prîao*

south ใต้ *tâi*

souvenir ของที่ระลึก *khăwng thîi ralúek*

soy sauce ซีอิ๊ว *sii-íu*

spanner, wrench กุญแจเลื่อน *kuncaeh lûean*

spare สำรอง *sămrawng*

spare parts อะไหล่ *alài*

spare tyre ยางอะไหล่ *yaang alài*

spare wheel ล้ออะไหล่ *láw alài*

speak พูด *phûut*

special พิเศษ *phísèht*

specialist (doctor) หมอเฉพาะทาง *măw chapháw thaang*

speciality (cooking) อาหารจานเก่ง *aahăan caan kèng*

speed limit ความเร็วจำกัด *khwaam reo camkàt*

spell สะกด *sakòt*

spices เครื่องเทศ *khrûeang thêht*

spicy เผ็ดร้อน *phèt ráwn*

splinter (wood) เสี้ยน *sîan*

splinter (glass) เศษแก้ว *sèht kâeo*

spoon ช้อน *cháwn*

sport กีฬา *kiilaa*

sports centre ศูนย์เครื่องกีฬา *sŭun khrûeang kiilaa*

spot (place) ที่ใดที่หนึ่ง *thîi dai thîi nùeng*

spot (stain) รอยเปื้อน *rawi pûean*

spouse คู่สมรส *khûu sŏmrót*

sprain เคล็ด *khlét*

spring (season) ฤดูใบไม้ผลิ *rúeduu bai mái phlì*

spring (device) สปริง *sapring*

square (shape) สี่เหลี่ยมจัตุรัส *sìi lìam catùrát*

square (shopping plaza) ศูนย์การค้า *sŭun kaan kháa*

square metre ตารางเมตร *taaraang méht*

squash (vegetable) สควอช *sakhwáwt*

squash (game) เล่นสควอช *lên sakhwáwt*

stadium สนามกีฬา *sanǎam kiilaa*

stain รอยเปื้อน *roi pûean*

stain remover ที่ลบรอยเปื้อน *thîi lóp roi pûean*

stairs บันได *bandayi*

stamp แสตมป์ *sataehm*

stand (be standing) ยืน *yuehn*

stand up ยืนขึ้น *yuehn khûen*

star ดาว *dao*

starfruit มะเฟือง *má-fueang*

start เริ่ม *rôehm*

station สถานี *sathǎanii*

statue รูปปั้น *rûup pân*

stay (remain) คงอยู่ *khong yùu*

stay (in hotel) พัก *phák*

steal ขโมย *khamoi*

steamed นึ่ง *nûeng*

steel เหล็กกล้า *lèk klâa*

stepfather พ่อเลี้ยง *phâw líang*

stepmother แม่เลี้ยง *mâeh líang*

steps ก้าว *kâo*

sterilize ฆ่าเชื้อ *khâa chúea*

sticking plaster พลาสเตอร์ *phlaasatôeh*

sticky tape เทปเหนียว *théhp nǐao*

stir-fried ผัด *phàt*

stitches (in wound) เข็ม *khěm*

stomach (organ) ท้อง *tháwng*

stomach (abdomen) ท้อง *tháwng*

stomach ache ปวดท้อง *puàt tháwng*

stomach cramps ตะคิวที่ท้อง *takhiu thîi tháwng*

stools (feces) อุจจาระ *ùtcaará*

stop (halt) หยุด *yùt*

stop (cease) เลิก *lôehk*

stop (bus-) ป้ายรถเมล์ *pâi*

stopover ค้างคืน *kháang khuehn*

store, shop ร้าน *ráan*

storey ขั้น *chán*

storm พายุ *phaayú*

straight ตรง *trong*

straight ahead ตรงไปข้างหน้า *trong pai khâng nâa*

straw (drinking) หลอดดูด *làwt dùut*

street ถนน *thanǒn*

street vendor

คนหาบของขายตามถนน *khon hàap khǎwng khǎi taam thanǒn*

strike (work stoppage) นัดหยุดงาน *nát yùt ngaan*

string เชือก *chûeak*

strong แข็งแรง *khǎeng raehng*

study เรียน *rian*

stuffed animal สัตว์สตาฟ *sàt stáaf*

stuffing ยัดไส้ *yát sâi*

subtitles บรรยาย *ban yai*

succeed สำเร็จ *sǎmrèt*

sugar น้ำตาล *námtaan*

suit สูท *sùut*

suitcase กระเป๋าเดินทาง *krapǎo doehn thaang*

summer หน้าร้อน *nâa ráwn*

sun ดวงอาทิตย์ *duang aathít*

sunbathe อาบแดด *àap dàeht*

Sunday วันอาทิตย์ *wan aathít*

sunglasses แว่นกันแดด *wâen kan dàeht*

sunhat หมวกกันแดด *mùak kan dàeht*

sunrise ดวงอาทิตย์ขึ้น *duang aathít khûen*

sunshade ในร่ม *nai rôm*

sunscreen ครีมกันแดด *khriim kan dàeht*

sunset ดวงอาทิตย์ตก *duang aathít tòk*

sunstroke เป็นลมแดด *pen lom dàeht*

suntan lotion โลชั่นกันแดด *lohchân kan dàeht*

suntan oil น้ำมันทากันแดด *nàmman thaa kan dàeht*

supermarket ซุปเปอร์มาร์เก็ต *súpôehmaakèt*

surcharge เงินเก็บเพิ่ม *ngoen kèp phôehm*

surf เล่นโต้คลื่น *lên tôh khlûehn*

surface mail เมล์ธรรมดา *meh(l) thammadaa*

surfboard กระดานโต้คลื่น *kradaan tôh khlûehn*

surname นามสกุล *naam sakun*

surprised ประหลาดใจ *pralàat cai*

swallow กลืน *kluehn*

swamp บึง *bueng*

sweat เหงื่อ *ngùea*

sweater เสื้อกันหนาว *sûea kan nǎo*

sweet หวาน *wǎan*

sweetcorn ข้าวโพดหวาน *khâo phôht wǎan*

swim ว่ายน้ำ *wâi náam*

swimming pool สระว่ายน้ำ *sà wâi náam*

swimming costume ชุดว่ายน้ำ *chút àap náam*

swindle โกง, หลอกลวง *kohng, làwk luang*

switch สวิทช์ *sa-wít*

synagogue สุเหร่าของยิว *suràw khǎwng yiu*

syrup น้ำเชื่อม *náam chûeam*

T

table โต๊ะ *tó*

tablecloth ผ้าปูโต๊ะ *phâa puu tó*

tablemat ผ้ารองจาน *phâa rawng caan*

tablespoon ช้อนโต๊ะ *cháwn tó*

table tennis ปิงปอง *ping pawng*

tablet PC แท็บเล็ท พีซี *tháeb-lét phii sii*

tablets ยาเม็ด *yaa mét*

tableware ชุดทานอาหาร *chút thaan aahǎan*

take (medicine) กิน *kin (yaa)*

take (photograph) ถ่ายรูป *thài rûup*

take (time) ใช้เวลา *chái wehlaa*

talk พูด *phûut*

tall สูง *sǔung*

tampon แทมปอน, ผ้าอนามัย *thaehmpawn, phâa anaamai*

tanned สีน้ำผึ้ง *sǐi nám phûeng*

tap ก๊อก *káwk*

tape measure สายวัด *sǎi wát*

tap water น้ำก๊อก *nám káwk*

taste รส *rót*

taste (verb) ชิม *chim*

tax ภาษี *phaasǐi*

tax-free shop ร้านปลอดภาษี *ráan plàwt phaasǐi*

taxi แท็กซี่ *tháeksǐi*

taxi stand ป้ายรถแท็กซี่ *pâi tháeksǐi*

tea (black) ชาดำ *chaa dam*

tea (green) ชาเขียว *chaa khǐao*

teacup ถ้วยน้ำชา *thûai nám chaa*

teapot กาน้ำชา *kaa nám chaa*

teaspoon ช้อนชา *cháwn chaa*

teat (bottle) จุกนม *cùk nom*

telephoto lens เล็นส์ส่องทางไกล *len sàwng thaang klai*

television ทีวี *thii wii*

telex เทเล็กซ์ *thehlèk*

temperature (heat) อุณหภูมิ *unhàphuum*

temperature (to have a) มีไข้ *mii khâi*

temple วัด *wát*

temporary filling อุดฟันชั่วคราว *ùt fan chûa khrao*

tender, sore ช้ำ *chám*

tennis เทนนิส *thehnít*

ten สิบ *sìp*

tent เต็นท์ *tent*

terminus สถานีปลายทาง *sathǎanii plai thaang*

terrace (patio) เทอเรซ *thehrêht*

terrace (houses) บ้านห้องแถว *bâan hâwng thǎeo*

terrible แย่มาก *yâe mâak*

texting สงเอสเอ็มเอส *sòng es-em-es*

thank ขอบคุณ *khop khun*

thank you, thanks ขอบคุณ *khàwp khun*

thaw ละลาย *lalai*

theatre โรงหนัง *rohng nǎng*

theft การขโมย (ของ) *kaan khamoi (khǎwng)*

there ที่นั่น *thîi nân*

thermometer (body) ปรอท *paràwt*

thermometer (weather) เทอร์โมมิเตอร์ *thoehmohmítôeh*

thick หนา *nǎa*

thief ขโมย *khamoi*

thigh ขาอ่อน *khǎa àwn*

thin (not fat) ผอม *phǎwm*

thin (not thick) บาง *baang*

think (ponder) คิด *khít*

think (believe) เชื่อ *chûea*

third (1/3) เศษหนึ่งส่วนสาม *sèht nùeng sùan sǎam*

third (place) ที่สาม *thîi sǎam*

thirsty หิว *hǐu*

this afternoon บ่ายนี้ *bài níi*

this evening เย็นนี้ *yen níi*

this morning เช้านี้ *cháo níi*

thread ด้าย *dâi*

throat คอหอย *khaw hǒi*

throat lozenges ยาแก้เจ็บคอ *yaa kâe cèp khaw*

thunderstorm พายุ *phaayú*

Thursday วันพฤหัสบดี *wan pharúehàt (sabawdii)*

ticket (admission) บัตร *budd*

ticket (travel) ตั๋ว *tǔa*

ticket office ที่ขายตั๋ว *thîi khǎi tǔa*

tidy เรียบร้อย *rîap rói*

tie (necktie) ไท, ผ้าผูกคอ *thai, phâa phùuk khaw*

tie (verb) ผูก *phùuk*

tights (thick) ถุงน่องหนา ๆ *thǔng nâwng nǎa nǎa*

tights (pantyhose) ถุงน่อง *thǔng nâwng*

time (occasion) เวลา, ที *wehlaa, thii*

times (multiplying) คูณ *khuun*

timetable ตาราง *taaraang*

tin (can) กระป๋อง *krapǎwng*

tin opener ที่เปิดกระป๋อง *thîi pòeht krapǎwng*

tip (gratuity) ทิป *thíp*

tissues กระดาษเช็ดปาก *kradàat chét pàak*

tobacco ยาสูบ *yaa sùup*

today วันนี้ *wan níi*

toddler เด็กเล็ก *dèk lék*

toe ปลายเท้า *plai tháo*

together ด้วยกัน *dûai kan*

toilet ห้องน้ำ *hâwng náam*

toilet paper กระดาษชำระ *kradàat chamrá*

toilet seat ที่นั่งส้วม *thîi nâng sûam*

toiletries เครื่องใช้ในห้องน้ำ *khrûeang chái nai hâwng náam*

tomato มะเขือเทศ *makhǔea thêht*

tomorrow พรุ่งนี้ *phrûng níi*

tongue ลิ้น *lín*

tonight คืนนี้ *khuehn níi*

tool เครื่องมือ *khrûeang mueh*

tooth ฟัน *fan*

toothache ปวดฟัน *pùat fan*

toothbrush แปรงสีฟัน *praehng sǐi fan*

toothpaste ยาสีฟัน *yaa sǐi fan*

toothpick ไม้จิ้มฟัน *mái cîm fan*

top up เติม *toehm*

torch, flashlight ไฟฉาย *fai chǎi*

total ทั้งหมด *tháng mòt*

tough ยาก *yâak*

tour ทัศนาจร, ทัวร์ *thátsanaacawn, thua*

tour guide มัคคุเทศก์, ไกด์ *mákkhúthêht, kái*

tourist class ชั้นนักท่องเที่ยว *chán nák thâwng thîao*

tourist information office สำนักให้ข้อมูลนักท่องเที่ยว *sǎmnák ngaan hâi khâw muun nák thâwng thîao*

tow ลาก *lâak*

tow cable ลวดลาก *lûat lâak*

towel ผ้าเช็ดตัว *phâa chét tua*

tower หอคอย *hǎw khawi*

town เมือง *mueang*

town hall ศาลากลาง *sǎalaa klaang*

toy ของเล่น *khǎwng lên*

traffic การจราจร *kaan caraacawn*

traffic light ไฟจราจร *fai caraacawn*

train รถไฟ *rót fai*

train station สถานีรถไฟ *sathǎanii rót fai*

train ticket ตั๋วรถไฟ *tǔa rót fai*

train timetable ตารางรถไฟ *taaraang rót fai*

translate แปล *plaeh*

travel เดินทาง *doehn thaang*

travel agent เอเย่นขายตั๋ว *ehyên khǎi tǔa*

traveler นักเดินทาง *nák doehn thaang*

traveler's cheque เช็คเดินทาง *chék doehn thaang*

treatment การรักษา *kaan ráksǎa*

triangle สามเหลี่ยม *sǎam lìam*

trim (hair) เล็ม *lem*

trim (haircut) ตัดผม *tàt phǒm*

trip การเดินทาง *kaan doehn thaang*

truck รถบรรทุก *rót banthúk*

trustworthy ไว้ใจได้ *wái cai dâi*

try on ลอง *lawng*

tube (of paste) หลอด *làwt*

Tuesday วันอังคาร *wan angkhaan*

tuna ปลาทูน่า *plaa thuunâa*

tunnel อุโมงค์ *ùmohng*

turn off ปิด *pìt*

turn on เปิด *pòeht*

turn over พลิก *phlík*

TV ทีวี *TV*

TV guide รายการทีวี *raikaan thii wii*

tweet ทวีท *tweet*

tweezers แหนบ *nàehp*

twin-bedded เตียงคู่ *tiang khûu*

Twitter ทวีทเตอร์ *ta-wít-er*

typhoon ไต้ฝุ่น *tâifùn*

tyre ยางรถ *yaang rót*

tyre pressure ลมยาง *lom yaang*

U

ugly น่าเกลียด *nâa klìat*

UHT milk นมยูเอชที *nom yuu èht thii*

ulcer แผลเปื่อย *phlǎeh pùeai*

umbrella ร่ม *rôm*

under ใต้ *tâi*

underpants กางเกงใน *kaangkehng nai*

underpass ถนนลอดใต้สะพาน *thanǒn lâwt tâi saphaan*

understand เข้าใจ *khâo cai*

underwear กางเกงใน *kaangkehng nai*

undress แก้ผ้า *kâeh phâa*

unemployed ว่างงาน *wâang ngaan*

uneven ไม่เรียบ *mâi rîap*

university มหาวิทยาลัย *mahǎawítthayaalai*

unleaded ไร้สารตะกั่ว *rái sǎan takùa*

up ขึ้น *khûen*

upload อัพโหลด *ap-lòod*

upright ตั้งตรง *tâng trong*

urgent ด่วน *dùan*

urgently อย่างรีบด่วน *yàang rîip dùan*

urine ปัสสาวะ *patsǎawá*

used bookstore ร้านหนังสือมือสอง *ráan nǎngsǔeh mueh sǎwng*

username ชื่อผู้ใช้ *chûe phûu chái*

usually มักจะ *mák ca*

V

vacate ปล่อยให้ว่าง *plòi hâi wâang*

vacation วันหยุด *wan yùt*

vaccinate ฉีดวัคซีน *chìit wáksiin*

vagina ช่องคลอด, จิ๋ม *châwng khlâwt, jhim*

valid ใช้ได้ *chái dâi*

valley หุบเขา *hùp khǎo*

valuable มีค่า *mii khâa*

valuables ของมีค่า *khǎwng mii khâa*

van รถตู้ *rót tûu*

vase แจกัน *jheakan*

vegetable ผัก *phàk*

vegetarian คนที่กินเจ *khon thîi kin ceh*

vein หลอดเลือดดำ *làwt lûeat dam*

velvet ผ้ากำมะหยี่ *phâa kammáyîi*

vending machine เครื่องขายของ *khrûeang khǎi khǎwng*

venemous มีพิษ *mii pít*

venereal disease โรคที่ติดต่อทางร่วมเพศ *rôhk thîi tìt tàw thaang rûam phêht*

vertical แนวตั้ง *naeo tâng*

via โดยทาง, ผ่าน *doi thaang, phàan*

video camera กล้องวิดีโอ *klâwng widii-oh*

video cassette คาสเซ็ทวิดีโอ *khaasét widii-oh*

video recorder เครื่องอัดวิดีโอ *khrûeang àt widii-oh*

view ทัศนะ, วิว *thátsaná, wiu*

village หมู่บ้าน *mùu bâan*

visa วีซ่า *wiisâa*

visit เยี่ยม *yîam*

visiting time เวลาเยี่ยม *wehlaa yîam*

vitamins วิตามิน *wítaamin*

vitamin tablets ยาเม็ดวิตามิน *yaa mét wítaamin*

volcano ภูเขาไฟ *phuu khǎo fai*

volleyball วอลเล่ย์บอล *wawllêhbawn*

vomit อาเจียร *aacian*

W

wait รอ, คอย *raw, khawi*

waiter บริกร, คนเสริฟ *bawríkawn, khon sòehf*

waiting room ห้องนั่งรอ *hâwng nâng raw*

waitress บริกรหญิง *bawríkawn yǐng*

wake up ตื่น *tùehn*

Wales เวลส์ *wehl(s)*

walk (noun) การเดิน *kaan doehn*

walk (verb) เดิน *doehn*

walking stick ไม้เท้า *mái tháo*

wall กำแพง *kamphaehng*

wallet กระเป๋าสตางค์ *krapǎo staang*

want, need ต้องการ *tâwngkaan*

wardrobe ตู้เสื้อผ้า *tûu sûea phâa*

warm อบอุ่น *òp ùn*

warn เตือน *tuean*

warning คำเตือน *kham tuean*

wash ล้าง *láang*

washing การล้าง *kaan láang*

washing line ราวตากผ้า *rao tàak phâa*

washing machine เครื่องซักผ้า *khrûeang sák phâa*

wasp ตัวต่อ *tua tàw*

watch เฝ้า *fâo*

water น้ำ *náam*

waterfall น้ำตก *nám tòk*

waterproof กันน้ำ *kan náam*

water-skiing สกีน้ำ *sakii náam*

way (direction) ทาง *thaang*

way (method) วิธี *wíthii*

we เรา *rao*

weak อ่อนแอ *àwn aeh*

wear ใส่ *sài*

weather อากาศ *aakàat*

weather forecast พยากรณ์อากาศ *phayaakawn aakàat*

website เว็บไซต์ *web-sai*

wedding งานแต่งงาน *ngaan tàeng ngaan*

Wednesday วันพุธ *wan phút*

week สัปดาห์ *sàpdaa*

weekday วันทำงาน *wan tham ngaan*

weekend วันสุดสัปดาห์ *wan sùt sàpdaa*

weigh ชั่ง *châng*

weigh out แบ่งชั่ง *bàeng châng*

welcome ยินดีต้อนรับ *yindii tâwn ráp*

well (good) ดี *dii*

well (for water) บ่อน้ำ *bàw náam*

west ตะวันตก *ta-wan tòk*

wet เปียก *pìek*

wetsuit ชุดดำน้ำ *chút dam náam*

what? อะไร *arai*

wheel ล้อรถ *láw rót*

wheelchair เก้าอี้มีล้อเข็น *kâo-îi mii láw khěn*

when? เมื่อไร *mûearai*

where? ที่ไหน *thîi năi*

which? ไหน *năi*

white ขาว *khǎo*

white wine ไวน์ขาว *wai(n) khǎo*

who? ใคร *khrai*

why? ทำไม *thammai*

wide-angle lens เลนส์มุมกว้าง *len(s) mum kwâang*

widow แม่ม่าย *mâeh mâi*

widower พ่อม่าย *pohh mâi*

wife เมีย, ภรรยา *mia* (formal)

Wifi (wireless connection) วายฟาย *wai-fai*

wind ลม *lom*

window (in room) หน้าต่าง *nâatàang*

window (to pay) เคาน์เตอร์ *khaotôeh*

windscreen, windshield กระจกหน้ารถ *krajòk nâa rót*

windscreen wiper ที่ปัดน้ำฝน *thîi pàt nám fǒn*

wine ไวน์ *wai(n)*

winter หน้าหนาว *nâa nǎo*

wire ลวด *lûat*

witness พยาน *phayaan*

woman ผู้หญิง *phûu yǐng*

wonderful ยอดเยี่ยม *yâwt yîam*

wood ไม้ *mái*

wool (cloth) ผ้าขนสัตว์ *(phâa) khǒn sàt*

word คำ *kham*

work งาน *ngaan*

working day วันทำงาน *wan tham ngaan*

worn (used) ใช้แล้ว *chái láeo*

worn out ขาดแล้ว *khàat láeo*

worried กังวล *kangwon*

wound บาดแผล *bàat phlǎeh*

wrap ห่อ *hàw*

wrench, spanner กุญแจปากตาย *kuncaeh pàak tai*

wrist ข้อมือ *khâw mueh*

write เขียน *khǐan*

write down จดลงไป *jod long pai*

writing pad กระดาษฉีก *kradàat chìik*

writing paper กระดาษเขียนจดหมาย *kradàat khǐan còt mǎi*

wrong ผิด *phìt*

Y

yarn (thread) ด้าย *dâi*

year ปี *pii*

yellow เหลือง *lǔeang*

yes (that's right) ใช่ *châi*

yes (female speaking) ค่ะ *khâ*

yes (male speaking) ครับ *khráp*

yes please (female) เอาค่ะ *ao khâ*

yes please (male) เอาครับ *ao khráp*

yesterday เมื่อวานนี้ *mûeawaan níi*

yoga โยคะ *yoo-khá*

you คุณ *khun*

youth hostel หอพักเยาวชน *hǎw phák yao-wachon*

Z

zip ซิป *síp*

zoo สวนสัตว์ *sǔan sàt*